LANGUAGE

Key Concepts in Philosophy

Key Concepts in Philosophy
Series Editors: John Mullarkey (University of Dundee) and
Caroline Williams (Queen Mary, University of London)

Language

Key Concepts in Philosophy

José Medina

continuum
LONDON • NEW YORK

Continuum
The Tower Building   15 East 26th Street
11 York Road   New York
London SE1 7NX   NY 10010

www.continuumbooks.com

British Library Cataloguing-in-Publication Data
A catalogue record for this book is available from the British Library.

ISBN: 0–8264–7166–8 (hardback)
0–8264–7167–6 (paperback)

Library of Congress Cataloging-in-Publication Data
Medina, José, 1968–
   Language / by José Medina
     p. cm. — (Key concepts in philosophy)
   Includes bibliographical references and index.
   ISBN 0–8264–7166–8 — ISBN 0–8264–7167–6 (pbk.)
   1. Philosophy, Modern. 2. Language and
Languages–Philosophy. I. Title. II. Series.
B804.M36 2005
121′.68—dc22   2005045478

Typeset by Servis Filmsetting Ltd, Manchester
Printed and bound in Great Britain by
MPG Books Ltd, Bodmin, Cornwall

To my friends and family for their constant support

CONTENTS

CHAPTER 1

COMMUNICATION AND SPEECH ACTS

What is language for? The main purpose of language is *communication*. This sounds like a commonplace truism, a trivial platitude; and yet it is a very rich insight that for a long time was virtually disregarded in the philosophical tradition. Until recently philosophers failed to elaborate this insight into a detailed account of the logic and structure of communication and of the different communicative functions of language. With the exception of W. v. Humboldt (1988), until the twentieth century the different aspects and purposes of communication received little attention, and as a result, the different communicative functions of language were left in the dark. In the absence of systematic elucidations of the complex and diverse communicative nature of language, researchers of language often took one single communicative function as primary and fundamental (sometimes even exclusive) without any argument, taking a part for the whole and producing one-sided and distorted accounts of language. Much of the research on language in the twentieth century can be understood as a battle against these oversimplications and oversights, a struggle to overcome the legacy of one-sided conceptions of language in different philosophical traditions. Many developments in linguistics, Communication Theory and Speech Act Theory have contributed to enrich our understanding of the communicative nature of language. In this chapter I will analyse and discuss these developments. Through an elucidation of the work of linguists and communication theorists such as Bühler, Jakobson and Habermas, I will offer an account of the different communicative functions of language. Drawing on Speech Act Theory, I will further develop the analysis of the different elements and functions of communication by looking at speech as *performance*. My discussion of the communicative structure of speech acts will closely follow the elucidations of linguistic performance offered by Austin (1975).

1.1 THE COMMUNICATIVE FUNCTIONS OF LANGUAGE

Karl Bühler (1933, 1934) gave a precise formulation to the traditional model of communication as containing three distinct elements: the speaker, addresser or sender of the message; the listener, addressee, audience or recipient of the message; and the world or object domain that is the topic of communication. Communication is thus conceived as a relation that binds together three elements – sender, recipient and topic. Accordingly, communication serves three distinct functions corresponding to these three relata. Bühler termed these communicative functions *expression, appeal* and *representation*. Each of these functions consists in a communicative orientation towards one of the three poles in the tripartite structure of communication. I will briefly specify what these three functions are, introducing other terms that linguists and philosophers have also used to describe them.[1] In the *representational, referential* or *descriptive* function, what takes centre-stage is what is talked about, the content or topic of communication; and the speaker and hearer are bracketed or relegated to the background. This function deals exclusively with what is represented or depicted in the communicative act. On the other hand, in so far as it focuses on the sender or addresser, communication also has an *expressive* or *emotive* function. Here what takes centre-stage is the expression of the speaker's subjectivity and attitudes (towards the topic or the audience of his/her speech act, for example). And finally, the *appellative* or *conative* function of communication is oriented towards the recipient or addressee and is intended to have an impact or produce an effect on him/her. The primary goal of communication in this function is to elicit a response in the audience: an emotional reaction, the performance of an action or whatever it might be.

For Bühler, language is a medium (or 'organon' as he calls it) that serves, simultaneously, three different but *internally related* communicative functions. Every communicative act, in so far as it must have the three necessary elements of communication, must involve all three communicative functions to some degree. But each of these functions sometimes becomes the explicit focus of communication. Therefore, we can find particular kinds of speech acts that exemplify these functions, for in them one particular communicative element takes precedence over the others and becomes the dominant element of the communicative exchange. Thus, for example, the representational or referential function is epitomized in *assertions* with a descriptive content such as 'The cat is on the mat', in which the transmission of information is the primary communicative goal. Although, of course, we can find a descriptive or representational informational content in communicative acts that are (arguably) not assertoric (such as the command 'Imagine the cat being on the mat'),[2] what is special about descriptive assertions is that they focus primarily and almost exclusively on the representational relation to the world or object domain that they describe. In the second place, the expressive or emotive function of language flavours all our utterances phonically, grammatically and lexically (as clearly marked in intonation, verbal tenses and voices and word choices). But this function is laid bare in *interjections* such as 'Oh!', 'Ouch!', 'Ugh!', 'Good grief!', 'Indeed!'. Interjections are words typically used in grammatical isolation to express emotion. In these peculiar forms of exclamation it is clear that what becomes the primary focus of communication is the speaker or sender him/herself; and the communicative act revolves around his/her emotive attitudes. Finally, the appellative or conative function of communication finds its purest forms in the *vocative* and the *imperative*, which give grammatical expression to this function. Vocatives are calls or interpellations directed at the person or thing being addressed, such as 'Hey you!', 'Girl, . . .', 'My friend, . . .', 'Oh cruel world, . . .'. The imperative is the grammatical mood used in commands and exhortations such as 'Listen!', 'Go!', etc. These communicative acts focus on the relation to the addressee. The communicative goal of the imperative is to make some kind of demand on the addressee; that of the vocative is to put the addressee in a particular communicative position, soliciting his/her attention and inducing a particular attitude or orientation in him/her.

Habermas (1992) has used Bühler's account of the tripartite structure of communication to classify the theories of meaning developed in the twentieth century. According to Habermas, theories of meaning fall into three categories, each of which privileges one communicative function. In the first place, *intentionalistic semantics* (championed by philosophers as different as Husserl and Grice) gives primacy to the expressive function of communication by tracing the semantic content of each speech act to the speaker in whom it originates. On this semantic approach, speakers are thought to be the well of meaning, for communicative contents are supposed to emanate from their subjective meaning-conferring acts and communicative intentions. On this view, all speech acts are, fundamentally, *expressive* speech acts. An alternative semantic framework can be found in *formal semantics*, which has received great theoretical development in the analytic tradition from Frege to Dummett. This is the second category of theory of meaning in Habermas' classification. Formal semantics gives primacy to the representational function of communication, and it explains meaning in terms of the referential relations or mappings between language and world (according to realists), or between language and our representations of the world (according to antirealists). On this view, all statements are understood as assertions or *constative* speech acts; and the content of a statement is claimed to be specifiable in its truth conditions or in its assertibility conditions, which characterize what the statement represents or depicts. Finally, a third category of semantic view is the *use-theory of meaning*, which Habermas claims to have been inaugurated by the later Wittgenstein and systematically developed by social pragmatics. According to Habermas (1992), this semantic perspective focuses on communicative interactions 'in which linguistic expressions serve practical functions' (p. 58). A use-theory of meaning gives primacy to the appellative or conative function in so far as it focuses on speech acts – such as commands – that purport to have a binding character and to establish normative expectations that regulate action. Habermas calls them *regulative* speech acts.

Habermas does not dismiss any of these theories and acknowledges that there is a lot to learn from each of them. But he argues that they can only offer one-sided accounts of meaning because they focus exclusively on one kind of speech act and one communicative function, disregarding the others. For Habermas, the challenge is to preserve the partial truths that these theories offer and to integrate them in a single framework. So he undertakes the synthetic work of unifying and systematizing their complementary insights and theoretical elaborations. He does this through Bühler's theoretical framework: it is his contention that Bühler's functional analysis of communication is what makes the synthesis and unification of theories of meaning possible. As he puts it, 'the discussion has essentially been dominated by these theories, for each of them has been able to appeal to a fundamental intuition. Bühler brings these intuitions together in his threefold functional schema' (1992, p. 58). Habermas draws on Bühler's classification of communicative functions for the development of his own Speech Act Theory. He proposes 'a validity-theoretic interpretation of Bühler's functional schema' (1992, p. 76). The central insight of the Habermasian theoretical development of Bühler's framework is that speaking is a matter of *claim-making*: when we speak we make a claim (various claims, actually) as to the *validity* of what we are saying. On this view, speech acts are essentially and fundamentally *validity claims*. According to Habermas, every speech act contains three different validity claims, even if only one of them is the explicit and primary focus of the communicative exchange in question. Habermas distinguishes three distinct dimensions of validity in speech corresponding to the three different elements of communication (speaker, world and addressee) and the three different communicative functions (expression, representation and appeal). Corresponding to the speaker and the expressive function, we have subjective correctness or authenticity. A second dimension of validity is objective correctness or truth, which relates to the world and the representational function. And a third dimension is intersubjective correctness, rightness or 'ought-validity', which concerns the addressee and the appellative function of communication. The statement 'The cat is on the mat', for example, contains a truth claim (that the described state of affairs actually obtains, that the representation is correct); but it also contains an authenticity claim (that the speaker is sincere in the expression of his/her belief); and a rightness claim, which concerns the appropriate reaction to the utterance, that is, what is to be done with it, how to act on the information provided (for example, as a warning, an admonition or a reproach that assigns blame and calls for an apology).

These validity claims are thematized in different kinds of speech acts: constative, expressive and regulative speech acts, respectively. Sometimes this is made explicit and linguistically marked, especially when there is a question as to what is meant by an utterance. So, for example, the statement 'The cat is on the mat' can be marked as a constative speech act by introducing it with 'I assert that . . .'; or as an expressive speech act by adding to it something like '. . ., I honestly believe'; or as a regulative speech act of a particular kind, say, by uttering the statement in a reproaching tone, or by adding '. . . where it shouldn't be', or 'I warn you that . . .'. But it is rare for these different kinds of speech act to be explicitly marked in language (we rarely say 'I assert so-and-so' instead of simply making the assertion). Typically it is the context that brings one validity claim to the foreground and makes it clear what kind of speech act we are dealing with.

Habermas emphasizes that in ordinary communication most validity claims are not fully and explicitly articulated, for their full and explicit articulation requires a process of argumentation in which these claims are justified or refuted and their validity settled. Validity claims are not vindicated until they are challenged and reasons for and against them are mobilized, discussed and balanced; otherwise, justificatory and refuting reasons remain implicit and inarticulate and the validity of claims is simply assumed. The process of challenging and vindicating validity claims is essential to the dynamics of communication as Habermas conceives it. If, from the perspective of its production, the essence of a communicative act is claim-making, from the perspective of its reception what is essential is *the 'yes/no' attitude of the interlocutor*, who can accept or reject the communicative offer in its different dimensions of validity. Discrepancies between the claim-making of a speaker and the 'yes/no' attitudes of his/her audience are to be resolved by rational argumentation, that is, by a process of giving and asking for reasons. According to Habermas, this is what distinguishes communicative action from other types of action: namely, that communicative action is oriented towards 'reaching an understanding' by rational means, as opposed to strategic action which aims simply at 'exerting influence'.[3] Habermas argues that communicative action, by its very dynamics, necessitates a process of justification in which the validity of claims gets settled. Discursive challenges prompt a justificatory process in which the role of the audience or challenger is to raise doubts or objections and ask for reasons to answer them, and the role of the speaker or claim-maker is to meet the argumentative challenges by providing convincing reasons and neutralizing contrary reasons. The goal of this justificatory process is the discursive vindication or 'redemption' (as Habermas puts it) of validity claims. Different validity claims are 'redeemed' by different *discourses*, which thematize different dimensions of validity and mobilize the relevant reasons for the justification of validity claims. Thus corresponding to constative speech acts and their claims to truth we have *theoretical* discourses; corresponding to regulative speech acts and their claims to rightness, *practical* discourses; and corresponding to expressive speech acts and their claims to authenticity or subjective correctness, *therapeutic* discourses. These three kinds of discourses refer to three distinct *worlds* or object domains corresponding to the three dimensions of validity. These worlds are the ontological correlates of truth, authenticity and rightness: an objective world, a subjective world and an intersubjective world. According to Habermas, our speech acts are communicative negotiations that involve these three different ontological domains. He claims that constative, expressive and regulative speech acts have distinct 'manners of referring' (1992, p. 76). Thus his Speech Act Theory provides a rich and complex ontological perspective according to which our communicative exchanges situate themselves at the cross-roads of three worlds. We will discuss the ontological significance of communication in connection with the referential function of language in later chapters (see csp. 4.3).

Habermas' account of communication has been criticized by many as overly rationalistic and overly idealistic for not taking into account the non-rational (and even irrational) aspects of communication, and for not paying sufficient and adequate attention to the interaction between the communicative and the strategic. Habermas has acknowledged and defended the (neo-Kantian) transcendental approach of his theoretical framework. He has argued that action presupposes the postulation of a regulative ideal, namely, an 'ideal speech situation' in which participants are only guided by communicative rationality, that is, by the force of the best reasons or arguments available. I will not get into this debate here.[4] Instead, I will focus on another sense in which Habermas' account of communication and its realization in speech acts may be inadequate or at least insufficient.

There is no question that, following Bühler, Habermas has developed a systematic account of communicative acts that is perfectly well rounded: a systematization in which everything comes in threes and fits together into a well-organized and aesthetically pleasing (especially for Hegelian sensibilities) tripartite structure. But it is far from clear that this systematization of the structural aspects of communication is exhaustive. Habermas' own earlier classifications contained other elements. In particular, his classification in *The Theory of Communicative Action* included a fourth validity claim: *intelligibility*. All speech acts contain a claim to linguistic validity, that is, the claim that something meaningful is being expressed, that the communicative act is intelligible. In his subsequent work, however, Habermas brackets this dimension and considers intelligibility as a general *presupposition* of communication, rather than as a distinct dimension of validity within it. But it is clear that we do in fact make validity claims concerning intelligibility and we can always challenge the intelligibility of our interlocutor's utterances. We often enter into a discursive process of explication, negotiation and justification in which the intelligibility of our speech acts is scrutinized. This communicative process has to be understood in terms of what has been termed in linguistics the *metalingual* function of communication, prompted by questions such as 'What do you mean?', or simply 'What?' or puzzled facial expressions that indicate lack of understanding. Through the exercise of this communicative function, meanings are spelled out, explicitly articulated and negotiated. This seems to be indeed a distinct communicative function.

To identify more systematically what is left out of the Bühlerian and Habermasian framework, we should go back to linguistics. There is a lot to learn from linguists who have elaborated and expanded on Bühler's threefold schema. Roman Jakobson, in particular, has developed a more refined and comprehensive analytic schema that identifies six basic elements in the process of communication and six distinct communicative functions corresponding to them. Besides the speaker, the hearer and the world or context that the speech act refers to, Jakobson distinguishes three other communicative elements in our linguistic performances: the *message* itself, that is, the string of sounds or marks that are used in the speech act; the intersubjective *contact* it produces, a contact that cannot be reduced to the subjectivities involved in the communicative act but consists, rather, in the relation between them; and the *code*, that is, the repertoire of linguistic tools and materials from which the message is composed, the linguistic medium on which the speech act relies for its significance. Expanding on Bühler's tripartite account of communication, Jakobson (1990)[5] provides the following diagram for the analysis of communicative acts (p. 73):

CONTEXT
ADDRESSER ——— MESSAGE ——— ADDRESSEE
CONTACT
CODE

Corresponding to these six elements of communication, Jakobson recognizes six distinct communicative functions. To the emotive, conative and referential functions identified by Bühler, Jakobson adds the *metalingual* function, the *phatic* function and the *poetic* function. The *metalingual* function is a glossing function that focuses on the code being used. Jakobson emphasizes that the problematization and discussion of the code are not only the specialized activities of professionals of language and communication, but also, and more importantly, the very common activities of ordinary speakers in their everyday communicative exchanges. Although modern logicians drew the distinction between 'object languages' (for speaking of objects) and 'metalanguages' (for speaking of language), Jakobson argues that this distinction is implicit in ordinary linguistic practices, and that metalanguages are not only the technical tools of linguists and logicians, but also the ordinary devices of everyday activities: 'Like Molière's Jourdain, who used prose without knowing it, we practice metalanguage without realizing the metalingual character of our operations' (1990, p. 75). For Jakobson, metalinguistic capacities are a crucial part of normal communicative competence: the cognitive and linguistic abilities involved in communication presuppose the ability to ask about the code, to engage in linguistic disputes and to elucidate and discuss the syntactic, semantic and pragmatic rules used in our communicative exchanges.[6]

A fifth communicative function on Jakobson's list is the *phatic* function. This function of communication focuses on the *contact* between sender and addressee. This communicative function of language teaches us that speaker and hearer cannot be conceived as distinct and separate poles of communication. What comes first in the communicative order is the intersubjective relation or social contact between interlocutors, which positions each of them *vis-à-vis* the others. It was Malinowski (1953) who discovered in his anthropological studies that there are communicative acts whose primary purpose is to establish and sustain contact with one's interlocutors. As Jakobson puts it, the whole point of utterances dominated by the phatic function is 'to establish, to prolong, or to discontinue communication, to check whether the channel works ("Hello, do you hear me?"), to attract the attention of the interlocutor or to confirm his continued attention ("Are you listening?" or in Shakespearean diction, "Lend me your ears!" – and on the other end of the wire

"Um-hum!")' (1990, p. 75). We share the phatic function of language with animals (for example, talking birds) that often use sounds to attract each other's attention and to establish and sustain the social contact required for all kinds of complex interactions. Jakobson points out that the phatic function 'is also the first verbal function acquired by infants; they are prone to communicate before being able to send or receive informative communication' (ibid.).

Finally, the sixth communicative function in Jakobson's account is the *poetic* function of language. This function is characterized by its 'focus on the message for its own sake' (1990, p. 76). The poetic function brings to the fore the material and aesthetic aspects of communication. Under this function, written marks and sounds are typically (though not necessarily) treated as uninterpreted signs: 'This function, by promoting the palpability of signs, deepens the fundamental dichotomy of signs and objects' (ibid.). This is one of the examples that Jakobson uses to illustrate the poetic function of language: '"Why do you always say *Joan and Margery*, yet never *Margery and Joan*? Do you prefer Joan to her twin sister?" "Not at all, it just sounds smoother." In a sequence of two coordinate names, as far as no problem of rank interferes, the precedence of the shorter name suits the speaker, unaccountable for him, as a well-ordered shape for the message' (ibid.). The choice of example is not accidental. Jakobson uses a common phenomenon in ordinary language to emphasize that the poetic function of language operates (although typically unconsciously) in the regular production of speech acts in everyday communicative contexts. He remarks that although poetry focuses heavily on this function,[7] 'any attempt to reduce the sphere of the poetic function to poetry [. . .] would be a delusive oversimplification. The poetic function is not the sole function of verbal art but only its dominant, determining function, whereas in all other verbal activities it acts as a subsidiary, accessory constituent' (ibid.).

With its focus on the message itself, the poetic function of language thematizes what is at the very core of the communicative act: the poetic act of communication arranges and rearranges the linguistic medium in multifarious ways, inexhaustibly creating new linguistic productions from the code and rearranging the code through these productions; it articulates the social contact or inter-subjective relation between speakers, positioning one *vis-à-vis* the other aesthetically, through language, in particular ways; and it also recreates linguistically the context (or world) that the interlocutors come to share on the basis of their poetic interaction. Arguably, this function constitutes the motor of language, the primary productive force in communication, in so far as it is responsible for linguistic creativity (the innovation or regeneration of language), for social productivity (the making and remaking of social relations through language), and for ontological generativity (the kind of radical production or creation of domains of reality described as 'world-disclosing'[8] or 'world-making'[9]). We will come back to the linguistic, social and ontological aspects of the poetic function in later chapters (especially in the discussion of linguistic creativity in Chapter 4). But before concluding this section, I want to draw attention to two important observations about the Jakobsonian account of the communicative functions of language.

In the first place, it is important to keep in mind that all the communicative functions of language appear in complex relations with one another, not in isolation. As pointed out above, even when one of the communicative functions of language is the focus of attention (e.g. in interjections, commands or descriptions), the others are also operating, if only tacitly, in the background. Jakobson emphasizes that the interrelations between the communicative functions of language are crucial for understanding all linguistic phenomena. Take, for example, the phenomenon of word choice: e.g. we can select one among the more or less similar nouns 'child', 'kid', 'youngster' and 'tot', and one of the semantically cognate verbs 'sleeps', 'dozes', 'nods', 'naps'. A particular word choice can be expressive or emotive, that is, it can be indicative of the speaker's subjective attitudes. It can also be conative in so far as it tries to suggest something to the recipient of the message. A word choice also has referential aspects or implications, for it offers a particular articulation of the referent designated and the scene depicted. It has also a metalingual facet in so far as it tries to avert misunderstandings and to maintain or create a shared code between interlocutors. It can also have a phatic dimension in maintaining a particular kind of contact with the interlocutor or audience. And finally, our choice of words typically also has a poetic dimension corresponding to its aesthetic aspects and the creativity involved in its production.

In the second place, it should be noted that Jakobson's account of the elements of communication and of communicative functions is a helpful organizational scheme that can be used to group all the studies, discussions and debates on language that can be found in the philosophical and scientific literature. I will so use it in the development of my narrative in this book. Jakobson's useful guide to the elements and functions of communication provides the key to the conceptual map I will try to articulate to navigate the vast array of theoretical positions, approaches and perspectives in Philosophy of Language, Semiotics and Communication Theory. The subsequent chapters should be read as discussing in detail the inner workings of different communicative functions and their complex and problematic interrelations. Through a discussion of the thorny debates about sense and reference, Chapter 2 will elucidate the knotty relationship between the expressive and referential functions of language. The discussions of the formation and transformation of different forms of intersubjectivity and community through language will elucidate the conative and phatic functions of communication (see Chapters 3 and 5). In a critical examination of philosophical issues concerning intelligibility and linguistic creativity, Chapter 4 will be concerned primarily with the metalingual and poetic functions of language. And finally, the discussion of the complex relationship between language and identity (including gender, sexuality, race and ethnicity) in the concluding chapter will involve all the communicative functions of language and their interrelations.

1.2 COMMUNICATION AND PERFORMANCE

There is a tight connection between communication and performance. We communicate through our acts; and the communicative functions of language cannot be carried out and fulfilled in any other way than performatively. The intimate bond between speech and action is precisely what the Wittgensteinian notion of a language-game is meant to underscore: 'I shall [. . .] call the whole, consisting of language and the actions into which it is woven, the "language-game"' (1958 §7); 'the term "language-*game*" is meant to bring into prominence the fact that the *speaking* of language is part of an activity, or of a form of life' (1958 §23). On Wittgenstein's view, to speak is to make a move in a language-game, that is, to do something in a normatively structured activity. Our utterances or linguistic moves are governed by rules (the rules of the game we are playing) and subject to normative assessments: they can accomplish or fail to accomplish something (they can be successful or unsuccessful, for example, in issuing a command, making a promise, telling a joke); and what they accomplish can be good or bad (e.g. a good or bad command, promise or joke). Things get done in and through our linguistic actions. Wittgenstein emphasizes the vast multiplicity of things that we do with language:

> Giving orders, and obeying them. Describing the appearance of an object, or giving its measurement. Constructing an object from a description (a drawing). Reporting an event. Speculating about an event. Forming and testing a hypothesis. Presenting the results of an experiment in tables and diagrams. Making up a story; and reading it. Play-acting. Singing catches. Guessing riddles. Making a joke; telling it. Solving a problem in practical arithmetic. Translating from one language into another. Asking, thanking, cursing, greeting, praying. (1958 §23)

And this is of course a list that has to be left open, for our linguistic activities or practices are living things that are always changing. The use of language is as unpredictable as human action, for indeed *an utterance is itself an act*. The point is not simply that speech relates to action, but rather, that speech itself *is* action. This point was elaborated in full by J. L. Austin's influential account of 'performative utterances'.

Although we have already made an incursion into Speech Act Theory with Habermas, let's now go to its origins with Austin and his account of *speech as action*. Austin revolutionized analytic Philosophy of Language by drawing attention to the close and constitutive link between language and performance. In the now classic paper 'Performative utterances' (1979) Austin developed his performative account as an argument against a well-entrenched bias in the philosophical tradition: the pervasive assumption that 'the sole business, the sole interesting business, of any utterance – that is, of anything we say – is to be true or at least false' (p. 233). Given this bias, Austin complains, in the Philosophy of Language all utterances have been assimilated to *declarative statements*; that is, they have been conceived as declarations or assertions whose contents are descriptions that have to be assessed in terms of their truth or falsity. Nondeclarative utterances, such as interrogatives and imperatives, have been considered to be derivative from and parasitic upon the declarative use of language, and even analysable into this primary use: for example, some had argued that 'What time is it?' or 'Give me a slab!' were shorthand for the declarative statements 'I want to know what time it is' or 'I want you to give me a slab', and that the longer sentences were contained, implicitly, in the shorter ones. In the opening pages of 'Performative utterances' Austin contends that in order to disarm this reductive approach (often called 'descriptivism' or 'assertionalism') and to undermine and eliminate the bias in which it originates, it is not enough to simply draw attention to the 'different uses of language' as 'the "use of language" movement' (also called 'ordinary-language philosophy') had been doing up to that point (see esp. p. 234). Austin uses a different tactic. Instead of emphasizing the wide range of non-declarative uses of language, he calls our attention to a kind of utterance that fits perfectly the descriptivist or assertionalist paradigm (having the appearance of being a declarative statement), but nonetheless resists the traditional analysis and cannot be adequately explained and evaluated as a description that aims at depicting some truth about the world: 'a kind of utterance that looks like a statement and grammatically, I suppose, would be classed as a statement, which is not nonsensical, and yet is not true or false' (p. 235).

Some of the examples that Austin gives in order to identify this peculiar class of utterances are: saying 'I apologize' after treading on someone's toes; saying 'I do' or 'I take this woman to be my lawful wedded wife' in a wedding ceremony; saying 'I name this ship *Queen Elizabeth*' in a christening ceremony with the bottle of champagne in hand; and saying 'I bet you sixpence it will rain tomorrow'. The peculiar feature of all these utterances is that, as Austin puts it, 'in saying what I do, I perform that action' (ibid.). These utterances *do* something; the utterances themselves are tantamount to the performance of an action: apologizing, getting married, baptizing and betting. They are *speech acts* properly so called. That is, they are *sayings* that are, at the same time, *doings*: 'if a person makes an utterance of this sort we should say that he is *doing* something rather than merely *saying* something' (ibid.). When I say 'I promise so-and-so', I am not describing myself as making a promise; I am actually making the promise as I speak, I am manufacturing it with my words; by the very pronouncement of those words by me, the promise gets made. Austin calls these linguistic acts *performative utterances* or simply *performatives*. He contrasts them with *constatives*: the declarative statements that are mere sayings or locutions whose function is to mirror the world, rather than to intervene in it by means of language. Austin's contrast between constatives and performatives is a contrast between two different types of linguistic acts: *locutionary* acts and *illocutionary* acts. We will come back to this contrast later in order to undermine it and ultimately abandon it; but as a ladder that we'll kick away and leave behind, this contrast will be useful and instructive, raising us to higher levels of understanding about the workings of language – as we shall see, this is in fact how Austin used the contrast.

While our declarative statements or locutionary acts aim at truth, it seems clear that truth is not the central and obvious value for the assessment of our illocutionary acts. If someone says 'I apologize' or 'I bet you a dollar that I can do it', 'That's true' and 'That's false' do not seem to be the appropriate reactions. Acknowledging the act performed and responding to it, for example by accepting the apology or taking up the bet, are appropriate reactions; but assessing the truth-value of the statement is not. When it comes to illocutionary acts, truth and falsity seem to be beside the point. So what is the point of performative utterances? What function do they serve if it is not truth-telling? The function and objective of illocutionary acts consist in the satisfactory performance of an act, the successful accomplishment of an action through language. According to Austin, performatives have a dimension of validity other than truth. The normative axis around which the production, reception and evaluation of illocutionary acts revolves is performative success or what Austin calls 'felicity'. Speech acts can be performed appropriately or inappropriately, successfully or unsuccessfully, that is, *felicitously* or *infelicitously*. Unlike the truth or falsity of locutionary acts, which relates to something entirely outside the utterance (i.e. the way the world is), the felicity or infelicity of illocutionary acts is a performative quality, that is, a quality that is immanent in our linguistic practices and performances and does not depend upon something extraneous that is mind-independent and language-independent. However, this does not mean that performing a speech act felicitously is simply a matter of making certain sounds. As Austin emphasizes, performing a speech act felicitously involves more than 'simply saying a few words' (1979, p. 236). Apologizing, making a bet, promising, getting married and all the other things that we do with words require much more than merely uttering certain words. For those words that we utter to have the appropriate force and to perform the relevant actions, an entire social machinery must be in place. For indeed speech acts are social acts embedded in and defined by social customs, practices, institutions and traditions. Austin emphatically rejects the idea that what is needed for our words to have performative force and to be able to accomplish an illocutionary act is some invisible extra element that is somehow behind the words – an inner act of 'the mind', 'the spirit' or some other 'backstage artiste' performing its magic behind the scenes (ibid.). According to Austin, it is not legitimate to say, with Euripides' Hippolytus, 'My tongue swore to, but my heart did not'; and if we allow people to say such things, 'we open a loop-hole to perjurers and welshers and bigamists and so on' (ibid.), undermining the normative force of our words and ultimately destroying the social institutions and the historical practices and traditions associated with them. As the old saying states, 'our word is our bond'. It is important to keep in mind that an insincere promise is still a promise, although an infelicitous one. Sincerity, having the intention or predisposition to follow through with the commitment being undertaken, is one of the conditions that have to be met for a promise to be felicitous. For Austin, the sincerity condition is immanent in the socio-linguistic practice of promising and is displayed in the normative attitudes exhibited by speakers towards one another in making and evaluating their promises. This seems to show that what creates and sustains the normative force of language is the *responsiveness* of linguistic agents, the fact that they hold each other responsible for the implications of their linguistic acts. This is what creates a tight link between certain words and certain normative expectations in speakers and hearers. Thanks to this sustained responsiveness, promising, like any other illocutionary act, is something that becomes normatively laden; and one of the norms that have been built into it is the sincerity condition.[10] That is why the statement 'I promise to do X but I do not have the slightest intention to do X' contains a performative contradiction, although it does not seem to be (on the surface, at least) logically contradictory.

There are all kinds of different conditions that have to be met for a speech act to be felicitous. And corresponding to these *felicity conditions*, there are indeed all kinds of ways in which an illocutionary act can go wrong. Some of these conditions have to do with the speaker, others with the audience and still others with facts about their surrounding context, present, past and future. For example, a promise is not made felicitously if the speaker is in no position to procure the thing being promised – a fact about the speaker that makes the promise unfeasible and taints the illocutionary act; a bet is not performed felicitously if no one takes it up – here we have the violation of a felicity condition that requires an appropriate response from the audience; and a couple does not enter into a marital relationship by saying 'I do' if the person who pronounces them a married couple has not been invested with the authority to perform a marriage ceremony – which involves the violation of a felicity condition that requires an antecedent social fact (namely, being socially invested with certain powers and functions). Felicitous illocutionary acts are a complicated business: they have to be preceded and followed by certain facts and conditions; and it is also required that they be uttered by the appropriate speaker in front of the right audience, in the right circumstances, following the proper procedure, etc.

Austin does not get tired of stressing the unlimited number of ways in which a speech act can go wrong, derail, be thwarted or simply fall short of felicity. I will not try to list all the different cases he mentions, but it is important to recognize some extreme cases of performative failure, which seem to constitute a special category. The problem with these cases of radical failure is not simply that they lack felicity; rather, they seem to be beyond felicity and infelicity altogether because the conditions for performative success or failure cannot be met and therefore the evaluation of the act as a performative attempt to do something with language, on a par with other attempts of this kind, is not appropriate. Unlike normal infelicities, these failures have a different normative standing; they are normative deviations of a more radical kind. Although Austin also calls these radical performative failures infelicities, he recognizes that there is something unusual about them and reserves a special name for them: 'We shall call in general those infelicities [. . .] which are such that the act [. . .] is not achieved, by the name of MIS-FIRES' (1975, p. 16). The attempt to do something with words can be carried out felicitously or infelicitously, but it can also fail completely, without producing any illocutionary act at all. In this case we have a misfire: the act that we purport to perform does not come off; it becomes 'void, without effect' (1979, p. 238). This is what happens 'if, for example, we do not carry through the procedure –

whatever it may be – correctly and completely' (ibid.). For example, a marriage is not performed at all by the marrying parties saying 'I do', if after their utterance the priest or city official drops dead without finalizing the ceremony. Another case of misfire occurs when the performative procedure used has no backing, for performative success requires that 'the convention invoked must exist and be accepted' (p. 237). Austin gives the following example: one does not divorce one's spouse simply by saying 'I divorce you' because uttering this sentence does not constitute an accepted procedure for performing such an act.

In order to draw a sharp categorical distinction between misfires and normal infelicities, Searle (1965, 1969) differentiates between two different kinds of speech-act rules: *constitutive* rules and *regulative* rules. Constitutive rules are preconditions or prerequisites that make the act what it is and are, therefore, absolutely necessary conditions without which the act would not obtain; in other words, they are conditions *sine qua non* for the performative production of an illocutionary act. On the other hand, regulative rules are felicity conditions properly so called, that is, norms for assessing felicity which enable us to measure the degree of performative success once the illocutionary act has been achieved. Searle's distinction between constitutive and regulative rules is designed to explain and ground the distinction between misfires and normal infelicities: whereas a violation of a constitutive rule aborts the purported speech act, the violation of a regulative rule results simply in infelicity, that is, in the defective character of the act achieved. This distinction presupposes that we can sharply distinguish between what is constitutive of an act and what is simply desirable and optimal in that act. But can we?

It appears that illocutionary acts can be performed felicitously, infelicitously and not at all; but there are special cases that are hard to classify. To use an example from Lycan (2000), if I say 'I apologize' in a deliberately unrepentant, jeering, sneering tone, 'is that a grievously infelicitous apology, or no apology at all?' (p. 177). Austin recognized an intermediate set of cases between misfires and normal infelicities that troubles any sharp distinction between constitutive and regulative rules. A special kind of infelicity occurs when the illocutionary act is accomplished but it turns out to be a pure sham or fraud, a charade. Here we have cases of performative deception, distortion or perversion. These radical cases of infelicity in which the act is nonetheless achieved (in some sense) Austin calls 'ABUSES'

(1975, p. 16; see also 1979, p. 239). I am abusing a performative procedure if, for example, I use the greeting 'I welcome you' when you enter my home, 'but then I proceed to treat you as though you were exceedingly unwelcome' (1979, p. 239). In the case of an abuse we do have a performative procedure that is being used yielding a particular result; however, the performative procedure is perverted in a radical way because instead of being used in the usual accepted way it has been abused or used fraudulently, as part of a swindle or charade. Austin also offers this more famous and more problematic example: imagine that in the christening of a ship 'some low type comes up, snatches the bottle [. . .], breaks it on the stem, shouts out "I name this ship the *Generalissimo Stalin*", and then for good measure kicks away the chocks' (pp. 239–40). Austin remarks that we would all agree that the ship has not been properly named *Generalissimo Stalin*, but 'we may not agree as to how we should classify the particular infelicity in this case' (p. 140). Is it an abuse or a misfire? Some may regard this case as an infelicitous christening; others may not view it as a christening at all.

Things are complicated further by the fact that abuses often go unnoticed. Abuses are not always so transparently performed as in Austin's example. There are cases of abuse in which the lack of felicity may be quite opaque and hard to detect. Think, for example, of the case of bigamy: after many years of 'marriage', a 'married' person may discover that his/her partner was already married and therefore unable to enter into another marriage. Or (perhaps less realistically) a happily 'married' couple may discover that the person who performed the marriage ceremony was an impostor posing as a priest or a city official, without genuine authority to celebrate the marriage. There are all kinds of violation of performative procedures that are hard to detect and often remain undetected. So even if we agree that these violations should render the act void, the act may nonetheless be *taken as valid*, although wrongly; and in being socially accepted, the act already acquires a social reality and it can yield real-life consequences that may be hard to erase. This shows that the question of annulling or declaring void a previously accepted illocutionary act that has already produced social consequences is not as easy and straightforward as it may seem. Once an abuse is publicly recognized, it is not at all clear that the only appropriate response is the complete annulment of the corresponding act; nor is it clear how we go about annulling an act and erasing its consequences. For example, in the legal arena, the courts could very well decide that one or both partners in an infelicitous marriage of the sort I just described may retain some (perhaps even all) the legal benefits of marriage; in some cases, they may even maintain the marital status; and even if the marriage is annulled and declared void, their relationship may nonetheless obtain some recognition under the law (especially if they have not been responsible for the abuse at all).

A more complex but more interesting case, which I have analysed elsewhere,[11] is the case of the different instances of same-sex marriage ceremonies that took place in the US in 2004. Some of them explicitly defied written laws (although at the same time complying with other laws, constitutional laws, claimed to be higher, as was the case in San Francisco), but others did not. In Massachusetts same-sex marriage ceremonies took place after being legalized by the legislature (which was forced to do so by the State Supreme Court), although their validity will surely be challenged in the future. There is certainly room for different normative attitudes in the assessment of these cases: some people deem these same-sex marriage ceremonies misfires, others abuses, others infelicitous acts of a regular kind and yet others felicitous acts that are simply adventurous and pioneer in their novel kind of felicity. But no matter how strongly we may feel about these cases, it is clear that the relevant legal, social and political practices are flexible enough to allow for disagreements and reasonable disputes, leaving different courses of action open to us. Without disregarding the constraints that emerge from established practices, social institutions and historical traditions, it is important to recognize that, within some limits, it is ultimately up to us how we carve the normative space that separates felicities from infelicities, abuses and misfires. The normative distinctions between felicity, infelicity and radical performative failures appear to be fixed, absolute and incontestable only when there is a background agreement about the norms of conduct which is taken for granted by (or simply forced upon) all the members of the linguistic practice. This apparently unquestionable normative order becomes unstable and sometimes even breaks down when there is no background consensus, or when this consensus is called into question. It is important to note the enormous normative weight that the consensus of a society carries in setting the norms of correct performance; but we need to ask how this consensus can be modified, amended and pluralized so as to make the regulations of our linguistic practices more flexible and less oppressive. We will discuss the normative relations between the social and individual aspects of linguistic performance in later chapters (see esp. Chapters 5 and 6).

1.3 KNOTTY PERFORMANCES: LOCUTIONARY CONTENTS, ILLOCUTIONARY FORCES AND PERLOCUTIONARY EFFECTS

How do we distinguish illocutionary acts from locutionary acts, performatives from constatives? Austin's pivotal distinction for the development of his theory of speech acts proved to be hopelessly elusive. All the grammatical criteria he considered failed to draw a sharp distinction between constatives and performatives. To begin with, he remarked that it seems to be the mark of a performative utterance that its verb appears in the first person singular present indicative: 'I *promise* that I will pay you back'. In fact, there seems to be an asymmetry between this verbal tense and the rest: while 'I promise' (uttered in the right circumstances) is an illocutionary act, 'I promised', 'He promises', 'They will promise', etc., are descriptions (not performances) of illocutionary acts. And this asymmetry is not accidental, for only the subject invested with the proper authority and in the present – that is, at the moment of the utterance – can accomplish the act in question by his/her very utterance; such an accomplishment performed by others or at other times can be descriptively recreated but not re-enacted by the speaker. For example, no one can *make* a promise for you; nor can anyone (including yourself) reach into the past or into the future to *make* a promise; indeed one can describe or predict such acts of promising, but the acts themselves have to be performed by the promising subjects. However, Austin is quick to point out that although this grammatical characterization does apply to a broad class of performative utterances, it leaves out another important class: 'There is at least one other standard form, every bit as common as this one, where the verb is in the passive voice and in the second or third person, not in the first' (1979, p. 242). Examples of this second grammatical class of performatives are 'Passengers are warned not to do so-and-so' and 'You are authorized to do so-and-so'. But, as Austin himself emphasizes, there are still many other performatives that are left out of these two standard grammatical groups. Moods other than the indicative are used to carry out linguistic actions: imperatives are used to issue orders, and interrogatives to ask questions. Clearly 'Shut the door' is as much an order as 'I order you to shut the door'. It is only that in the case of the imperative we have a performative utterance without a performative verb that makes explicit the kind of illocutionary act that the utterance accomplishes. But the attempt to find a grammatical characterization of performative utterances collapses completely when we realize that even the most typical grammatical form of constatives (with the verb in the indicative mood and in the third person) can be used for performatives. For, as Austin points out, a constative can become a performative under the right circumstances: for example, 'This bull is dangerous' can be a warning written in a notice for the public; and we can also find more laconic forms of this warning such as 'Dangerous Bull' or simply 'Bull'.

Austin concluded that there is no set of grammatical features that define performative utterances and can distinguish them from constatives. But he proposed a test that seems to mark off performatives from constatives: the so-called '*hereby* criterion'. According to this criterion, a statement is a performative if we can interpolate 'hereby' before the main verb. This criterion works well for the two standard grammatical forms that Austin discusses: 'I *hereby* promise to pay you back', 'Passengers are *hereby* warned that they should not do so-and-so', 'You are *hereby* authorized to do so-and-so'. On the other hand, constatives do not pass the test at all. As Lycan (2000) puts it, '"The cat is hereby on the mat" is nonsensical or at least false, because the cat is (or is not) on the mat regardless of my saying that it is. My saying it does nothing to make it so' (p. 178). But what about the warning 'Dangerous bull'? And what about the imperative 'Shut the door'? These *shortened* or *implicit* performatives do not seem to pass the test. But it has been argued that the 'hereby' should be interpolated before the performative verb that makes explicit the kind of speech act that they perform, that is, that the test should be applied to the *lengthened* and *explicit* versions of performative utterances. Thus 'Shut the door' can be classified as a performative because it is equivalent to 'I [hereby] order you to shut the door' where 'hereby' can be appropriately inserted; and similarly, a sign saying 'Dangerous bull' passes the test because it is equivalent to 'You are [hereby] warned that this bull is dangerous'. This way of applying the 'hereby' criterion can also make sense of harder cases such as cryptic one-word performative utterances. For example, 'Hooray!',

'Shame!' and 'Damn!' can arguably be analysed into, respectively, 'I [hereby] cheer', 'I [hereby] castigate you' and 'I [hereby] curse'. But with the requirement that the test be applied to the lengthened and explicit version of the performative utterance in question, the test seems to become useless because all utterances can pass it, *including constatives*!: 'I *hereby* state that the cat is on the mat'. But there is something to be learned from this expansion of the test: all utterances *are* in fact performative, or at least contain a performative element; for every time we use language, we *do* something with it, we perform a linguistic action. For example, when I make an assertion, I perform an act of asserting.

We can do all kinds of things with language with or without saying what we are doing (e.g. cheering, castigating, cursing, etc.). There are two ways in which we can carry out an illocutionary act, *implicitly* or *explicitly*. The performative utterances with which Austin began his discussion constitute a special (particularly sophisticated) class of performatives, namely, those that contain a performative preface in which a verb makes explicit the speech act that is being performed. But speech acts are constantly being performed without such fanfare. Austin uses this important distinction between implicit and explicit performatives to show that constatives actually constitute a particular kind of performative utterances, whose performative character is also codified and made explicit by performative verbs: 'I state that . . .', 'I assert that . . .', 'I judge that . . .', 'I report that . . .', etc. And just as constatives eventually turn out to be a subclass of performatives, their truth conditions turn out to be a subclass of felicity conditions. On this view, truth is a kind of felicity, a subcategory within it that has fascinated philosophers because of the special metaphysical and epistemic features that it seems to have. On Austin's view, an assertion, like every locution, is an illocution, that is, a linguistic act that can go well or be thwarted, being felicitous or infelicitous, successful or unsuccessful, depending on whether or not it accomplishes what it sets out to do. And what an assertion sets out to do is to describe a state of affairs, to offer a representation of the world; and this communicative goal can be accomplished well or badly, or not at all (if there is a representational abuse or misfire).

But how do we know in any given case what a speech act sets out to do? How do we know its force and communicative function? 'If I get tired I'll go home.' Is that a threat or a promise? 'The kitchen should be cleaned up.' Is that an order, an insinuation or just an observation? In some cases we just don't know with certainty and precision what the speech act is trying to accomplish, and the illocutionary force of the utterance remains vague and interpretable in various ways;[12] in other cases it is made sufficiently clear by the context what kind of illocutionary act is being performed (e.g. the authority of the speaker or the presence of penalties can make clear that something is an order rather than a mere suggestion); and yet in other cases, the illocutionary force is explicitly marked in the utterance itself by a performative verb. The function of explicit performative verbs is precisely to specify the communicative point of the utterance and to make clear 'how far it commits me and in what way, and so forth' (Austin 1979, p. 245). Which illocutionary forces are explicitly codified in language and which ones remain implicit depends on social needs and values. In some cases it is considered advantageous and appropriate to mark overtly and unequivocally the linguistic action being performed, while in other cases this is deemed counterproductive or inappropriate – a deception is not achieved by declaring 'I hereby deceive you'; nor is an insult accomplished with the formula 'I insult you'.[13] As Austin remarks, this is 'one way in which language develops in tune with the society of which it is the language' (ibid.).

So, in the end, performatives do not constitute a distinctive class of utterances at all; all utterances are performative utterances! And thus Austin's original distinction between performatives and constatives turns out to be a distinction, not between different kinds of utterance, but rather, between two different components present in every utterance:[14] *illocutionary force* and *locutionary content*. Just as every speech act (including constatives) has a particular force, we can also say that every speech act has a particular content, even if this content is not contained (or explicitly expressed) in the utterance itself, but is simply implied by it.[15] Rather than winding up with semantic relativism or subjectivism, Austin's critique of 'the true–false fetish' lead us to conclude that *objective validity* is a crucial dimension of performative utterances, a dimension that is part and parcel of performative felicity. As Austin puts it, performative utterances typically exhibit 'a general dimension of correspondence with fact' (p. 250); and this means that their felicity conditions typically include truth conditions.

Thus Austin concludes his famous essay 'Performative utterances' emphasizing these two components of language, force and content, which are present (virtually) in every utterance. He proposes a two-factor account of language as an alternative to traditional uni-dimensional accounts that focused exclusively on content. But things get much more complicated. To begin with, Austin introduces a third element or aspect of language: *the perlocutionary*. A perlocution is what is achieved *through* the locution or linguistic act, but *not in* it. A perlocutionary act is not guaranteed by the utterance itself, but is rather produced by its reception, by what is done with it. Perlocutionary acts are, therefore, essentially effects, results, conse-quences of speech acts. For example, convincing, scaring and upset-ting are perlocutionary effects of utterances. I may be able to achieve these effects through my speech acts, but they are in no way guaran-teed by the acts themselves – they are not achieved in them – for they are an outcome that depends on the reception of the audience, that is, on the reaction of the interlocutor(s): whether you are convinced, scared or upset depends on you, on how you receive and are affected by the utterance. Accordingly, it is not appropriate to say 'I hereby convince you that so-and-so', 'I hereby scare you' or 'I hereby upset you'. Other perlocutionary acts are alarming, amazing, amusing, annoying, boring, frightening, etc. Thus the study of speech acts has to be further complicated to include a third component: to the illo-cutionary force and the locutionary content of utterances we have to add their perlocutionary effect. Some suggested a conservative solution to this Austinian complication of the study of language, namely: to confine semantics to the study of locutionary contents, as traditionally done, and to develop a new discipline to study illo-cutionary forces and perlocutionary effects. According to this con-servative suggestion, instead of restructuring the goals and methods of semantic theory, we should keep doing semantics in the same way as before but with the supplementation of a substantial addition: *pragmatics*, which is put in charge of the illocutionary and perlocu-tionary. It has been suggested that what is needed is the following *division of labour* betwen semantics and pragmatics: the former would elucidate how things are depicted by our utterances, and the latter would take care of the things – the acts – achieved in and through them. As a conclusion to this chapter, I will try to show that this neat division of labour does not work and that a sharp separa-tion between semantics and pragmatics is ultimately untenable. My argument will provide a bridge to the next chapter which will continue the discussion of the complex relations between semantics and pragmatics through an elucidation of the debates between theories of sense and reference.

Both illocutionary force and perlocutionary effects can affect the semantic content of utterances. Meaning cannot be simply reduced to locutionary content without further ado. I will try to show that the content, force and effect of speech acts interact in complex ways: they are not isolated and autonomously packaged ingredients of utterances that can be analysed independently of one another. If I succeed in showing this, it will follow that semantic theory cannot have the luxury of analysing the contents of utterances in a way that completely disregards their illocutionary forces and perlocutionary effects (for example, in terms of their truth conditions, or in terms of their justification or verification conditions).[16] In the first place, the illocutionary force of an utterance makes a semantic contribution to the content of a statement: you don't understand the statement, at least not completely, if you don't know whether it is a suggestion, a mere observation, a warning, an order, a threat, etc. If you don't understand distinctions of force in a language, the linguistic competence you have achieved so far is still deficient and your capacity to process meanings in that language will be limited. So illocutionary force seems to be *a kind of meaning*, perhaps not independent of, but distinct from and not easily reducible to locutionary or propositional meaning. But what exactly is the semantic significance of the illocutionary force of utterances?

Some have denied that there is any genuinely *semantic* difference between 'p', on the one hand, and 'I state that p', 'I recommend that p', 'I order that p', etc., on the other. Defenders of this view claim that the performative prefaces of explicit performatives are *force labels* that make no semantic difference, arguing that force and content are independent variables that operate autonomously from one another. According to this view, there is only a difference of style between implicit and explicit performatives: explicit performatives are just formal, inflated and verbose equivalents of the simpler statements. Since there is only a stylistic difference, it is argued, we should conclude that the performative prefaces add no content whatsoever; they simply make explicit something that is already there, said or unsaid. However, this analysis of force and its explicit formulation has become implausible and unsatisfactory, for it has proven to be increasingly difficult to deny that linguistic expressions of force can make semantic contributions to the meaning of utterances. One of the recalcitrant linguistic phenomena that this view fails to explain is the problem of adverbial modifiers: there is indeed a semantic difference between 'I willingly admit that so-and-so' and 'I reluctantly admit that so-and-so'. Moreover, performative prefaces can be richly structured and contain long adverbial clauses which seem to be full of content: e.g. 'Mindful of the penalties for those who withhold information in a court of law, I state that . . .'; or 'Considering the possible repercussions of my words for your wellbeing, I have to inform you that. . .'.

Many philosophers and linguists have recognized the semantic significance of illocutionary force, but the semantic contribution of the illocutionary aspects of an utterance has proved to be difficult to explain in a satisfactory way. One possibility is to treat performative utterances as oblique contexts (in some ways similar to indirect speech) with embedded statements. According to this view, it is the illocutionary meaning that dominates the embedded locutionary meaning, as suggested by the grammatical structure of explicit performatives in which an embedded statement is subordinated to the performative preface. In this way the locutionary or propositional content is presented as protected – sheltered and filtered – by the illocutionary meaning expressed in the performative preface. The central flaw of this analysis is revealed by the problem of the impossibility of perjury: after saying 'I state that I did not do it' in a trial and being proved to have lied, the witness can always say 'But what I said was true: I did state that I did not do it; the fact that I did do it is irrelevant'. But of course one cannot evade a perjury charge so easily – the normative weight of our words goes deeper. The perjury problem is indicative of a more general problem that appears when the embedded propositional content of a performative utterance is neutralized by its illocutionary force, for this makes speech acts self-justifying and at the same time normatively thin or even empty, making it possible to escape discursive commitments of all sorts. This was recognized by Cohen (1964). The so-called Cohen's problem emphasizes how hard it is to formulate the truth conditions of explicit performatives so that the commitment to the truth conditions of the subordinate clause is preserved. No consensus on a satisfactory treatment of this problem has yet been reached in the literature.[17]

There is an alternative approach to illocutionary force that results in a semantic view that falls entirely outside the Austinian framework of Speech Act Theory. On this approach, the illocutionary ingredient and the locutionary or propositional ingredient are treated as coordinated elements of an utterance, rather than the latter being conceived as subordinated to the former. That the relation between the illocutionary and the locutionary aspects of an utterance is one of coordination or conjunction, instead of subordination, means that in explicit performatives speakers engage in two distinct semantic activities: saying something and describing themselves as performing that linguistic act of saying. On this view, an explicit performative can be semantically analysed into a double act with a double set of commitments. Utterers of explicit performatives do two things simultaneously: they commit themselves to the propositional content of the saying and they commit themselves to their own description of the saying. In this vein, Cresswell (1973) and Bach and Harnish (1979) argued, *pace* Austin's insistent denial, that performative verbs are descriptive and that they are used by speakers not only to perform linguistic actions but also to describe themselves as performing them. The problem with this view is that it involves an assimilation of the performative dimension of language to its descriptive dimension; and thus it falls back into descriptivism and its 'true–false fetish', explaining the performative element of an utterance in truth-conditional terms. But isn't, say, baptizing someone or something more than simply saying that you do so? Isn't marrying someone (genuinely) more than simply describing a performance (accurately)? Don't these linguistic acts involve producing things with language, instead of simply describing those things as if they were states of affairs that may or may not obtain independently of the utterances that describe them?

It has become increasingly clear that a theory of meaning must provide an account of the semantic significance of the illocutionary aspects of language, and yet no fully satisfactory account has been developed either within Speech Act Theory or outside it (e.g. in Truth-Conditional Semantics, Verificationism or Assertibilism). Moreover, a theory of meaning must not only take into account the illocutionary force of utterances, but must also pay attention to their perlocutionary effects. The perlocutionary dimension of language also has semantic significance. The effects of an utterance on its audience or receptors can also affect its meaning. This semantic relation between an utterance and its effects can be established in various ways: sometimes it is produced *ad hoc* in the very context of the utterance, without relying on established usage or coined connotations; other times it depends on a *history of use*, that is, on the consolidation of semantic associations through a long chain of similar speech acts with similar effects. These are semantic *implications* of a special kind. Grice (1957, 1968, 1969, 1975) termed the former kind of implied meaning *'conversational implicature'* and the latter kind *'conventional implicature'*. I now turn to these two kinds of conveyed meanings and invited inferences in order to complete this preliminary elucidation of the different areas in the field of semantics. As Grice did, I will spend more time on the richer phenomenon of conversational implicature in which connoted meanings are created *in situ* by speakers, in contrast with conventional implicature which is a matter of coined connotations (e.g. the contrastive connotation of 'but'). It is not surprising that Grice's semantic theory is particularly helpful here since it revolves entirely around the perlocutionary dimension of language, that is, around the reception of speech acts and its impact on the hearers. Gricean semantics remains the most elaborate account of the semantic significance of perlocutionary effects on the audience.

The great insight behind Gricean semantics is that in ordinary conversational exchanges there is much more to the meaning of an utterance than what appears on the grammatical and logical surface: utterances often convey things other than what they literally mean and they often imply things other than what they strictly entail (from a logical point of view). For example, if someone says 'There's the door' in the context of a heated dispute, and even more pointedly as a reply to the interlocutor's threat that he might quit the conversation, the speaker is clearly suggesting that the hearer can leave the room if he/she so wishes. The utterance is not properly understood if it is taken literally by the hearer as a mere indication of the location of the exit and entrance to the room. The conveyed meaning of this utterance is that the interlocutor can abandon the conversation and part company any time he/she wants. The adequate understanding of this meaning requires the processing of what has been termed 'an invited inference'.[18] But why should we interpret the utterance as conveying a meaning that is not explicitly expressed, as suggesting the possibility of departure to the interlocutor? Grice's answer is that, taken literally and without any added suggested meaning, the utterance would make little sense: it would make no contribution to the conversation whatsoever and, therefore, it would be of no value. The speaker must know that indicating the location of the door provides no new or relevant information; and, therefore, he/she must mean something else, he/she must be trying to convey something different with his/her utterance: that is, he/she must be inviting us to draw an inference that will lead us to a different semantic content. We wonder 'Why is the speaker indicating where the door is at this point?'; and a plausible interpretation is that his/her indication may be a way of reminding us of the possible use of the door, perhaps even a way of encouraging its use. So what happens in our example is that we rule out the literal interpretation of the statement 'There's the door' in the context of a dispute (which does not concern the door at all) because it violates the maxims that typically regulate our communicative exchanges, in particular, the so-called *Maxim of Relevance*: 'Say things that are to the point'; or 'Speak so as to advance the conversation'.

The Maxim of Relevance is one of the most useful rules for conversational exchanges and one of the most often used in the studies of Gricean pragmatics. But there are other conversational maxims that Grice specified and used in his analyses. Here are some formulations of those maxims (from Grice 1975, p. 159): 'Make your contribution to the conversation as informative as possible, but not more informative or less informative than is required' (Maxims of Quantity); 'Do not say what you believe to be false', and 'Do not say that for which you lack adequate evidence' (Maxims of Quality); 'Avoid obscurity', 'Avoid ambiguity', 'Be brief', 'Be orderly' (Maxims of Manner). According to Grice, all these different maxims are corollaries of the most fundamental principle of communication that governs all conversation. This is what he called the *Cooperative Principle*, which reads as follows: 'Make your conversational contribution such as is required, at the stage at which it occurs, by the accepted purpose or direction of the talk-exchange in which you are engaged' (1975, pp. 158–9).

The central premise of the Gricean approach is that the communicative intentions of a normal speaker under normal circumstances conform to the Cooperative Principle and the conversational maxims that derive from it. According to Gricean semantics, the speakers' conversational contributions are governed first and foremost by these general rules for cooperative communication, rather than by the semantic conventions that fix word-meanings and sentence-meanings.[19] On this view, the intended meanings of speakers can depart – sometimes even wildly (e.g. in ironic utterances) – from the conventional meanings available in the linguistic tradition. Grice's analyses of intended meanings puts a lot of weight on the speaker's communicative intentions, undermining the traditional emphasis on linguistic conventions, which on his view become mere tools to be used and bent in all kinds of ways. This way of privileging intended meanings produced *ad hoc* over previously established semantic conventions gave rise to the opposition between *speaker's meaning* and *conventional meaning*, to which we will return in Chapter 5 (see 5.1). But how do interlocutors know when the speaker's intended meaning conforms to the conventional meanings of the words he/she is using, and when his/her main communicative intent is to convey something different? Grice identified the most common way in which a departure from conventional meanings can be detected and processed. This is what he called '*flouting*': a blatant violation of a conversational maxim, a violation that is done deliberately and openly. This kind of patent violation of conversational maxims is essential for the production of the implicatures that are – arguably – behind linguistic phenomena such as sarcasm and humour and behind figures of speech such as metaphor.[20] In ordinary contexts flouting is the most common mechanism that triggers the process of figuring out conversational implicatures. The example examined above ('There's the door') was an instance of flouting: it was the Maxim of Relevance that was flouted. Consider the following example in which a conversational implicature is produced by flouting the Maxim of Quantity. Imagine that someone asks me, a philosophy professor, 'Is Peter a promising graduate student? Are his essays good?'; and I reply, 'His spelling and grammar are impeccable'; or perhaps 'He has beautiful handwriting'. What the sentence I utter literally means according to standard semantic conventions may or may not be true, but that is immaterial; for the most important message I am trying to convey goes beyond the conventional meanings of the words I use. I am trying to imply that my assessment of Peter's philosophical competence is very poor: indeed, if a remark about Peter's spelling, grammar or handwriting is all (or the best) I can say about his intellectual skills, his philosophical capacities must be extremely deficient![21] I could have added 'That's all I can say', or 'That's the best compliment I can give him', in order to mark more clearly my intended meaning and to make perspicuous the kind of inference I am inviting my interlocutor to make. But often this kind of clarification or explicit marking is not necessary.

One of the central features of conversational implicatures is that they are *cancellable*, that is, they can be voided by the speaker if he/she so wishes. For example, the implicature about Peter's philosophical skills could be cancelled by adding, 'Don't get me wrong. He may be a very good philosopher too. I just don't have sufficient evidence yet to judge one way or the other'. In this way an otherwise reasonable suggested inference can be forestalled by the speaker. A second crucial feature of conversational implicatures is that they are supposed to be *computable* or *workable*, that is, they must be graspable by normal speakers in normal circumstances from their basic knowledge about communication and their shared background. According to Grice, our capacity to understand the intended meanings of speakers depends more heavily and more directly on our general linguistic competence than on our mastery of linguistic conventions.[22] This means that a pragmatic account of how conversational implicatures are computed or processed requires an account of what it means to be a competent participant in conversation. But it is important to note that the alleged feature of conversational implicatures in question is that they are *in principle* computable from conversational maxims; and this does not mean that *all* competent speakers will be able to understand *all* suggested or invited inferences. Of course not all conversational implicatures are as easily workable as the ones I have used to illustrate the Gricean approach. It is not uncommon to find hearers who are at a loss in deducing the speaker's meaning and must ask for help to work out the implicature. If a conversational maxim is flouted and we are not capable of repairing the patent violation on our own, we can solicit help from the speaker to identify his/her communicative intention by asking 'What do you mean?' or 'Why do you say that?' But in many cases of flouting (especially those carefully drafted by deft speakers) the patent violation is easily repairable and explicit cooperative repair work is not needed.

Grice's idea was that the Cooperative Principle and all the different conversational maxims that derive from it constitute an axiomatic system through which conversational implicatures can be worked out. This axiomatic system is supposed to capture the linguistic competence of ordinary speakers – their capacity to participate in conversation – by formulating the tacit principles that are implicit in people's minds and operate unconsciously in the cognitive processes that accompany the production and reception of speech acts. In this way the second feature of conversational implicatures, their computability, is unpacked. The two central complaints that have been raised against Gricean semantics concern precisely this second feature and the kind of axiomatic system that Grice proposes to explain it. In the first place, a criticism that has been repeatedly formulated is that the Gricean account of the processing or working out of conversational implicatures is implausible because of its enormous *complexity*. Critics have argued that we should be suspicious of the vast amount of complex reasoning posited by Grice's theory which is supposed to take place almost instantaneously. Those who defend the Gricean approach have replied that, as Lycan (2000) for example puts it, 'in many walks of life we do a great deal of reasoning very quickly and subconsciously' (p. 194); and perhaps this is one of those apparently simple cognitive capacities that turn out to be incredibly complex when they are formulated explicitly. The critics of Gricean semantics, however, are not satisfied with the intricate cognitive architecture that needs to be postulated and claim that it results in an unacceptable overintellectualization of linguistic competence.

In the second place, it has also been argued that the Gricean account of the processing or working out of conversational implicatures is *underdescribed*, that it is ultimately inadequate because of its *lack of specificity*: we are given an intricate and open-ended list or template of conversational maxims, we are offered little guidance for its application and we are wished good luck in identifying the relevant maxim for any given case. According to the Gricean account, the processing of a conversational implicature involves two stages: a first negative stage in which the hearer detects that the speaker's meaning diverges from conventional meaning ('The speaker couldn't possibly mean *that*'); and a subsequent positive stage in which the hearer tries to unravel the speaker's hidden reasoning and thus to identify his/her intended meaning ('She must be thinking this-or-that and trying to hint at this-or-that'). Sperber and Wilson (1986) and Davis (1998) have objected that Grice gives us very little help with the positive stage of this process: his maxims enable us to recognize that something is up, but it remains a mystery how exactly we are able to work out what that something – that insinuated content – is. The specific meanings produced by conversational implicatures are harder to figure out than it may seem. Davis (1998) contends that the importance of this problem is often underestimated and even entirely missed because in the examples discussed in the literature we *already know* what would normally be implicated by the utterance in question and, therefore, we don't see the need to ask how the positive calculation that leads us to the implicated meaning is worked out. Davis complains that we are being asked to presuppose too much and that, being heavily dependent on tacit knowledge, this approach becomes question-begging – presupposing rather than explaining already acquired linguistic skills and semantic knowledge.[23] But this may be a genuine problem only for those who are in search of radical presuppositionless explanations that start from scratch, instead of a less ambitious kind of pragmatic explanation that starts *in media res*.

Whatever we want to make of these problems, the unexplained complexity of conversational implicature as a semantic phenomenon is undeniable: it is certainly true that implicature is an obscure and complicated business with the deceiving air of familiarity and transparency, which results from the fact that it is an extremely common phenomenon in the production and reception of situated meanings in communicative exchanges. It is often unclear how we can go about representing the inference that enables us to understand an implicature, and yet this is grasped immediately and effortlessly by most speakers. And this does not happen only with exceptional cases. Sometimes we are at a loss to explain even the most common implicatures, not being clear even whether a maxim has been flouted (let alone which one). Take, for example, the conveyed or suggested meanings often associated with 'and'. Many conjunctions are read in a causal way: 'Mary heard the joke and laughed'. In most conversational contexts we would interpret this sentence as saying that Mary laughed *at* the joke, that is, that her laughter was provoked by what was said: we would understand that she laughed *because* of the joke and not for some other reason, even though no causal connection between the two events (but only their occurrence) has been explicitly stated. Other conjunctions connote a temporal order, although the temporal sequence is not logically entailed by the conjunction. Consider the sentence 'John and Mary fell in love and they got married'. In most conversational contexts, upon hearing this sentence, we would think that falling in love and getting married are not simply two things that happened to John and Mary in whatever order, but that they happened one after the other (perhaps even in a causal order as well, one because of the other). It could be argued that the implicature in this case is produced by our social conventions, for there is a social expectation that things normally happen in that order: nowadays, in most of the Western world, people typically get married *after* they fall in love (or are expected to do so). But consider the sentence 'John and Mary got married and they fell in love'. In most contexts we would still read a temporal order into the conjunction and one that corresponds with the word order, although in this case our interpretation is not supported by the standard social expectation but actually violates it.

It remains a mystery why it is so natural for us to understand conjunctions in temporal and causal ways.[24] Other things being equal, speakers assume that the grammatical order mirrors the causal and temporal orders. And indeed, why would speakers choose an order for their sentences that runs contrary (or is somehow at odds with) the causal and temporal orders of the events their sentences depict? Perhaps, for this reason, every choice of sentence order is tacitly understood as a tendentious choice which means something; perhaps the selected order acquires connotations by contrast with other possible orders that could have been chosen. In this sense, the implicatures concerning sentence order may be like the implicatures produced by word choice. Take, for example, the choice of the connective 'but' as opposed to 'and': 'but' performs the same function as 'and' except for carrying a contrastive connotation; so if someone says 'He is in the military, but he is smart', the conventionally implicated meaning is that there is an opposition between the things conjoined by 'but', being in the military and being smart. So perhaps the causal and temporal connotations of 'and' are *conventional implicatures* like the contrastive connotation of 'but'. Perhaps, the suggestion goes, these causal and temporal connotations have been built into the very meaning of 'and'; perhaps we are dealing with implicatures that have been conventionalized by continually reading conjunctions causally and temporally over time. If and when an implicature is conventionalized, we do not need to go through an inference to create the implicated meaning anew in each conversational context. There is no need for the inferential computation of conventional implicatures because they have become encoded, that is, they have been written into the semantic conventions that govern the meaning of a term or expression. We don't have to postulate any tacit reasoning in this case because conventional implicatures don't need to be worked out from contextual clues, unlike conversational implicatures. And this is the first crucial feature of *conventional* implicatures: they do *not* have to be *computable* or *workable contextually*.

However, the causal and temporal connotations of 'and' do not seem to exhibit the second crucial feature of conventional implicatures, namely, that they are *non-cancellable*. After saying 'He is in the military, but he is smart', you don't undo the implicated opposition simply by adding 'But I don't mean to say that military men are not smart'. Similarly with the so-called 'illocutionary implicatures' that derive from the conventions governing the illocutionary force of speech acts. Since the performance of a speech act (e.g. promising) implies the satisfaction of its felicity conditions (e.g. having the appropriate intention), these conditions are conventionally implicated in the utterance that accomplishes the linguistic action (e.g. my promise implicates that I have the intention to do what I promise). Illocutionary implicatures are part of the meaning of the performative verbs that codifies the illocutionary force of the corresponding speech acts (e.g. part of the meaning of 'promising' is 'having the intention of carrying out the act promised'). These conventional implicatures are clearly non-cancellable: again, I cannot say without contradiction 'I promise I will pay you back, but I have no intention of doing so'. By contrast, the causal and temporal connotations of 'and' *are* cancellable. It is not uncommon to find them created and then cancelled for humour, satire or some other effect: 'Mary heard the joke and laughed, although not at the joke.'; 'John and Mary fell in love and they got married, although not in that order'. It is instructive that the implicatures involved in the causal and temporal readings of 'and' are difficult to explain and hard to classify. These problems suggest that there may not be a sharp line between conversational and conventional implicatures: there is traffic between them as well as intermediate cases.[25]

The wide range of cases of conveyed meanings underscores the fact that the field of semantics is very broad and diverse and includes many phenomena that were initially relegated to the field of pragmatics. We can now recognize that many phenomena that were initially taken to be *merely* contextual matters (such as conversational relevance), or *merely* stylistic matters (such as word choice and sentence order), actually have deep semantic significance. We are able to recognize this although we are not yet able to offer a detailed explanation of the semantic significance of these phenomena, or to identify the semantic mechanisms that operate in the pragmatic contexts of linguistic interaction.[26] The broad and diverse range of cases of conveyed meanings shows that the issues concerning semantic content are not easily separable from the pragmatic issues concerning illocutionary force and perlocutionary effect. There are also other kinds of tacit meanings quite different from Gricean implicatures that problematize the relations between semantics and pragmatics in important ways. Of particular importance in this respect is the category of *semantic presupposition.* Consider the following sentences:

(1) Peter realized that he had no money.
(2) John stopped harassing Mary.
(3) It was Grandma who ate the ice-cream.

They carry the following *semantic presuppositions*:

(1′) Peter had no money.
(2′) John was harassing Mary.
(3′) Someone ate the ice-cream.

It is interesting to note that the negations of the sentences (1), (2) and (3) also carry the same semantic presuppositions. Not all sentences and their negations carry their corresponding semantic presuppositions with the same strength.[27] But whatever their strength, semantic presuppositions are unlike conversational implicatures and like conventional implicatures in being typically non-cancellable. On the other hand, they have a more direct connection with the literal meanings of words and sentences than implicatures of either kind have; so much so that they have been traditionally assimilated to logical entailment by strong programmes in logical analysis. It remains an open question even today how semantic presuppositions are processed or worked out by speakers: from logical principles, from semantic rules or from pragmatic principles of communication? Are they a special kind of logical entailment, analytic truths about meaning derivable from definitions, or a new form of pragmatic implication? This philosophical debate was opened by Peter Strawson (1950), arguing against Bertrand Russell (1905), that the use of the definite description 'The present King of France' does not *entail* the existence of a present king, but merely *presupposes* it.

According to Russell, a statement in which the description is used –
such as 'The present King of France is bald' – tacitly contains a false
claim entailed by the referring expression – namely, that there is one
and only one person who is presently the King of France – which
makes the whole statement false. By contrast, Strawson argued that
the statement 'The present King of France is bald' is neither true nor
false, but rather it lacks truth-value entirely, because it is not even a
valid candidate for semantic evaluation, for truth and falsity; and
the same should be said, he argued, for 'The present King of France
is not bald'. Strawson insisted that sentences containing empty referential expressions are not semantically evaluable – neither true nor
false – because the conditions for their semantic evaluation have not
been met: they have presuppositions that have not been fulfilled and
you cannot say something is true or false when the presuppositions
of what you are trying to say do not obtain, just as you cannot sell
a piece of land that doesn't exist and if you try to do so, the alleged
'sale' would be neither good nor bad, fair nor unfair, but void and
therefore, strictly speaking, not a sale at all.

How should we treat the existential claims that seem to be
somehow contained in referential expressions such as definite
descriptions? How does the reference of terms and expressions – or
the lack thereof – affect the truth and falsity of the sentences in
which they figure, or even the possibility of those sentences having a
truth-value at all? These questions will be addressed in the next
chapter, where, through a discussion of reference and truth, we will
examine the semantic evaluation of words and sentences as well as
the pragmatic conditions for such evaluation. This discussion will
continue and complete the analysis of the complex and problematic
relations between semantics and pragmatics initiated in this chapter.

CHAPTER 2

MEANING, SENSE AND INTERPRETATION

2.1 TWO TRADITIONS IN PHILOSOPHY OF LANGUAGE

Different semantic traditions in Philosophy of Language have accumulated many puzzles and paradoxes over the centuries. Arguably, many of these problems have been solved or dissolved with the turn to *pragmatics* in the twentieth century, facilitated and defended by philosophers as different as Wittgenstein, Strawson, Donnellan, Grice and Habermas. In this section, after a brief discussion of the different semantic traditions that have been developed in the history of philosophy, I will elucidate some of the central problems in semantics, how they have been treated by different semantic theories and how they have been reconceptualized after the pragmatic turn. When we address semantic problems through a study of the pragmatics of communication, the central phenomenon that needs to be explained is how particular speakers interpret each other in particular contexts of communication. In the second section of this chapter I will discuss different philosophical paradigms of interpretation in analytic and Continental philosophy and the problems they raise (especially problems of semantic indeterminacy that will be the focus of the next chapter).

Charles Taylor (1985) identifies two different semantic traditions in the history of philosophy: the *designative* tradition and the *expressive* tradition. The designative tradition focuses on what terms designate or denote, that is, on word–object relations, on the representational relations between language and the world, thus privileging the referential or representational communicative function of language. As Taylor discusses, the full elaboration of the designative tradition was motivated by epistemological considerations stemming from the scientific revolution and the development of modern science. People thought that science required a systematic account of the relations between language and the world, so that natural languages could be purified of subjective biases and scientists could rely on an *objective* medium for the description and explanation of natural phenomena in the world. This designative or referential approach to language was thus informed by *objectivism*, an epistemic attitude or orientation that treats the whole of reality as an object of scientific investigation, an object to be described and scrutinized for the purpose of knowledge acquisition. In applying an objectivist, cognitivist and descriptivist stance to language and its relation to the world, the designative tradition offered an account of meaning that could eliminate the mystifications of religious and spiritualist conceptions of language; but the ultimate result of the exclusive focus on the referential and representational aspects of meaning was an incomplete and one-sided account of language.

As Taylor explains, there are two crucial philosophical movements that contributed to the development of the designative tradition in the seventeenth and eighteenth centuries: *naturalism* and *nominalism*. On the one hand, naturalists such as Condillac treated language as a natural phenomenon that could be fully explained empirically. Naturalists developed exhaustive accounts of language from its genesis to its current form. On these accounts, linguistic phenomena (including the very origin of language and, with it, the origin of humanity) were treated, not as elusive spiritual phenomena, but as empirical objects of investigation that should be investigated by using an observer's stance and the scientific method. These naturalistic accounts are the predecessors of contemporary accounts of language in biological and behavioural terms.[1] On the other hand, nominalism also played a large part in demystifying the religious conceptions of language that had been developed in medieval philosophy, and in undermining the inflated ontological picture of reality offered by those conceptions. Nominalists argued that language, and not reality itself, is the home of the universal. It was argued that the meaning of a general term is a 'nominal essence' and not a language-independent essence or universal entity corresponding to the term. Nominalists reversed the order of explanation and, rather than conceiving of the use of abstract terms as grounded in pre-existing abstractions, they contended that generalities are the product of language use, that is, of using terms with general applicability to refer to a wide range of objects or properties. It is our groupings and the powers of abstraction of our mind that were claimed to produce the universal (rather than the latter being the parameter to assess the adequacy of the former). Hence the creative power that was assigned to definitions, through which we correlate names with objects and general terms with ideas. The central goal of the no-nonsense nominalism of the seventeenth century was to demystify language. It is in this sense that we must understand Hobbes' and Locke's project of grounding our picture of the empirical world in the firm foundations of clear and unequivocal definitions. It is also in this sense that we must understand the nominalist emphasis on the liberating power of definitions. Nominalism was the centrepiece of what has been called 'the *disenchantment* of the world'.[2]

With nominalism the designative tradition strove to overcome subjective and anthropomorphic projections and to achieve greater degrees of objectivity so that language can serve as an adequate medium for the representation of objective reality. But although the accomplishments of the designative tradition and its contributions to the Philosophy of Language are indisputable, this tradition has been criticized for missing the *constitutive* aspects of language because of its narrow focus on designation. The designative tradition depicted language as a crucial instrument of knowledge, a very important representational tool, but nothing more than a tool. By contrast, the *expressive* tradition developed by Romantic philosophers in the nineteenth century emphasized that language has more than instrumental value: it has a *constitutive* value, for it constitutes who we are, how we think and how we live. On the Romantic view of the expressive tradition, language, far from being a mere tool that we use, is part of who we are: it defines our humanity and sets the parameters of the life we lead.

The central difference between the designative and the expressive tradition is the difference between two competing strategies in semantic theory: *extensionalism* and *intensionalism*. What characterizes the semantic perspective of the designative tradition is an extensional approach that identifies the meaning of a term with its *extension*, that is, with what the term is true of, with the region of the world that corresponds to it (whether it is an individual or set of individuals, a property or a set of properties). In contrast with the extensionalism of the designative tradition, the expressive tradition argues that meanings do not reside in what exists out there independently of language, but rather, in what is created or constituted by language. As an alternative to the objectivist attitude centered around denotation or extension, the expressive tradition proposes a subjectivist attitude that focuses on the connotations of terms. On this subjectivist view, the meaning of a term is given in its *intension*: the concept it expresses, not the range of entities it refers to. By focusing on intensions and the subjective aspects of language, the expressive tradition depicts language as an expression of human subjectivity, an unfolding of human perspectives. Thus the expressive tradition gives centre-stage to the expressive function of language. On the expressive view, instead of the mind being 'the mirror of nature',[3] it is actually the world out there as it appears to us – as it is depicted in language – that is a reflection of the creative activity of the human mind and its use of language. This view was elaborated by German Romantic philosophers. Of special importance here is the ground-breaking work on language of Hamann, Herder and Humboldt, which set the agenda of the expressive tradition.[4] It is because of the crucial significance of these figures in the expressive tradition that Taylor named it 'the H-H-H' or 'the Triple-H tradition'. As we will see below, this tradition has been further elaborated in contemporary philosophy in different ways by many other philosophers – many other H's – whose perspectives on language are also expressive – especially, Husserl (1970) and Heidegger (1962, 1971).

The expressive tradition offers an account of language use as *an expressive activity*, an activity that articulates the world around us and defines our humanity. Rejecting the picture of passive copying or mechanical reproduction contained in some representational accounts of meaning (especially those of empiricists), the expressive tradition emphasizes that language use involves spontaneity and creation. Romantic philosophers argued that the use of language requires more than the passivity and receptivity underscored by the image of language or mind as a 'mirror of nature'. On the Romantic view, language use is an expressive activity that is reflective, normative and systematic or holistic. Let me briefly elucidate the kind of reflectiveness, normativity and systematicity or holism that Romantic philosophers identified as the central features of language.

Herder called attention to these features in his essay 'On the origin of language' (1772, English translation 2002). In this essay Herder criticizes Condillac's fable of two children in the desert who invent language by using cries and gestures as signs. Herder complains that this mythical account takes for granted the relation of signification, assuming those untouched by language know what a sign is and what it is for a sign to stand for something. But an account of the origin of language cannot simply assume these semantic capacities without being question-begging. On naturalistic accounts à la Condillac the word–object relations of semantic associations are depicted as automatic and mechanical. But Herder emphasizes that the meaningful use of signs involves *reflective awareness*. According to Herder, signifying involves a complex kind of discrimination, namely, the reflective recognition of something *as* something. So the core of Herder's indictment of the designative tradition is that it disregards the expressive dimension of language as a vehicle of reflective awareness. In the second place, Herder's critique of Condillac also emphasizes that naming and using names constitute a *normative* activity. Establishing semantic relations is not a matter of mere mechanical association; it is, rather, a matter of setting up normative relations. The relation between signs and what they designate is not a rigid connection, but a relation subject to normative assessment, a relation that can be correct or incorrect; for a sign may or may not fit the object for which it stands, and it may fit it in different ways. In the third place, Herder also called attention to the expressive activity of language use as a complex structuring activity that has a *holistic* dimension. Semantic relations are not isolated correlations between sounds and objects; they presuppose distinctions or contrastive discriminations. We recognize something as a robin as opposed to other birds and we refer to it as such on the basis of that contrast; we talk about birds as opposed to other animals, and about animals as opposed to plants, and about living things as opposed to inanimate objects, etc. The holistic picture of language underscores that meanings are systematic: they are repeated over time on different occasions, in different contexts and in relation to other meanings, and their interrelations form a *system*, a system of significations that supports any of the particular discriminations we make in language. This emphasis on the contrastive aspects of meaning leads to an *intensional holism* according to which the meaning of a term is given through other terms by holistic relations within language. On this holistic picture there are no autonomous semantic atoms, for the meaning of any linguistic unit in a system of signs depends on the entire conceptual schema contained in that linguistic framework.

With his empirical and theoretical studies of language Humboldt gave further elaboration to the view of language as an expressive structuring activity. He offered a powerful conceptualization of the holistic aspects of language with his famous and influential metaphor of 'the *web* of language'. Humboldt contended that language is like a web of interconnected items, and that the meshing of these interconnected elements is produced by our linguisitic actions or speech acts. According to Humboldt, it is essential for an adequate understanding of language that we recognize that the web of language is being perpetually recreated in speech, that is, continuously extended, altered and reconfigured in our linguistic performances and practices. As he famously put it, language is first and foremost *energeia*, not *ergon*, an activity, not a product.[5] There are indeed products of our linguistic activities, but these tentative and ever-changing fruits of our practices are webs that we weave as we go and can never amount to a finished and complete system. This provocative *practical holism* has far-reaching implications (some of which will be explored in later chapters). In the first place, this view underscores the open character of discursive practices and the tentativeness of their products, turning our linguistic negotiations into an infinite task. In the second place, this holistic view also emphasizes that we lack control over the language we use: our speech can never be entirely under our conscious control because we cannot master the entire web that constitutes the background of our speech (among other reasons because the entire web is never given). In the third place, the practical dimension of Humboldt's holism calls attention to the creativity of our agency: whether consciously or unconsciously, in control or out of control, our linguistic practices structure our lives and disclose the world around us.

The creativity of language as a structuring activity consists both in *articulation* and in *constitution*. Besides giving articulation to our world, language has also the power to make us who we are. It is in this sense that Humboldt claimed that language realizes man's *humanity*, calling attention to the constitution of human emotions as a central function of language. And it is in connection with this point that Taylor enters his central thesis about the historical development of the Philosophy of Language. According to Taylor, it is the expressive conception of language developed by Romantic philosophers that explains why language has acquired the significance it has in contemporary philosophy. Taylor's claim is that the expressive tradition is responsible for the centrality that language has come to occupy, for thanks to this tradition language came to be viewed as the key to understanding who we are, the key to solving philosophical puzzles about our humanity. It is in the constitutive aspects of language that its centrality resides: language has the power to constitute *specifically human emotions* and *specifically human social relations*. Taylor elaborates on these two creative aspects of the constituting function of language.

On the one hand, he explains, language is responsible for the constitution of *distinctively human concerns*: a range of ideals such as equality and justice and an entire range of emotions such as shame, love, hate, friendship, pride, etc., would not exist without language; they have been linguistically constituted. Taylor contends that nonlinguistic animals may feel anger, but not the complex human emotion of indignation; for – unlike gut feelings that are experienced directly, non-discursively – distinctively human emotions involve linguistic mediation: they have an essential discursive dimension in which their peculiar reflexivity and normativity reside. Human emotions that have been linguistically constituted involve reflective awareness and the recognition of normative standards that set the parameters of accountability. Human concerns are thus linguistically disclosed and they could not possibly be recognized if they were neither articulated nor acknowledged in our expressive activities. On the other hand, Taylor emphasizes, following the H-H-H tradition, that language is also responsible for the creation of *public spaces*. Language puts matters out in the open between interlocutors and thus creates a common vantage point from which they can survey the world together. Language is therefore responsible for the constitution of a dialogical perspective, an '*entre nous*' or 'being together'. Taylor observes that the philosophical tradition has been afflicted by a peculiar blindness to the public spaces created by language. He argues that the fact that sociality has been the blind-spot of the Philosophy of Language for a long time is the consequence of an epistemological tradition that has privileged the monological standpoint of the detached observer. With its emphasis on the linguistic creation of public spaces, the expressive tradition inaugurated a *dialogism* that underscores the social dimension of language and the impact of discursive practices in the constitution of human communities. This dialogic perspective has yielded many fruits in contemporary Philosophy of Language in the works of philosophers as different as Bakhtin, Wittgenstein, Foucault, Habermas, Rorty and Brandom, to name but a few.

Taylor teaches us that we value language in the way we do because we are Romantic. In this sense, in so far as it views language as central, contemporary philosophy is Romantic at its core. And this is true not only of hermeneutic approaches in Continental philosophy that are explicitly expressive, but also of central figures in the analytic tradition, starting with Gottlob Frege (1848–1925) – German philosopher, mathematician and logician, and one of the forefathers of the analytic tradition. Although Frege has been depicted by some as the champion of the designative tradition, his contributions to the Philosophy of Language are much more complex and interesting. Taylor argues that Frege should be given credit for introducing into the designative view some of the expressive elements underscored by the Romantic tradition: in particular, the holistic aspects of language use as a structuring activity. Indeed, with the introduction of the so-called *context principle*: 'Only in the context of a sentence does a word have meaning',[6] Frege depicted language use as an expressive activity that has irreducible holistic aspects. This holistic view constituted an important departure from pure designativism. This is how Taylor describes the 'major breaches' in the designative view produced by Frege's elucidations of language as a holistic structuring activity:

> What Frege shows to be wrong with a pure designative theory of meaning is that it ignores the activity underlying meaningful uses of language. Only in the context of a sentence does a word have meaning, because it takes a sentence to do what we do with words, that is, in highly general terms, say something. The designativist, one who tries to explicate meaning in terms of the things designated by the terms, has to take account of this activity, because it affects how words relate to things. In the assertion, we must distinguish two important roles, *referring and saying something of a referent*, and the way words relate to what we might think of as their designata is different in these different roles. (1985, p. 251; emphasis added)

As Taylor puts it, Frege contributed greatly to 'the decline of pure designativism'. The purely extensional or referential approach faced recalcitrant problems which suggested that intensions had to be accommodated in a full account of meaning. Perhaps the most influential attempt to combine the extensional and intensional aspects of meaning in a unified semantic theory came from Frege. To his semantic theory and its impact on the literature I now turn.

2.2 FROM FREGE TO DONNELLAN: REFERENCE, NAMES AND DESCRIPTIONS

Frege's famous essay 'On sense and reference' begins with the challenge of explaining the cognitive value of identity statements such as 'The Evening Star is the Morning Star'. Frege realizes that a purely extensional approach fails to meet this challenge because it cannot identify any difference between identity statements of the form 'A is B' and identity statements of the form 'A is A'. From a purely extensional point of view, all identity judgements are tautological statements of self-identity that do not contain any new information that is not already available to those who grasp the meaning of the terms involved. But of course there is a cognitive difference between tautological statements of self-identity such as 'Venus is Venus' and informative identity statements such as 'The Evening Star is the Morning Star'. The latter can convey new information. And in fact, the identity between the first star we see in the evening and the last star we can see in the morning was an empirical discovery in astronomy, a piece of information that was not available by means of semantic analysis, for it was not contained in the meanings of the terms used to describe the heavenly body that appeared in the evening and in the morning (not a star but the planet Venus, as it turned out). Informative identity statements of this kind are *not analytic but synthetic*: they involve more than linguistic analysis; they involve the synthesis of empirical information about the world. Similarly, the identity statement 'Smith's murderer is Jones' can also express a discovery, for example, in the resolution of a murder mystery. One may know the referent of the name 'Jones' and one may also know in some sense what the reference of 'Smith's murderer' is supposed to be (the person who killed Smith), but that is not sufficient to solve the murder mystery. 'Smith's murderer is Jones' expresses knowledge of the world, not of language – hence the mystery. Being able to grasp this kind of identity requires more than knowledge of meaning, which is why detectives or empirical investigators of any kind need much more than semantic analysis.

Frege's genius was to see that we cannot explain the informative character of identity statements with a single and monolithic notion of meaning. In order to solve the puzzles concerning the cognitive value of identity statements, Frege argued, we need to recognize that meaning is a broad semantic category with multiple dimensions, and we need to develop fine-grained distinctions to identify the different semantic ingredients that make up the meaning of a term. The elements that make up the significance of a term are the components of the communicable content of the term, that is, the components of the communicative contribution that the term makes to the sentences in which it figures. They are ingredients of what is shared in communication. In this sense Frege distinguishes between the reference (*Bedeutung*) and the sense (*Sinn*) of a term: the reference is what the term designates, the thing out there; the sense is the mode of presentation of the thing picked out, the way in which the referent or designatum is depicted. This distinction allows for the possibility of terms or expressions having the same reference but different senses; and this is exactly what happens to the descriptions 'The Evening Star' and 'The Morning Star': they have the same reference, but there is a semantic gap between them because they contain different modes of presentation of the same object.[7] Co-extensional terms that have different senses or intensions refer to the same entity through different paths, so to speak; and one may have travelled both paths without realizing that they lead to the same thing, for this thing is encountered in a different way, under a different aspect, in each case. In other words, one may not know that two senses are senses of the same referent, modes of presentation of the same entity. And this reveals the distinctive cognitive value of identity statements of the form 'A is B', for identity through different modes of presentation is not the same as tautological self-identity: the former conveys new information by connecting different senses or modes of presentation with the same referent, while the latter does not do anything of the kind.

The Fregean distinction between reference and sense revolves around the difference between the *objective* and the *intersubjective* aspects of communication. For Frege, the reference or *Bedeutung* is what is objective and independent of particular speakers and perceivers, whereas the sense or *Sinn* relates to how things appear to us or are depicted in language. Senses are intersubjective presentations or appearances and, therefore, they are dependent upon subjects to whom the referent or designatum is presented. But Frege emphasizes that senses are not purely subjective. Those purely subjective connotations that we associate with the terms we use constitute a third semantic element: what Frege calls 'the associated idea' (*Vorstellung*). Frege describes the associated idea as an idiosyncratic representation 'often imbued with feeling'. My idea of a referent, he says, 'is an internal image, arising from memories of sense impressions and acts, both internal and external, which I have performed' (1952b, p. 29). By contrast, Frege emphasizes that what defines a sense is that:

> [It] may be the *common property of many people*, and so is not a part or a mode of the individual mind. For one can hardly deny that mankind has a *common store of thoughts* which is transmitted from one generation to another. In the light of this, one need have no scruples in speaking simply of *the* sense, whereas in the case of an idea one must, strictly speaking, add whom it belongs to and at what time. (Ibid.; emphasis preserved and added)

Frege's tripartite distinction *Bedeutung–Sinn–Vorstellung* corresponds to three different semantic levels: the objective, the intersubjective and the subjective. For Frege, only two of these levels, the objective and the intersubjective, have cognitive significance for communication because only these can be part of sharable and communicable contents. The semantic level of *Bedeutung* relates to an objective common world; the level of *Sinn* corresponds to an intersubjective 'common store of thoughts'; but the level of *Vorstellung* does not correlate with anything common or intersubjectively shared. The subjective and idiosyncratic level of the associated ideas always remain personal: 'If two persons picture the same thing, each still has his own idea' (p. 30). Frege explains these three semantic levels and their different significance for communication with the analogy of someone observing the Moon through a telescope. He compares the object of observation, the Moon itself, with the *Bedeutung*; the representation of the Moon in the telescope, the image on the lens, with the *Sinn*; and the retinal image in the eye of the observer with the *Vorstellung*. The way the Moon appears through the telescope is publicly accessible to anyone who looks through the telescope; and the object itself is presumably out there to be inspected through different telescopic observations and in many other ways. In this sense, both the object and its intersubjective representations – the referent and its modes of presentation – are the subject-matter of our astronomical studies. However, the retinal image drops out: it is quite irrelevant for the purpose of our intersubjective investigations. On this view, the objective level of reference and the intersubjective level of sense are the aspects of our communicative and investigative practices that a theory of meaning must explain, the only rightful provinces of semantic theory.

As we saw, it is Frege's principle that only in the context of a sentence does a word have meaning. If we accept this context principle, we have to conclude that terms do not have reference and sense in themselves but only by virtue of the use we make of them in assertions. This was exactly Frege's thought: terms have sense and reference only in so far as they make a contribution to the significance of the sentences in which they are used. Given the dual aspect of the meaning of a term, we have to distinguish between *two distinct contributions* that a term can make to the assertoric content of a statement: they can contribute to make the statement *true* or *false*, or they can contribute to make the statement express a *thought*. The reference of a term is the contribution it makes to the truth-value of sentences; its sense is the contribution it makes to thoughts expressed by sentences. In this way sentence meaning is also analysed into two distinct components. Since for Frege the most basic unit of significance is the complete sentence, it is only appropriate that sentences have a double semantic life, like their semantic ingredients. Whole sentences also have *Sinn* and *Bedeutung*: their sense is the thought they express; their reference is their truth-value.

Frege uses a *substitutional approach* to identify the sense and reference of terms through their contributions to the sentences in which they figure. According to this substitutional approach, two terms or expressions have the same reference just in case they are interchangeable *salva veritate*, that is, just in case they can be substituted for one another without altering the truth-value of any sentence in which they are used; and two terms or expressions have the same sense just in case they are mutually replaceable *salva significatione*, that is, just in case they can be substituted for one another without altering the thought expressed by any sentence in which they are used. So the expressions 'Venus', 'Evening Star' and 'Morning Star' all have the same reference because they can be used interchangeably without altering the truth of sentences; but they have different senses because when they are substituted for one another, the thoughts expressed in sentences are altered. It is important to note that what we have said so far about substitution is valid only for free-standing assertions such as 'The Evening Star is very bright' or 'The Morning star is Venus', but not for embedded uses of these expressions in indirect speech ('S/He said that so-and-so') or in the ascription of so-called propositional attitudes[8] ('Jones believes/desires/intends/doubts, etc., that so-and-so'). For example, 'Jones believes that the Evening Star is Venus' may change in truth-value if we replace 'the Evening Star' or 'Venus' with 'the Morning Star', for Jones may believe that the Evening Star is Venus, but he may not believe that the Morning Star is Venus, or that the Evening Star is the Morning Star. So it is clear that embedded contexts require a special treatment, for sentences embedded in other sentences make a peculiar referential contribution to the truth-value of the whole sentence: not through their own truth-value and the reference of their component terms, but through the thought they express and the senses of their component terms. Embedded sentences have an *indirect reference*. As Frege puts it, the peculiar *Bedeutung* of embedded sentences is not their customary reference, their truth-value, but rather, their *customary sense*: the thought they express. For when we describe the speech of others or their mental contents, we are talking about – referring to – thoughts; we are not talking about – referring to – the truth-value of those thoughts.

Frege's substitutional approach takes his holistic view a step further: it shows that the most basic unit of significance is not the isolated sentence, but an entire cluster of interrelated sentences, that is, *an inferential pattern*. Thus, in Frege's semantic analyses, we are led from terms to sentences and from sentences to patterns of inferences. This gives a peculiar twist to the holistic view of language. This particular version of semantic holism is *inferentialism*. Frege's inferential holism had an extraordinary impact in early analytic philosophy[9] and it continues to have a noticeable impact today in contemporary Philosophy of Language.[10]

Frege's inferential holism complicates semantic issues substantially. How do we know, on this view, whether the terms we use are significant, whether they really have sense and reference? Frege points out that very often we don't really know; we just take it for granted. In ordinary language the reference of our terms is simply a *presupposition* of communication. Frege observes that usually when we talk, 'we presuppose a *Bedeutung*' and 'we can of course be mistaken in the presupposition' (1952b, p. 31). He remarks that 'in order to justify speaking of the *Bedeutung* of a sign, it is enough, at first, to point out our intention in speaking or thinking' (p. 32). But ultimately, on Frege's view, it is only through an exhaustive analysis of the inferential relations between our sentences that we can determine the reference and sense of our terms. In ordinary language we have terms that don't refer to anything real (e.g. 'The Tooth Fairy', 'Odysseus') and terms that don't have a clear sense or that have many senses (e.g. 'the blessed', 'the ignorant'). Frege argues that for the purpose of scientific investigation it would be ideal to have a language in which every term has reference and a univocal sense. This is what the logical notation that Frege proposed, his *Begriffschrift*, [11] tried to provide: a transparent notation in which each sign is correlated with one referent or designatum and one mode of presentation. It was Frege's hope that with this logical notation we could avoid ambiguity, plurivocity and lack of reference; and our reasoning and investigations would proceed with perspicuity, unimpeded by semantic obstacles. On the other hand, Frege observed that ordinary language falls short of this semantic perspicuity. In particular, he remarks, in ordinary language we should expect to find significant sentences without reference, that is, without truth-value, 'just as there are parts of sentences having sense but no *Bedeutung*' (ibid.). For example, Frege says, 'Odysseus was set ashore at Ithaca while sound sleep' is a sentence with sense but without reference, for it expresses a thought but it has no truth-value. According to Frege, the sentence cannot say anything true or false because it doesn't talk about the world, about things that have objective existence; but the sentence expresses a thought that 'remains the same whether "Odysseus" has a *Bedeutung* or not'; and 'one could be satisfied with the sense, if one wanted to go no further than the thought' (p. 33). But sometimes we are interested in the reference of our terms and sentences, and we want to go beyond mere senses, beyond thoughts and modes of presentations. Frege asks: 'why do we want every proper name to have not only a sense, but also a *Bedeutung*? Why is the thought not enough for us?' 'Because, and to the extent that, we are concerned with its truth-value', he answers (ibid.). According to

Frege, there is no objective semantic level in fictional discourse, no *Bedeutung*, because there is no interest in objective reality and no concern for the truth. Given the lack of objectivity, there are no truth claims in the realm of the fictional. What distinguishes science, by contrast, is the concern for truth: 'The question of truth would cause us to abandon aesthetic delight for an attitude of scientific investigation' (ibid.). In science the objective dimension of speech takes centre-stage: we talk about the world and we say something true or false about it; in this sense 'judgments can be regarded as advances from a thought to a truth-value' (p. 35). But the objective semantic level of reference often disappears when we abandon scientific discourse.

Frege's project was to develop a logical notation that could guarantee that terms have reference and that sentences have truth-value. He observed that there are no guarantees for the objective dimension of meaning in our ordinary uses of language. But we shouldn't hastily conclude in the light of these observations that Frege viewed ordinary language as logically defective, and art and fictional discourses as inferior to science, or that he envisioned his notation as a logical tool for revising and correcting the semantics of ordinary language. Contemporary interpretations of Frege's works have disavowed the revisionary implications of his philosophy.[12] On a non-revisionary reading, Frege's contrast between ordinary language and his logical notation is not the contrast between an imperfect language and an ideal language, but rather, a contrast between different communicative tools for different communicative purposes. On the Fregean view, while a logical notation should be especially well equipped to advance from thoughts to truth-values in a systematic way, ordinary language is suitable for sharing thoughts for purposes other than the systematic evaluation of truth (amusing oneself, bonding with others, encouraging, discouraging, etc). Frege thought that ordinary language was not appropriate for science, that is, for the study of truth in a systematic way. But it is not clear that this makes his logical notation superior in a general sense, for presumably this notation is not appropriate for many other communicative purposes for which ordinary forms of expression are more apt. But be this as it may, the fact is that for many decades philosophers – even influential figures as prominent as Russell – read Frege as proposing a strong version of logical revisionism.

Fregean semantic theory has traditionally been taken to be a very strict and restrictive view of meaning that encourages us to exercise semantic suspicion with respect to our ordinary modes of expressions, which, after all, could *at most* be apt for communication at the intersubjective level of sense, but not at the semantic level of reference. Moreover, the Fregean view can be taken to cast doubt on ordinary language even at the semantic level of sense: for, how can there be a mode of presentation of a non-existing *Bedeutung*? How can something that does not exist be presented in any way at all? Are the senses of non-referring terms intrinsically misleading and defective? As a reaction to this restrictive semantic view, philosophers developed more liberal views of meaning, views in which even fictional discourse could have *Bedeutung*. Some argued that we can make true or false claims in fictional discourse and fictional names can have reference. They would say that 'Odysseus came back to Ithaca' is a true claim and anyone who denies it does not know his/her Greek mythology; and 'Othello killed Desdemona' is also a true claim and those who deny it don't know their Shakespeare. On this view, we can talk about an objective reality in the realm of imagination; we can say that fiction refers to an objective reality, albeit a reality constructed by us. Some idealist philosophers such as Meinong[13] went further and attributed objective reality not only to fictional entities that we cannot find in the empirical world, but also to contradictory entities whose existence is logically impossible, such as the round square. Meinong's thought was that the referents of denoting phrases such as 'The golden mountain' or 'The round square' must have some kind of existence – if not in the physical world of our experience, then in some other world – for otherwise the sentences in which they figure would be meaningless; and not only do we succeed in communicating meaningfully about these things, but we can also say true things about them, such as 'The round square does not exist'. The central problem with this liberal semantic view is that it results in *ontological inflation*, in the proliferation of worlds. In other words, this semantic approach opens the door to a multiplication of entities and realities that is hard to contain within reasonable limits.

It is at this point that Russell arrives on the scene. He took his challenge to be the overcoming of an unacceptable false dilemma: the dilemma between semantic realism and semantic idealism. The two horns of the dilemma that Russell wanted to overcome were the following: an overly restrictive view of meaning à la Frege that ties the domain of what is significant to the domain of what actually exists, and denies full meaning to expressions without denotation; and an overly liberal view of meaning à la Meinong that postulates not only a sense but also a reference for every grammatically correct denoting phrase. This is how Russell explains his realist commitments and his problem with the inflated ontology of an idealist semantic view such as Meinong's:

> To maintain that Hamlet, for example, exists in his own world, namely, in the world of Shakespeare's imagination, just as truly as (say) Napoleon existed in the ordinary world, is to say something deliberately confusing [. . .]. There is only one world, the 'real' world: Shakespeare's imagination is part of it, and the thoughts that he had in writing Hamlet are real. So are the thoughts that we have in reading the play. But it is of the very essence of fiction that only the thoughts, feelings, etc., in Shakespeare and his readers are real, and that there is not, in addition to them, an objective Hamlet. When you have taken account of all the feelings roused by Napoleon in writers and readers in history, you have not touched the actual man; but in the case of Hamlet you have come to the end of him. (1993, p. 169)

In his landmark essay 'On denoting' (1905) Russell criticizes the ontological inflation of Meinong's semantics, but he also criticizes the more austere Fregean view. Russell endorses the realist view that there is only one world, one objective reality, to which our terms can refer and which can make our statements true or false. But he wants to defend his realism without imposing strong ontological restrictions on the domain of the meaningful, for the domain of meaningful discourse exceeds the domain of what exists. We do talk meaningfully about things that don't exist; and *pace* Frege, Russell maintains that our claims about non-existent things can be semantically evaluated; they have a truth-value: they are false. According to Russell, a non-referring denoting phrase implicitly contains, in itself, a false claim and it is for this reason that the whole sentence in which that phrase figures is false. This is what his theory of descriptions sets out to explain.

Through his theory of descriptions Russell explains how the referential failures of denoting phrases such as 'the round square' or 'the present king of France' can be reduced to false claims. The starting-point of Russell's theory is the distinction between two kinds of -

referential expressions: *names*, which pick out a particular without the mediation of any semantic content; and *definite descriptions*, which are denoting phrases that delineate the contours of an entity that may or may not exist. This semantic distinction rests on the logical atomism that connects Russell's Philosophy of Language with his ontology and epistemology. In 'On denoting' Russell emphasizes the importance of the semantic analysis of denotation for the Theory of Knowledge. He points out that the two kinds of denoting phrases he distinguishes correspond to the two basic kinds of knowledge we have: *knowledge by acquaintance* and *knowledge by description*. Denoting through names is the appropriate kind of reference for 'the things we have presentations of', that is, the things we know by acquaintance and can refer to directly. On the other hand, 'the things we only reach by means of denoting phrases' and don't have direct knowledge of are things we can only denote by means of descriptions (1905, p. 478). Some things can be epistemically accessible to us both by acquaintance and by description, but there are other things that we can only know by description because direct acquaintance is not possible. For example, for us, Napoleon is a historical entity that we can only talk about and know through descriptions, although of course this was not the case for his contemporaries. But there are also other particulars that no human can be acquainted with: for example, 'The center of mass of the Solar System' denotes an entity that is humanly accessible only by description.

For Russell, names are the logical and semantic atoms of language; they are the most basic unit of significance, which refer directly to simple particulars in the world. These logical atoms that get their semantic content through acquaintance are also basic epistemic atoms, for they constitute the building blocks of all knowledge. Descriptions, on the other hand, also have a crucial epistemic significance on this view, for they are the linguistic tools that enable us to extend the scope of our thinking and reasoning so as to cover hypothetical entities that may or may not exist: 'All thinking has to start from acquaintance; but it succeeds in thinking *about* many things with which we have no acquaintance' (p. 480). It is thanks to descriptions that our thinking can operate in the broader realm of the possible, instead of being restricted to the realm of the actual.

On Russell's view, there can be no names of non-existent objects, for by definition a name is a label that is directly linked to a particular with which we are in immediate contact. So 'Odysseus' or

'Hamlet', for example, may look like names, but, according to Russell, they cannot be real names because they have no reference. These expressions, Russell reasons, must contain hidden descriptions which delineate particulars that fail to exist. In fact, for Russell, all ordinary names have a descriptive component and should be distinguished from names properly so called from a logical point of view. So he introduces the technical expression 'logically proper names' that he reserves for those terms without descriptive content that are directly connected to a referent. According to Russell, the best candidates we have in ordinary language for this category of referential expressions are indexicals such as 'This' and 'That' which have a direct reference.[14] In sharp contrast with names, descriptions delineate profiles that may or may not be satisfied by anything that exists. Descriptions do not contain a designation within themselves or a direct link to a referent. Russell emphasizes that these 'denoting phrases never have any meaning in themselves' (ibid.), but only in the propositions in which they occur. Russell observes that the main source of confusion in philosophical accounts of descriptions has been to assume that the object of analysis should be the descriptions themselves as designators, while in fact what we need is an analysis of propositions containing descriptions. What logical analysis must uncover, Russell contends, are the *propositional functions* through which descriptions refer.

We need a logical analysis of two kinds of descriptions: indefinite and definite. Indefinite descriptions such as 'I met *a* man' constitute an attempt to refer to something or other, but do not pick out a particular thing or definite individual. According to Russell, these descriptions make an *existence claim*: they claim that something or other exists that satisfies the description, that fits the mould constructed by the description. This existence claim is the proposition through which the description may or may not refer to something or other. But this propositional function has only an indefinite reference and it remains opaque as to what entity in particular satisfies the description. So, for example, if I talk about 'a frog', I assert that there is at least one thing in the world that is a frog, but there may be more than one frog in the world. Thus, the statement 'I saw a frog' contains two distinct claims: that there exists at least one thing that is a frog and that I saw it. But there may be more than one thing that satisfies the description: there may be many frogs and I may have seen more than one. Definite descriptions, on the other hand, constitute attempts to refer to something in particular, a particular individual that fits the profile delineated by the description. But how do definite descriptions manage to pick out a definite particular? Unlike indefinite descriptions, which make only an existence claim, definite descriptions also make a *uniqueness claim*: that there is *exactly one* thing that the description is true of. So the propositional function contained in a definite description consists in the combination of two distinct claims, an existence claim and a uniqueness claim. This complex propositional function can have a definite reference; it may denote a particular. It is through the complex proposition or concatenation of claims 'There is *at least* and *at most* an x that is so-and-so' that a definite description ('The so-and-so') can refer to a definite particular. The two hidden claims that are implicit in a definite description can also be expressed as follows: 'The F' asserts that there is an x that is F, and for any y that is F, y = x; that is, there is at least and at most an x that is F.

According to Russell's theory, descriptions are propositional functions that may or may not be true of something. Their reference or lack or reference depends on the truth or falsity of the claims they implicitly make when they are used in a sentence. A definite description can fail to refer for two reasons corresponding to the two claims contained in it: it can lack denotation because there is not a single thing that fits the description – an *existential failure*; or because there is more than one thing that fits the description – a *uniqueness failure*. For example, the description 'The author of *The Odyssey*' can fail to denote for two reasons: because *The Odyssey* was a popular poem in the oral tradition that no one wrote; or because it was written by more than one person. The upshot of Russell's theory is that descriptions are conceptual expressions that can be empty or not empty depending on the truth or falsity of their hidden claims. Russell's logical analysis has the virtue of offering solutions to the semantic puzzles about descriptions that had been accumulated in the philosophical tradition. As he emphasizes, his theory can explain the significance of descriptions that lack denotation without indulging in ontological inflation. This theory shows that we don't need to postulate non-existent entities corresponding to definite descriptions without denotation. We can talk meaningfully about the round square even though such a thing cannot exist because we have manufactured a denoting phrase that is necessarily empty, a description that no entity can satisfy because it contains two incompatible predicates. On the other hand, other definite descriptions without denotation such as 'The present King of France' are simply contingently empty because the propositions through which they try to refer happen to be false. So we don't need to postulate either logically impossible entities or contingently non-existent entities. In fact, according to Russell's theory, we do not need to postulate entities of any kind corresponding to the definite descriptions that are meaningfully used in assertions, for the significance of these expressions does not lie in their denotation but in the general statements they implicitly make, their hidden claims about existence and uniqueness.

Another puzzle-solving virtue that Russell exploits in the presentation of his theory is that it can show that assertions containing definite descriptions without denotation do not violate the Law of Excluded Middle (or any other logical law regulating the inferential relations between truth and falsity). Since a sentence can only be either true or false and nothing else, when a sentence is false, its negation must be true and vice versa. However, it would be wrong to conclude from the falsity of 'The present King of France is bald' that 'The present King of France is *not* bald' is true. This inference would be wrong because what makes the first sentence false is not the hair on the French King's head; rather, what makes it false is that there is no King of France today. The philosophical confusion in the analysis of this sentence arises, according to Russell, because the sentence has the deceiving appearance of making only one claim, when in fact it makes two other claims implicitly: the definite description makes the complex double claim that that there is at least and at most one person who is the present King of France; and then the complete sentence makes the claim that that person is bald. In this case the sentence as a whole is false because the existence claim contained in the definite description fails. So an assertion containing a definite description involves the conjunction of three distinct claims and, therefore, it can be false for three different reasons. To use another example, 'The author of *The Odyssey* was Greek' could be false in three ways or for three reasons: perhaps because *The Odyssey* was a popular poem that no one wrote; perhaps because Homer co-wrote it with other people; or perhaps because Homer was not Greek.

Russell's theory assimilates the referential failures of descriptions to false claims that are implicitly asserted, and their referential successes to implicitly asserted true claims. In his influential article 'On

referring' (1950) Strawson offers a powerful critique of this assimilation and Russell's semantic approach. Strawson agrees that Russell
has identified the conditions that, from a logical point of view, make
the denotation of definite descriptions possible, but he rejects the
idea that that these conditions are implicitly stated in the descriptions. He argues that they are *presuppositions* we make when we use
definite descriptions, but they are not part of the assertoric content
of these descriptions. According to Strawson, the presumptions concerning existence and uniqueness that definite descriptions typically
bring with them are simply *implied, not asserted*: they are *presuppositions of our use*. As Strawson puts it, the referential use of a definite description implies (without logically entailing) that 'the
existential conditions described by Russell are fulfilled', but to use
the definite article 'the' in this way 'is not to *state* that those conditions are fulfilled' (p. 222). The principal mistake that Strawson identifies in Russell's theory is the assimilation of referring to asserting:
'To refer is not to say you are referring. [. . .] referring to or mentioning a particular thing cannot be dissolved into any kind of assertion.
To refer is not to assert, though you refer in order to go on to assert'
(p. 223).

Strawson illustrates his critique of Russell and his alternative
analysis of the 'uniquely referring use' of language with the following example: 'Suppose I advance my hands, cautiously cupped,
towards someone, saying, as I do, "This is a fine red one." He,
looking into my hands and seeing nothing there, may say: "What is?
What are you talking about?" Or perhaps, "But there's nothing in
your hands"' (ibid.). As Strawson goes on to point out, it would be
absurd to say that the complaint 'But there's nothing in your hands'
denies or contradicts what the speaker *said*, whether explicitly or
implicitly: what is being denied or rejected is not one of the claims I
asserted, for I asserted nothing about there being an object in my
hand; what is being denied or rejected is a presupposition of my
utterance, a precondition that must be satisfied before I can make a
semantically evaluable assertion. The violation of this presupposition or precondition does not result in the falsity of the assertion, as
Russell thought, but rather, in the impossibility of evaluating the
truth-value of the assertion: the sentence cannot be deemed either
true or false because it is not semantically evaluable at all. According
to Strawson, we should elucidate the logic of referring by examining
the presuppositions we make in our referential uses of language; and

we don't need to postulate hidden claims that are implicitly asserted through the deep logical structure of sentences in order to explain our referential successes and failures. 'The general moral of all this', Strawson remarks, 'is that communication is much less a matter of explicit or disguised assertion than logicians used to suppose' (ibid.).

Strawson's thesis that what semantic analysis uncovers is not hidden contents and assertions, but the presuppositions of our use of expressions, puts the relationship between ordinary language and semantic analysis in a new light. According to Strawson, semantic analysis should not be conceived as a revisionary logical analysis that can reveal what our sentences *really* mean, digging up from the level of deep syntax their real semantic contents, which are disguised by the misleading grammatical structures of ordinary language at the surface level. Instead, semantic analysis should be conceived as a *pragmatic* analysis of our uses of language that brings to the fore presuppositions that are part of the taken-for-granted background that supports the significance of our uses of language. In this sense, Strawson's view facilitates the *shift from semantics to pragmatics*, or more precisely, from a formal semantics that operates in abstraction from particular contexts of use to a context-sensitive semantic approach that analyses meanings through pragmatic elucidations of language use. Strawson's analysis makes clear that the presuppositions of uniquely referring expressions are *pragmatic* presuppositions, for they derive from the pragmatics of their *use*. Strawson emphasizes that referring is not something that linguistic expressions – whether names or definite descriptions – can do for themselves. It is not language that refers; referring is something we do, something we use language to do: '"Mentioning", or "referring", is not something an expression does; it is something that someone can use an expression to do' (p. 219).

As Strawson points out, it is very important to keep in mind that the semantic analysis of linguistic expressions can take place at three different levels: (1) at the level of *signs*, where we find the expressions themselves as linguistic units; (2) at the level of *uses*, where we find semantic *types* regulated by rules, habits or conventions; and (3) at the level of *utterances*, where we find instances of use, *tokenings* of semantic types in particular contexts. According to Strawson, meaning and reference cannot be found at the level of signs or expressions, for independently of particular uses and instances of those uses, expressions remain uninterpreted strings of signs and can have neither meaning nor reference. As Strawson emphasizes, expressions by themselves cannot be said to refer to anything, and sentences by themselves cannot be said to be true or false. However, on this view, general uses or types do have a general meaning, although they do not have reference until they are uttered in particular occasions of use. Strawson describes the meaning of referential expressions and sentences at the level of use, independently of their denotation and truth-value, as follows:

> To give the meaning of an expression (in the sense in which I am using the word) is to give general directions for its use to refer to or mention particular objects or persons; to give the meaning of a sentence is to give *general directions* for its use in making true or false assertions. [. . .] to talk about the meaning of an expression or sentence is not to talk about its use on a particular occasion, but about the rules, habits, conventions governing its correct use, on all occasions, to refer or to assert. So the question of whether a sentence or expression *is significant or not* has nothing whatever to do with the question of whether the sentence, *uttered on a particular occasion*, is, on that occasion, being used to make a true-or-false assertion or not, or of whether the expression is, on that occasion, being used to refer to, or mention, anything. (1950, pp. 219–20)

So, on Strawson's view, it is important to realize that there is nothing general about the reference of our linguistic expressions, when they have one (just as there is nothing general about the truth-value of sentences, when they have one): referring is a matter of particular instances or occasions of use, the tokenings of semantic types in particular contexts. Strawson underscores the important fact, entirely neglected in Russell's theory, that the same referential expressions and complete sentences may have different reference and different truth-value (if they have one at all) on *different occasions of use*. Thus, for example, 'The present King of France is bald' may have been *true* when uttered in the reign of Louis XIV and *false* when uttered in the reign of Louis XV – and, by contrast, the utterance of this sentence today does not amount to a semantically evaluable claim, a proper candidate for truth or falsity. In short, according to Strawson's analysis, truth and reference have to be elucidated at the *pragmatic levels of use*: both the general level of rules for use and the concrete level of particular instances and contexts of use. The upshot of Strawson's view is that there can be *no semantics without pragmatics*.

Strawson's semantic elucidations of descriptions at the level of use try to establish that *referring* cannot be reduced to *asserting* because these are two radically different uses of language. His pragmatic analysis underscores that there is a crucial distinction between two different uses of language that Russell's theory of descriptions overlooked: this is the distinction between 'using an expression to make a unique reference' and 'asserting that there is one and only one individual which has certain characteristics' (p. 223). Strawson emphasizes that we have to make a clear distinction between *referential uses* and *ascriptive* or *attributive uses* of language: *identifying* something (mentioning or calling attention to it) and *saying something about it*. These two uses of language correspond roughly to the grammatical categories of the subject and the predicate of a sentence. And they are governed by two distinct kinds of linguistic conventions: rules for referring and rules for ascribing or attributing. Ironically, Keith Donnellan (1966) used Strawson's distinction between referring and attributing to develop a theory of descriptions that aims to refute not only Russell, but also Strawson himself.

Donnellan's theory of definite descriptions follows Strawson in drawing attention to particular occasions of use and the contexts in which they take place. But Donnellan argues that Strawson's analysis of definite descriptions is as flawed as Russell's because it reduces all occurrences of descriptions in all contexts to *one single use*, with only one set of presuppositions and only one correct analysis, while in fact, he argues, there are *two distinct uses* of definite descriptions: the *referential* and the *attributive* use.

In the *attributive use* of a definite description the information contained in the description is all important; as Donnellan puts it, it occurs *essentially*: the description is intended to pick out *whoever* or *whatever* happens to be the so-and-so. Adapting one of Donnellan's famous examples, imagine a criminal psychiatrist who in the course of a criminal investigation and in the light of the evidence accumulated utters the claim 'Smith's murderer is insane'. In this forensic context the psychiatrist is using the description 'Smith's murderer' attributively to refer not to any particular suspect, but to whoever happens to have committed the crime. The psychiatrist may very well suspect someone in particular, say Jones, to be the author of the murder, but in uttering the claim in the forensic context he/she is using the description attributively to talk about *whoever* happens to fit the description, whether it is Jones or someone else. Let's adapt another of Donnellan's examples: imagine that at a party someone says 'The person drinking a martini will be in trouble'. If the description is used attributively, then the utterance talks about *whoever* happens to be drinking a martini. In this example of the attributive use the property of drinking a martini has become essential, all important, perhaps because the consumption of alcohol is prohibited at that party or because the speaker found out that martini drinks are poisoned. What characterizes this use of definite descriptions is that the *attribute* used in the description (rather than any referent in particular) is the focus of attention, the topic of communication.

In the *referential use* of definite descriptions, by contrast, the information contained in the description is not at all important, but accidental. As Donnellan puts it, it occurs *instrumentally*: the description is used as a mere tool or instrument to pick out something or someone *in particular*, whatever the most accurate description of that object or person happens to be. Referential uses of descriptions can be characterized as *indexical* or *deictic* uses, that is, as attempts to *point* at something or someone in particular, where the description is simply used as a way of drawing attention to that particular referent. So, for example, imagine that someone watching Jones on trial for the murder of Smith makes the comment 'Smith's murderer is insane', using the definite description referentially to talk about Jones. In this scenario the speaker's claim is still to be understood as a claim about Jones even if it turns out that he did not murder Smith: the speaker is not interested in talking about whoever turns out to have assassinated Smith, but about Jones *in particular*. Similarly, if at a party someone asks 'Who is the man drinking a martini?' because he/she is curious about the man holding a martini glass, he/she is referring to *that man*, that man in particular and that man only, and not to whoever happens to be drinking a martini at the party. Imagine the speaker confesses 'I am attracted to the man drinking a martini'. If he/she is using the description referentially, his/her confessed attraction to *that man* will be in no way diminished if it is discovered that the man was actually drinking water out of a martini glass.[15] Nor did the speaker unknowingly confess an attraction to that other man who, unbeknown to him/her, happened to be drinking a martini in a paper cup. When a description is used refe-rentially, it is used to refer to a particular someone or something, whether or not that person or object turns out to fit the description in the end, all things considered. In this use of descriptions the ref-erential success does not depend on the correctness of the descrip-tion employed. In the attributive use, by contrast, it is quite a different matter.

For Russell, all descriptions were attributive, whereas, for Strawson, they were all referential. Donnellan contends that both accounts are one-sided. With his distinction between attributive and referential uses Donnellan dissolves the dispute between Russell and Strawson as to whether what characterizes definite descriptions is an element of generality or an element of particularity. Different ele-ments are emphasized in different uses of descriptions: generality in the attributive use (*whatever* or *whoever* is the so-and-so) and partic-ularity in the referential use (*that one and that one only*). Donnellan argues that a single analysis will not be able to account for both uses because different semantic assumptions attach to these uses and different consequences concerning reference and truth follow from these assumptions. Consider what happens when *nothing* satisfies the description: for example, if no one murdered Smith because he committed suicide, or if no one was drinking a martini at the party. In the attributive use the definite description lacks reference and the sentence in which it figures lacks truth-value: the psychiatrist didn't succeed in talking about the psychological profile fitting the perpe-trator of a murder because the murder didn't take place; and the person at the party preoccupied with martini-drinking didn't succeed in saying something true or false about whoever was violat-ing the prohibition of alcohol consumption or whoever was in danger of being poisoned because no one was. However, the incor-rectness of these descriptions does not have the same consequences when they are used referentially. Even if the intended referent does not fit a description used referentially, the speaker still refers to that referent and the claim he/she makes still has truth-value: the person at the trial still referred to Jones and claimed he was insane, which is either true or false, even if Smith committed suicide and 'Smith's murderer' is an empty description true of no one; and the person at the party still managed to pick out the man he/she was interested in and also managed to say something about him, even if the man didn't fit the description he/she used, strictly speaking. Donnellan has identified two uses of descriptions that are indeed quite different and exhibit a different logic. But what makes the difference? What is ultimately responsible for these different semantic presuppositions and consequences? What determines whether our use of a definite description is referential or attributive?

According to Donnellan, the beliefs of the speaker and the audience can play a role in shaping which description is selected and how it is used, but beliefs don't determine whether a description is used attributively or referentially on a particular occasion. Someone can use a description referentially even if he/she believes it to be false. For example, a speaker can refer to someone as 'the King' even if he/she believes him to be an impostor, thinking perhaps that the audience would recognize that man as the King and the description (though incorrect, according to him/her) would thus function as a successful instrument to pick out that person. But the referential use is also independent of the beliefs that the audience happens to have about the referent; and a definite description can be successfully used to refer to something or someone in particular even if the audience does not believe the description to be correct: for example, even if everybody (speaker and audience included) thinks the man being referred to as 'the King' is not the legitimate king, they may still find it advantageous to refer to him under that description (say, to avoid being accused of treason or disloyalty by those who call that person 'the King'). Although beliefs play a role in our use of descriptions, Donnellan contends that they are not what makes the difference between the referential and the attributive use. The basis of this crucial semantic distinction, he claims, resides in the *communicative intentions* of the speaker: 'whether or not a definite description is used referentially or attributively is a function of the speaker's intentions in a particular case' (Strawson, 1950, p. 297). The attributive use presupposes the intention to talk about whoever or whatever has certain attributes; and the referential use presupposes the intention to refer to someone or something in particular, whatever attributes that person or object turns out to have in the end. Donnellan's claim that a referential intention is both a *necessary* and a *sufficient* condition for a referential act has far-reaching implications for the notion of reference. Let's explore what follows from the claim that referring requires a referential intention on the part of the speaker.

In the first place, it follows from the claim that a referential intention in the speaker is a *necessary* condition for a referential act that we have to distinguish sharply between *referring* and *denoting*. On this view, there cannot be an act of referring without an intention to refer; we cannot refer to someone or something without knowing it. So, if a description picks out an unintended object, this is not an object that the speaker refers to: this object is part of the denotation of the description, but not part of the speaker's reference. 'Denoting and referring should not be confused', Donnellan insists (p. 293). If, for example, in 1960 a political analyst made the claim 'The Republican candidate for president in 1964 will be a Conservative', he/she would be talking about whoever became the candidate (that is, about an abstract political profile and not its instantiation) and, therefore, he/she would not be referring to anybody in particular. Donnellan contends that it would make no sense to say 'that the speaker had referred to, mentioned, or talked about Mr. Goldwater'; for, on his view, 'while the definite description used did *denote* Mr. Goldwater (using Russell's definition), the speaker used it *attributively* and did not *refer* to Mr. Goldwater' (p. 293).

In the second place, from the claim that the speaker's referential intention is a *sufficient* condition for the act of reference it follows that referring requires no particular belief about the intended referent. On Donnellan's view, a referential act requires the intention to refer *and nothing else*; in particular, referential intentions are claimed to be *independent of beliefs* about the referent. Thus, on this view, the truth or falsity of the beliefs that the speaker may have about the referent are deemed semantically irrelevant. The suggestion is that there are *pure referential intentions* that are completely unaffected by cognitive states and utterly independent of the truth or falsity of all the beliefs that the speaker may happen to have. Consider Donnellan's example of someone asking 'Is the man carrying a walking stick the professor of history?' According to Donnellan, the referential use of the description 'the man carrying a walking stick' is successful, given the appropriate intention to refer, even if the description rests on a mistake; and there may be a whole range of mistaken beliefs to which the description gives expression: from small mistakes of detail – perhaps the man is not carrying a walking stick, but an umbrella – to important mistakes that affect the identity of the referent – perhaps the intended referent is not a man but a woman. But Donnellan argues that even the most radical mistake does not necessarily annul the referential act. Imagine, for example, that what the speaker intends to refer to is not a man at all, but just a rock that looks like a man from a distance. Even this radical cognitive failure, Donnellan contends, does not necessitate referential failure: 'in this case, I think I still have referred to something, to the thing over there that happens to be a rock but that I took to be a man' (p. 296). Interestingly, though, although the cognitive failure may not affect the referential success of the description, it does affect the *truth-value* of the claims that are made using this description, for the error in categorization involved in the description reveals that a host of attributes are inapplicable to the referent and that, therefore, the ascription of these attributes do not amount to *true or false* claims; they would be simply altogether misleading and inappropriate claims: we cannot say of a rock that it is or is not the history professor, just as we cannot say that it is male or female, single or married, etc. Donnellan seems to acknowledge this when he recognizes that it is unclear whether a question about a referent described with a deeply mistaken category can be answered at all: 'in this case it is not clear that my question can be answered correctly. This, I think, is not because I have failed to refer, but rather because, given the true nature of what I referred to, my question is not appropriate' (ibid.).

But what happens in the case of a hallucination, or when the referent ceases to exist without the speaker knowing it? Does the speaker still refer to something? Is there still an intended referent in this case? Doesn't Donnellan's view involve the postulation of imaginary and non-existing entities? Avoiding ontological inflation à la Meinong, Donnellan acknowledges possible cases of referential failure: 'There is finally the case in which there is nothing at all where I thought there was a man with a walking stick; and perhaps here we have a genuine failure to refer at all' (ibid.). But Donnellan insists that what causes the referential failure is something more radical than a mistaken belief or an inaccurate description that nothing fits. On his view, a referential failure is due to communicative circumstances that depart radically from and fail to support the speaker's referential intention, irrespective of his/her beliefs and the accuracy of his/her words: 'This failure of reference, however, requires circumstances much more radical than the mere nonexistence of anything fitting the description used. It requires that there be nothing of which it can be said, "That is what he was referring to." [. . .] the failure of reference and truth value does not come about merely because nothing fits the description he used' (ibid.).

Driving a wedge between beliefs and referential intentions, Donnellan insists that there may be referential success even in the face of radical and massive cognitive failures. But Donnellan's thesis of *belief-independence* is highly problematic. How are we supposed to divine referential intentions in the light of their alleged belief-independence? After all, referring is something we do jointly in communicative situations, and its success requires a process of negotiation and interpretation through which we reach a mutual understanding as to what is being talked about. In other words, from a communicative standpoint, what matters is not simply the speaker's reference, but how he/she manages to communicate his/her referential act to an interlocutor: what matters is joint reference or co-reference, the convergence of the referential acts of speaker and hearer in communicative exchanges. On this view, an account of reference must pay attention not only to the production of speech but also, and simultaneously, to its reception. From this point of view, a theory of reference must involve nothing less than a full-blown *theory of interpretation* that can explain how mutual understanding can be achieved in communication. This interpretative turn in semantic theory calls into question the independence between belief and reference, between the intensional and the extensional aspects of meaning. Contemporary theories of interpretation both in Anglo-American and in Continental philosophy have underscored the interdependence between belief and meaning: they have emphasized that we cannot make sense of the things we refer to independently of how we conceive of them and of the beliefs we hold to be true about them. Different theories of interpretation (such as those of Quine, Davidson, Gadamer and Ricoeur) have developed different holistic views of the relationship between belief and meaning, emphasizing – in different ways – that truth and reference go together, that we cannot understand the referential aspects of language independently of its attributive or predicative aspects: we cannot understand what it is to refer to something unless we understand what it is to make a true claim about it. It has been argued that these dimensions of language, the referential and the attributive, are necessarily interdependent. In the next section I will briefly introduce two different philosophical approaches to interpretation, two frameworks that offer competing accounts of the complex relations between truth, sense and reference, as they appear in communicative attempts to achieve mutual understanding. These are the

neo-empiricist framework of Quine and Davidson and the hermeneutic framework articulated by Gadamer (among others).

2.3 INTERPRETATION AND TRANSLATION: NEO-EMPIRICIST AND HERMENEUTIC APPROACHES TO LINGUISTIC UNDERSTANDING

What makes co-reference possible? What accounts for the possibility of speakers' jointly referring to the same thing in communicative
exchanges? What are the conditions of possibility for sharing reference and sense? When we look at these semantic notions from the
shared perspective of interlocutors or partners in conversation, it
seems clear that our referential successes and failures as well as our
attributive or predicative successes and failures are to be understood
as *interpretative successes* and *failures*, that is, as accomplishments
and breakdowns that are part and parcel of the interpretative negotiations that take place in the process of communication. We need to
understand how the reference and sense of our words and the truth
and meaning of our claims emerge from interpretative negotiations;
we need to understand how reference, sense and truth become entan-
gled in processes of interpretation, and how we can best navigate
their complex relationships. In what follows I will identify the central
claims and assumptions of two philosophical models or accounts of
interpretation. First, I will discuss a *neo-empiricist* account that has
been extremely influential in contemporary Philosophy of Language
in the analytic tradition; and then I will sketch an alternative
account developed in Continental philosophy, a *hermeneutic*
approach that will be further discussed in 4.2.

In his influential essay 'Two dogmas of empiricism' Quine (1951)
critically questioned some of the most central notions and assumptions in Philosophy of Language and Epistemology within the neo-
empiricist tradition of the twentieth century defended by logical
positivists such as Rudolf Carnap.[16] One of the dogmas of empiricism Quine attacked (the most important for our purposes) was the
dogma that there is an *analytic–synthetic distinction* we can draw
among our statements, that is, that our statements can be divided
into two classes: those that are true or false by virtue of their
meaning – *analytic* statements, such as 'A bachelor is an unmarried
man' or 'A rabbit is a large-eared, hopping lagomorph' – and those
that are true or false by virtue of the empirical facts – *synthetic* statements, such as 'Pedro is a bachelor' or 'A rabbit just hopped by'.

Quine argues that our knowledge of language and our knowledge of the world cannot be sharply separated; and we cannot neatly classify statements in terms of what makes them true, language or the world. Quine's argument tries to show that there are no judgements that are true solely by virtue of language, or of linguistic conventions; and there are no judgements that are true solely by virtue of the empirical world, that is, of facts experienced without the mediation of language. According to Quine, all statements have both a linguistic and an empirical component; and although one of these components may predominate over the other, there are no cases in which either the linguistic or the empirical component is null, as had been claimed about the analytic truths of definitions and the core empirical truths of sense-data statements, respectively. Our knowledge of meaning has an unavoidable empirical component, and our knowledge of the world has an unavoidable linguistic component. On the one hand, I cannot be said to grasp the meaning of the term 'rabbit' unless I hold certain true empirical beliefs about rabbits. And, on the other hand, I can have no knowledge of rabbits unless I have at least a partial understanding of what 'rabbit' means. What 'rabbit' means and what a rabbit is are matters that cannot be extricated; they are in fact two sides of the same issue. Hence the unavoidable interdependence of belief and meaning: we need to be able to identify the meanings expressed by words while at the same time identifying the beliefs expressed by statements. We need a *methodology* that enables us to tackle these two tasks simultaneously. Quine tries to elucidate the methodology of interpretation by examining the practice of *translation*. For Quine, translation is a paradigmatic and especially perspicuous form of interpretation, because in translation the language to be interpreted is made sense of in a different language, that of the interpreter. More specifically, the Quinean model focuses on a special case of translation that he terms *radical translation*, in which the objective is the construction of a translation manual for a new language.

But where do we begin? How do we embark on the complex task of interpretation or translation? How do we get started on this messy business of understanding each other if we cannot separate our linguistic knowledge and our empirical knowledge, if we have to identify meanings and beliefs simultaneously? How do we manage to refer to the same things while figuring out what we are saying about those things? Quine argues that the process of interpretation or translation from one language into another must begin with what he calls *'stimulus meaning'*, that is, the sensory stimulations associated with words and sentences. For Quine, it is very important that we identify the stimulus meaning of a word with a pattern of stimulations,[17] and not with the object(s) that trigger those stimulations – for we have to be able to associate similar stimulations with different objects in order to apply generic terms such as 'rabbit', and different stimulations with the same object in order to apply a proper name to an individual that may cause quite different stimulations in different situations. The stimulus meaning of a sentence is a set of surface irritations of our receptors that prompt our assent or dissent to a sentence: 'any treatment of language as a natural phenomenon must start with the recognition that certain utterances are keyed to ranges of sensory stimulation patterns; and these ranges are what stimulus meanings are' (1969, p. 157; see also 1990, p. 3). Quine describes the stimulus meaning of a sentence as an ordered pair of two different components: the 'affirmative stimulus meaning', which is the class of those stimulations that prompt assent to the sentence; and the 'negative stimulus meaning', which is the class of those stimulations that prompt dissent to the sentence. Of course not all sentences in a language are directly tied to stimulation patterns that prompt assent or dissent on the occasion of their utterance. Those that are Quine calls *'occasion sentences'*. They play a crucial role in the process of translation: they are the starting points of this process. According to Quine, the empirical task of constructing a translation manual for a language must begin with the identification of occasion sentences in that language, and with the development of interpretative hypotheses about the meaning of these sentences, that is, about the stimulation patterns associated with them.

Quine describes occasion sentences as those sentences that 'command assent or dissent only if queried after an appropriate prompting stimulation' (1960, pp. 35–6). But although occasion sentences are directly tied to stimulus meanings, *collateral information* can also play a role in prompting assent or dissent to these sentences. Assent and dissent can be prompted by something other than the occurrence of the relevant stimulations; they can be prompted by related and prior observations as well as by background knowledge. For example, if the translator or linguist queries the speaker by asking 'Rabbit?', it is possible that the speaker may assent to the query even if he/she has not seen a rabbit in the present environment.

As Quine puts it, he 'may assent on the occasion of nothing better than an ill-glimpsed movement in the grass, because of his earlier observation, unknown to the linguist, of rabbits near the spot' (1960, p. 37).[18] According to Quine, we cannot eliminate the role that collateral information plays in our verbal behaviour, given the unavoidable holistic relations that exist among our beliefs. However, he contends that the role of collateral information can be minimized by focusing on observational terms and sentences that are relatively invariant from occasion to occasion. Some stimulus meanings are less susceptible than others to the influence of intrusive information. Quine (1960) points out that although even the stimulus meaning of an observational term like 'red' could be 'made to fluctuate a little from occasion to occasion by collateral information on lighting conditions' (p. 42), this term does have a high degree of invariance. According to Quine, there is a continuum of degrees of observability and invariance of stimulus meaning, with terms such as 'red' at one extreme, terms such as 'bachelor' at the other extreme and terms such as 'rabbit' somewhere in between. Quine argues that the translator or linguist should focus on a particular subclass of occasion sentences, namely, *observation sentences*, which are those occasion sentences whose stimulus meaning is relatively invariant under the influence of collateral information.[19]

Quine develops his arguments about meaning and translation through the thought experiment of *radical translation* in which a field linguist faces the problem of how to interpret the linguistic input of a newly discovered language. In all his different formulations[20] of this thought experiment Quine imposes the same constraints on the construction of a translation manual. The only data available to the linguist are native utterances and their concurrent observable circumstances. So, for instance, the linguist hears a native utter 'gavagai' in the presence of a rabbit and he/she formulates different hypotheses as to what the term may designate: the entire animal, its parts, its colour, its movement, etc. To test these hypotheses the linguist utters 'gavagai' in different circumstances and waits for the native's assent or dissent. In this way some hypotheses get refuted and others confirmed. The linguist will continue in this fashion, confirming hypotheses about individual sentences as well as about grammatical trends, until he/she designs a translation manual which enables him/her to interpret any arbitrary sentence that the natives can utter. The problem is that no matter how much evidence is available to the linguist and no matter how well his/her translation manual fits this evidence, we can always construct an alternative manual that fits the evidence equally well. In other words, it is in principle possible for two radical translators following the same procedure to come up with incompatible translation manuals. Quine draws two conclusions from this argument: first, the thesis of the *indeterminacy of translation*,[21] namely, that the meaning of a sentence is not determined by facts, but it is relative to the translation manual of our choice; and second, the thesis of the *inscrutability of reference*,[22] namely, that the reference of a word is not determined by facts, but is relative to the apparatus of individuation of our choice, that is, to the ontology built into our translation manual.

Quine generalizes the conclusions of his thought experiment and argues that *radical* indeterminacy is a *basic* and *unavoidable* feature of language. Quine's indeterminacy thesis concerns not just the peculiar activity of a radical translator, but all language use. As he puts it, 'radical translation begins at home'.[23] Although we use the same marks and sounds as other people in our linguistic community, the task of interpreting their speech is no different from radical translation: in order to understand speakers of the same language, we also have to be able to translate their meanings into our language. And the fact that we are using the same marks or sounds does not make any difference because meanings are not attached to marks or sounds: there are no meanings independently of the system of beliefs in which they figure; and therefore meanings are *relative* to belief systems and to the particular speakers who hold them. Ordinarily when we say that we use the *same* words, we are not talking necessarily about synonymous terms, but about *homophonic* terms, that is, terms that look and sound the same, but for all we know may have quite different meanings, since their meanings derive from the network of interlocking beliefs in which they are embedded.

To describe the complex system composed by the beliefs expressed in the sentences we utter or think, Quine uses the metaphor of *the web of beliefs*. According to the Quinean view, in speaking or thinking we are weaving our beliefs into a complex web or network; and our meanings are the nodes in that web or network. On this view, all our beliefs are interrelated; and their inferential relations form a system in which everything is affected by everything else. The most theoretical beliefs at the centre of the web still have an empirical component in so far as they are indirectly related to the edges of the web through a complex chain of beliefs with which they are in contact or interwoven. Even the most directly sensory beliefs at the fringes of the web, even observation sentences, have a theoretical aspect in so far as they are related to many other beliefs in a chain that goes to the very centre of the web. On this view, communication consists in connecting webs of beliefs; and it is therefore of the utmost importance that these webs overlap. Translation requires a mapping of beliefs from one web onto another. And it is important to note that, for Quine, the ordinary kind of translation that is supposed to take place in everyday communication is also *indeterminate*, as indeterminate as radical translation: we can narrow down the range of interpretative hypotheses about our interlocutor in the light of the evidence we have about his/her verbal behaviour, but we cannot eliminate all competing hypotheses; there is always room for alternative hypotheses that accommodate equally well all the instances of observation sentences and the patterns of stimulations that go with them.

Following Quine, Donald Davidson tries to develop a systematic account of interpretation as a mapping between webs of beliefs. Building on the assumptions and conclusions of Quine's account of translation, Davidson tries to formulate a general methodology for the construction of a theory of interpretation that could, in principle, enable us to understand *any* language whatsoever. The general methodology that Davidson sets out to articulate is supposed to have *universal applicability*. This general methodology of interpretation, Davidson argues, can be used to construct theories of interpretation applicable not just to any natural language (English, Spanish, Chinese, etc.) or dialect, but to any *idiolect*, that is, any personal use of language to express one's own system of beliefs: e.g. English-as-spoken-by-Mary, or Spanish-as-used-in-Pedro's speech and writing. According to Davidson, belief systems or *webs* are expressed in idiolects; and, therefore, the central goal of the methodology of interpretation should be to teach us how to construct a theory of interpretation for an idiolect. Davidson sets himself a challenge modelled on Quine's discussion of radical translation, namely, to offer an account of '*radical interpretation*', which presents us with the challenge of constructing a theory of interpretation from scratch for a speaker we have never encountered before.[24] How do we go about accumulating evidence for a new idiolect and systematizing this evidence into a theory of interpretation that can enable us to understand any arbitrary sentence in that idiolect?

Davidson and Quine hold similar holistic views of language and interpretation. For Davidson, as for Quine, the interpretation of meaning and the interpretation of belief go hand in hand because one's meanings are determined by what one holds to be true. Davidson's account of interpretation (like Quine's account of translation) starts with the thesis of the *interdependence of belief and meaning*, according to which we can only identify the meanings of someone's words by individuating the beliefs that his/her sentences express.[25] On Davidson's view, to say that the expressions of two speakers have the *same meaning* is to say that there is a substantial overlap between the beliefs held by these speakers which contain those expressions. For example, both the speaker I am interpreting and I attach the same meaning to the term 'robin' if and only if we have sufficiently similar beliefs about what we call robins. If there is no significant overlap between our beliefs about robins, the semantic congruity disappears: the identity of meaning is lost. It cannot be the case that the speaker means the same thing as I do by the term 'robin' and yet he/she denies that robins fly, that they have wings, that they are birds, etc. If he/she denies too many of the beliefs I hold to be true of robins, I should start concocting other interpretative hypotheses that may capture better the meaning that he/she attaches to the term 'robin'. For example, if I discover that the speaker gives his/her assent to the sentences 'Robins have big ears', 'Robins have big teeth', 'Robins hop around in the grass', etc., then I should conclude that by 'robin' he/she means rabbit (what I mean by 'rabbit' in my idiolect). On this view, our meanings emerge from the networks of sentences we hold true; and, therefore, interpretation must be a matter of comparing and contrasting systems of beliefs from which meaning emerges, a matter of connecting idiolects in a systematic way. In order to establish these systematic correlations between idiolects, Davidson proposes to focus on *assertions*, taking for granted the semantic capacity of holding something to be *true* and taking the very notion of *truth* as unproblematic and intuitively understood.[26] What we need in order to develop a methodology of interpretation, Davidson argues, is a way of systematically relating the sentences held true by the speaker and those held true by the interpreter.

Davidson argues that in order to produce the systematic mappings between sentences required for a theory of interpretation, we need a *recursive device* that can be applied to an infinite number of sentences and can give us an infinite number of mappings between sentences in different idiolects. Davidson finds this recursive device in Tarski's *convention T*,[27] which uses the predicate 'true' as a disquotational device that correlates two sentences: '"p" is true if and only if q'. This biconditional combines indirect and direct speech to establish the logical equivalence between a quoted sentence and an unquoted sentence. This convention can be applied in the task of interpretation by replacing the quoted sentence '"p"' with a sentence in the language we try to interpret and 'q' with a sentence in our language. An application of Tarski's *convention T* is called a T-sentence; and it is the formulation of an interpretative hypothesis that expresses a semantic equivalence: a sentence that is cited and a sentence that is asserted are claimed to be logically equivalent, that is, extensionally synonymous or intersubstitutable *salva veritate*. The so-called *object language*, that is, the target language that we are trying to interpret, may or may not be the same as the *metalanguage* used by the interpreter to explicate meanings. Thus we can find T-sentences that correlate two different languages: '"La nieve es blanca" is true if and only if snow is white', or '"Es regnet" is true if and only if it rains'. But we can also find T-sentences that are one-to-one mappings between sentences in the same language, or more accurately, between sentences in homophonic idiolects: e.g. '"Snow is white" is true if and only if snow is white'. When dealing with homophonic idiolects, the correlated sentences themselves may be homophonic: '"Robins are cute" is true if and only if robins are cute'; but they may not be: '"Robins are cute" is true if and only if rabbits are cute'. For, indeed, speakers who use the same marks and sounds can certainly express different meanings in their assertions. Whether the correct interpretative hypothesis has the form '"p" is true if and only if q' or '"p" is true if and only if p' – e.g. whether 'robin' should be interpreted as meaning robin or rabbit – depends on how similar the idiolects of speaker and interpreter are, that is, how much overlap there is between the signs expressing their systems or webs of beliefs.

On Davidson's view, interpretation is a holistic process in which we identify the meanings that speakers attach to their words by examining their beliefs. On this view, what determines the meanings of the individual words of a speaker are all the sentences the speaker in question holds true taken together. So translation is a process of interpretation through which we try to get into the belief system of another by constructing a *theory of truth* for it.[28] But how do we go about constructing a theory of truth to interpret the assertions of a new interlocutor? How do we proceed in the *radical* interpretation of a new idiolect? When I meet my interlocutor for the first time I know nothing about his/her belief system, about the array of sentences he/she holds true. According to Davidson, I have no option but to assume that his/her belief system is very much like my own, that for the most part there is a *massive overlap between our beliefs*. This is what Davidson calls *the principle of charity*, a methodological maxim that regulates interpretation, guiding how we go about comparing and contrasting belief systems and correlating idiolects. The principle of charity says that we must assume that speakers believe mostly true beliefs and, therefore, for the most part their belief systems overlap. For Davidson, this is a methodological constraint on interpretation, an unavoidable presupposition of our interpretative practices: interpretations must be *charitable* in order to be meaningful interpretations at all; *charity* is a condition of possibility of interpretation. As Davidson (1984) puts it: 'we cannot take even a first step towards interpretation without assuming a great deal about the speaker's belief. [. . .] the only possibility at the start is to assume general agreement on beliefs' (p. 196). This is what his principle of charity commands, that we interpret the speech of others in a way that maximizes agreement. This principle doesn't eliminate the possibility of disagreement; but it shows that we can only make sense of local disagreements against the background of a massive agreement.

For Davidson, the principle of charity is a transcendental principle of interpretation that characterizes every interpretative act, including those involved in self-interpretation. According to this principle, interpretation requires the assimilation of any belief system one encounters to one's own at the present time, for a valid act of interpretation must produce maximum agreement with what I believe right now. And this methodological assumption must hold true also when I interpret my past speech and writing: I must assume that my belief system has not changed radically, that I have not changed my mind on most matters. We will come back to this issue in Chapter 5.

As the implications of the principle of charity reveal, the Davidsonian view of interpretation results in a *monological view* of communication. This monological view faces two central problems that will be explored in the next two chapters. In the first place, this view seems doomed to *meaning scepticism* (which, of course, Quine, Davidson and their followers are willing to embrace as a true insight about the nature of meaning). In following Quine and Davidson, the interpreter may not need to be sceptical about his/her own present meanings, but he/she must be sceptical about anyone else's meanings, including those of his/her own past self. Are *shared* meanings possible at all on the Quinean and Davidsonian view of interpretation? Is semantic scepticism inescapable? We will discuss these questions in Chapter 3 (see also 5.1). On the other hand, a second central problem that the Davidsonian framework of interpretation raises concerns the *social aspects of language*. We need to ask whether shared conventions are required by communication and whether or not any durable semantic sharing can result from it. On the Quinean and Davidsonian view, since each interpreter must translate everyone else's speech into his/her own idiolect, the mutuality of linguistic understanding in communication seems to be lost: there is no guarantee for reciprocal exchanges and genuine sharing in communication. Revisiting the central theses of the Quinean and Davidsonian accounts of translation and interpretation, we will discuss the *social* aspects of language and whether communication involves *mutual* understanding. This discussion will be initiated in Chapter 3 and completed in Chapter 5.

Before closing this chapter, I want to introduce an alternative philosophical approach to interpretation, which will be at the same time an alternative to the monological view of communication that derives from Quine and Davidson. This alternative can be found in *hermeneutics*, a philosophical framework developed by some of the most central figures in twentieth-century German philosophy. Hermeneutics – the art and science of interpretation – was originally concerned with the interpretation of sacred texts, but it acquired a much broader significance with Wilhelm Dilthey and Martin Heidegger. The hermeneutic tradition began with the insights that interpretation is holistic and circular: *holistic* because any part of the text or message to be interpreted is dependent on the interpretation of the whole; and *circular* because any interpretation rests on a prior interpretation, that is, a pre-interpretation, pre-conception, pre-judgement or prejudice that orients and structures the interpretative act. These pre-judgements or pre-orientations may come from the interpreter him/herself, from his/her predecessors or from a cultural tradition. This circular movement of interpretation going back to a pre-orientation or pre-judgement is the so-called *hermeneutic circle*.[29] It has been argued that the circle of interpretation may not be vicious. Dilthey and Heidegger generalized the notion of the hermeneutic circle and presented it as an unavoidable feature of all human knowledge and all interpretative activity. Dilthey (1989, 1996) conceptualized the human sciences as interpretative sciences and articulated a methodology of interpretation that provided guidelines and criteria for understanding what authors and native informants mean by their words. Heidegger's hermeneutics (1962), on the other hand, elaborated an account of the *existentialist* dimension of interpretative phenomena. On the Heideggerian view, what characterizes the encounter between interlocutors or between an interpreter and a text is an *ontological entanglement* in which what is at stake is the very being, the very existence and life, of those involved in the interpretative encounter. Heidegger conceived of interpretation as an 'ontological event', that is, an existential and transformative interaction between interpreter and text that becomes itself part of the history of what is understood – just as, for example, the interpretation of the law transforms its application and becomes incorporated in the law, transforming the lives of those who interpret it and apply it as well as the life of the law itself. For Heidegger, interpretative encounters are mutually transformative in a deep sense: they involve more than a change of belief or any other minor modification that does not change who we are; they involve ontological or existential transformations that reorient our beings, changing our orientation towards life and death.

These central hermeneutic themes in Dilthey and Heidegger were elaborated by Hans Georg Gadamer in his seminal work *Truth and Method* (1989). Gadamer argued for the hermeneutic thesis that prejudices or pre-judgements are an unavoidable part of all judgements. On Gadamer's view, any text or speech has a fundamental historical dimension and we should inquire into its historical presuppositions which make the text or speech what it is and support its intelligibility. In this hermeneutic inquiry what we find as the precondition of interpretable texts and utterances is a *historical tradition* that provides a horizon of understanding in which things become intelligible. For Gadamer, traditions have both *enabling and constraining effects* in the process of interpretation: they enable us to understand meanings, but they also constrain the range of meanings that our interpretative sensibilities are capable of registering, making us blind to varieties of signification that lie outside the scope of the tradition. In Gadamer's hermeneutics, understanding is conceived as the continuation of a historical tradition; and, therefore, it inevitably remains historically situated and conditioned by a tradition. But Gadamer's hermeneutics also emphasizes the *dialogical openness* of the interpreter, which makes it possible for prejudices to be challenged and for horizons to be broadened. Prejudices are unavoidable but they can always be critically questioned; and the interpretative scope of a tradition – the range of meanings to which it is open – can always be broadened. In fact, for Gadamer, a genuine communicative encounter is always an opportunity for broadening one's horizon, a potential site for the critique of prejudices and an occasion for self-transformation. This view of communication is elaborated in Gadamer's *dialogical model* of conversation and of the interpretation of texts.

According to Gadamer, what characterizes a genuine conversation is the dialogical openness of its participants: 'it is characteristic of every true conversation that each opens himself to the other person, truly accepts his point of view as worthy of consideration and gets inside the other to such an extent that he understands not a particular individual, but what he says' (1989, p. 347). On this view, the genuine communicative attitude of a partner in conversation involves a loss of individuality and a loss of control. For this reason, Gadamer remarks that it is a mistake to talk, as we do, of 'conducting a conversation', for it would be more appropriate to say that 'we fall into a conversation' (p. 345). What characterizes true conversational partners is their interpretative *vulnerability*, that is, their willingness to take communicative risks, their openness to be exposed to new meanings and to be interpreted in new ways. This vulnerability is completely missed by the monological account of linguistic understanding in terms of replication or reproduction. Gadamer rejects this account as a distorted model of communication. He argues that it is a mistake to think that understanding consists in getting inside another person's mind and reliving his/her experiences. This monological model of communication depicts the meanings of the different contributions to the conversation as already fixed in the minds of the contributors even before they spoke, as if those meanings belonged to the private realms of individual speakers, rather than to the public space between them. On this monological model, there is no real partnership in conversation, there is no mutuality in conversational exchanges. But for Gadamer what characterizes the understanding reached in conversation is precisely its *mutuality*: to reach an understanding in a conversation is to reach a meeting point, to come to an agreement, to be mutually transformed. Understanding is an accomplishment that can only be mutual. For Gadamer, a genuine conversation is a transformative encounter; and if an understanding is achieved in it, it is a mutual achievement that touches the lives of those involved. For, according to Gadamer, understanding is not first and foremost an intellectual process of interpretation, but a lived experience: 'an accomplishment of life. For you understand a language by living in it' (p. 346).

Gadamer applies his hermeneutic view of conversation to the interpretation of texts. According to Gadamer, reading and understanding a text exhibits the same logic and dynamic as a conversation. The mutuality of the understanding reached in conversation is also present in the understanding of a text, for, according to Gadamer, the interpretation of a text is a conversation between the text and its interpreter. The understanding of a text does not consist simply in the reproduction of the original communicative intention of its author. On Gadamer's conversational model of interpretation, the understanding of a text involves a process of negotiation regulated by the *logic of question and answer*: the text and the interpreter pose certain questions to each other and they try to answer each other in a mutual effort of reaching out. Gadamer develops his dialogical account of the interpretation of texts and his critique of the monological model through an elucidation of the understanding of texts involved in translation from another language. According to Gadamer, the activity of translation shows perspicuously the inadequacy of the monological view: 'the translation of a text [. . .] cannot be simply a re-awakening of the original event in the mind of the writer, but a recreation of the text that is guided by the way the translator understands what it said in it. No one can doubt that we are dealing here with interpretation, and not simply with reproduction' (p. 347). The explicit interpretative effort of the translator in bridging 'the gulf between languages' also 'shows clearly the reciprocal relationship that exists between interpreter and text, corresponding to the mutuality of understanding in conversation' (p. 349). But, as Gadamer emphasizes, this is not specific to translation but is in fact characteristic of the interpretative encounter with any text (whether in one's native language or not): 'The translator's task of re-creation differs only in degree, not qualitatively, from the general hermeneutical task presented by any text' (ibid.).

Gadamer summarizes the core insight of his dialogical model of interpretation as follows: 'Interpretation, like conversation, is a closed circle within the dialectic of question and answer' (p. 351). What the interpretation of a text demands from a reader or translator is that he/she becomes a partner in conversation, which requires not only dialogical openness, but also *involvement*: he/she needs to ask questions and try to provide answers to the questions posed by the text. This interpretative encounter is a process of mutual interrogation. The interpreter will leave a mark in the text,[30] but the text will also leave a mark on the interpreter. Thus in the reading and understanding of a text we can see the ontological or existential entanglement and the mutual transformation characteristic of interpretative encounters. This mutually transformative understanding is what Gadamer calls a *'fusion of horizons'*, the coming together of the horizons of partners in conversation (whether these partners are people or texts). He describes this 'fusion' as 'the full realization of conversation, in which something is expressed that is not only mine or my author's, but common' (p. 350).

Gadamer and the hermeneutic tradition offer a dialogical view of communication that contrasts sharply with the Quinean and Davidsonian monological model. But the dialogical model is not without problems. Perhaps the most central problem that this model faces is linguistic *relativism*. By putting the emphasis on the *perspectival* character of interpretation, hermeneutic approaches seem to invite a certain relativism of perspectives. The first issue that relativism raises is whether there can be objectivity in communication. Can our interpretative practices exhibit *any* degree of objectivity? The dialogical view of hermeneutic approaches typically emphasizes that interpretation necessarily has a subjective or intersubjective dimension. What this view rejects is an *absolute* notion of objectivity: objectivity as something that is mind-independent and language-independent, an absolute perspective or lack of perspective – *the view from nowhere*.[31] But it is not the case that the dialogical view of interpretation is incompatible with every notion of objectivity. And indeed there are hermeneutic philosophers (most notably Habermas) who have tried to reconcile the notions of objectivity and intersubjectivity in their accounts of communication.[32] A second issue involved in the philosophical debate about relativism is the issue of *the limits of intelligibility*: Are there insurmountable limitations on communication and linguistic understanding? Are there limits to translation and interpretation? Are there languages that are untranslatable for us? Are there concepts that are beyond the scope of our interpretative capacities? Some have argued that the possibility of interpretation and understanding is not always a given, and that in some cases a 'fusion of horizons' may not be possible until certain conditions are met. In the extreme case, it has been argued, we may find languages so far apart, so radically different and historically distant, that they cannot be translated into one another; we may find texts that have become unreadable and speakers who have become uninterpretable. But even when the possibility of interpretation has not been lost – even when there is a 'fusion of horizons', a meeting of the minds or of the traditions involved – things can be lost in translation, meanings can be missed in interpretation. These problems associated with linguistic relativism will be discussed in Chapter 4 (see 4.3).

CHAPTER 3

INDETERMINACY AND LANGUAGE LEARNING: COMMUNICATION AS THE MEETING OF MINDS

In his sceptical reading of the *Philosophical Investigations*, Kripke (1982) found a strong convergence between Wittgenstein's and Quine's indeterminacy arguments about meaning. Following Kripke, many commentators have argued that, despite important differences of detail and orientation, the two philosophers are of one mind on essentials:[1] Wittgenstein's and Quine's indeterminacy arguments, they claim, support the same holistic view of language and a similar pragmatic approach to semantics. In this chapter I will try to show that the surface similarities between Wittgenstein's and Quine's arguments hide deep differences and that their arguments ultimately lead to incompatible views of language. Besides elucidating these influential views on the indeterminacy of meaning, I will also argue that everyday contexts of communication subject our linguistic interactions to substantive constraints in such a way that our meanings can acquire certain degrees of determinacy, even if some degrees of indeterminacy still subsist. Through contextual constraints the meanings of our situated linguistic interactions can become *contextually determinate*, that is, determinate enough for the communicative exchange to be able to proceed successfully. Contextual determinacy is achieved when the participants in communication narrow down the set of admissible semantic interpretations through a process of negotiation in which different interpretations are tacitly or explicitly rejected. It is important to distinguish between this contextually achieved form of determinacy that only comes in degrees and the idea of *absolute determinacy* advocated by meaning realists, which involves the *thesis of semantic uniqueness*, namely, the thesis that there is only a single interpretation that fixes the meaning of a term. Unlike absolute determinacy, *contextual determinacy* does not preclude the possibility of alternative interpretations within a *constrained* set; and, therefore, it admits certain degrees of indeterminacy even in smooth and successful communicative exchanges. However, these degrees of semantic indeterminacy have to be distinguished from the *radical indeterminacy* defended by meaning sceptics, which involves the *thesis of cognitive egalitarianism*, namely, the thesis that *all* rival interpretations are equally belief-worthy or equally rational to accept.

3.1 MEANING SCEPTICISM

In the *Philosophical Investigations* (1958; hereafter PI) we can find a whole battery of indeterminacy arguments that Wittgenstein uses to disarm different views of meaning. For the sake of brevity, I will focus on the Regress Argument as it appears first in the critique of ostensive definition and later in the rule-following discussion. With this argument Wittgenstein tries to establish that neither ostensive definitions nor interpretations can fix meaning. First, Wittgenstein emphasizes that ostensive definitions are used to introduce very different kinds of words: 'one can ostensively define a proper name, the name of a colour, the name of a material, a numeral, the name of a point of the compass and so on' (PI §28). So, far from fixing meaning, ostensive definitions are utterly ambiguous, for they 'can be variously interpreted in *every* case' (ibid.). One might think that the indeterminacy of an ostensive definition can easily be dispelled by disambiguating the ostension with a sortal, that is, with a classificatory term that specifies what *sort* of thing the word defined is supposed to name, saying for instance 'This *colour* is called so-and-so' (PI §29). But Wittgenstein replies that sortals can also be variously interpreted according to different classificatory systems; and since they are not self-explanatory, 'they just need defining [. . .] by means of other words!' (ibid.). But in order to guarantee the univocity of these further words, more defining is needed. So we are thus led to a regress. 'And what about the last definition in the chain?', Wittgenstein asks (ibid.). We can always interpret the terms used in the last definition in different ways. So the upshot of the argument is that meaning cannot be fixed by definition, for no matter how much is added to the definans, the definiendum remains indeterminate.

A similar Regress Argument can be found in the discussion of the continuation of a numerical series according to the rule '+ 2' (PI §§186–98). We tend to think that an algebraic formulation of this rule can fix what counts as the correct continuation of the series. But an algebraic formula can be variously interpreted, and therefore different continuations of the series can be regarded as correct applications of the same formula (PI 146). We are likely to reply that it is not the mere expression of the rule, the algebraic formula, but its *meaning*, that determines correct usage. It may appear that if we fix the interpretation of the rule, we thereby fix its meaning and hence its applications. We may think that how the formation rule '+ 2' is to be applied to the series of natural numbers can be fixed by giving the following interpretation: 'write the next but one number after *every* number' (PI 186); and we may think that all the numbers in the series follow from this sentence. To this suggestion Wittgenstein responds: 'But that is just what is in question: what, at any stage, does follow from that sentence. Or, again, what, at any stage we are to call "being in accord" with that sentence (and with the *mean*-ing you then put into that sentence – whatever that may have consisted in)' (PI 186). The interpretation of the rule does not really get us any further, for it can in turn be understood in different ways: it is in fact just another formulation of the rule, like the algebraic formula, and it can also be variously interpreted. So Wittgenstein concludes that 'any interpretation still hangs in the air along with what it interprets, and cannot give it any support. Interpretations by themselves do not determine meaning' (PI 198).

So, according to Wittgenstein's arguments in the *Philosophical Investigations*, definitions and interpretations leave meaning indeterminate.[2] *Prima facie* these indeterminacy arguments seem very congenial with Quine's arguments for the indeterminacy of translation and the inscrutability of reference examined above (see 2.3). And there is indeed something that Wittgenstein's and Quine's indeterminacy arguments have in common: they play a similar *negative* role against *meaning realism*. That is, these arguments undermine the view that the meaning of a word or a sentence is a definite predetermined *thing* that can be preserved in translation and that can be fully captured in an interpretation. But after rejecting meaning realism, Wittgenstein and Quine part company and they use their indeterminacy arguments to develop very different views of language.

As we saw, Quine generalizes the conclusions of his indeterminacy arguments and concludes that *radical* indeterminacy is a *basic* and *unavoidable* feature of language. By contrast, for Wittgenstein, our linguistic practices are not radically indeterminate. According to Wittgenstein, radical indeterminacy arises when we adopt a detached and absolute perspective, that is, when we become persuaded by decontextualized philosophical theories that distort language use by searching for unassailable *foundations*. Wittgenstein's indeterminacy arguments constitute an attempt to refute semantic foundationalism by showing that there are no 'superlative facts' that determine meaning, that these facts are philosophical fictions (cf. PI §192). With these arguments Wittgenstein tries to clear the way for a fresh approach to the everyday use of language. As he puts it, his goal is to get rid of semantic foundations or 'philosophical superlatives' and to go 'back to the rough ground' of our ordinary linguistic practices (PI §107). It is because we have been 'held captive' by a foundationalist picture of language that we have unreasonable expectations with respect to the meaning of our words (PI §115). And when we realize that these expectations cannot be fulfilled, we are tempted to conclude that meaning is *radically* indeterminate because it cannot live up to our philosophical standards. But the *radical* indeterminacy of meaning disappears when we stop looking for semantic facts that uniquely determine meaning and go back to the ordinary contexts of everyday communication. So, according to Wittgenstein, *radical* indeterminacy is the result of an unnatural foundationalist standpoint and, therefore, we should be suspicious of any philosophical theory that makes language radically indeterminate. Hence, if we agree with Wittgenstein, we should also be suspicious of the Quinean conception of language that derives from the model of radical translation.

We realize that indeterminacy arguments are not as troublesome as they seem when we notice that these arguments only play with *logical possibilities*. Most (if not all) of the logical possibilities considered by indeterminacy arguments are *equally* valid candidates for the interpretation of a term *in the abstract*, but not in particular situations where the state of the linguistic interaction and the knowledge available to participants, as well as various socio-historical circumstances affecting the use of the term, impose all kinds of interpretative restrictions. So, contextual factors heavily constrain semantic interpretations, rendering many logical possibilities unreasonable. As Laudan (1990) has suggested in the Philosophy of Science, indeterminacy arguments establish the *thesis of non-uniqueness*, that is, the thesis that for any interpretation there is always the *possibility* of an alternative interpretation that is logically compatible with our entire body of knowledge. But these arguments fall short of establishing the *thesis of cognitive egalitarianism*, that is, the thesis that *all* rival interpretations are equally belief-worthy or equally rational to accept. In other words, we can accept that our interpretations are *underdetermined* without being forced to conclude that they are *radically indeterminate*, for *underdetermination does not warrant radical indeterminacy*. The auxiliary assumption that enables us to go from underdetermination to indeterminacy is the assumption that there must be isolable semantic foundations that render our meanings fully determinate and fixed.

According to the semantic foundationalism of meaning realism, in the absence of semantic foundations, anything goes: that is, any semantic interpretation is equally valid; and hence meaning is radically indeterminate. It is only when we have been antecedently persuaded by semantic foundationalism that it makes sense to argue that in the absence of semantic foundations there is no determinacy whatsoever. Wittgenstein's diagnosis of meaning scepticism unmasks this foundationalist assumption and questions its plausibility or reasonableness. In order to show how gratuitous this assumption is, the next step is to sketch a nonfoundationalist picture of meaning in which *underdetermination does not warrant indeterminacy*. This picture blocks the inferential moves that meaning sceptics want to make with their indeterminacy arguments, showing that the impossibility of semantic foundations by itself does not warrant semantic scepticism. At the core of this nonfoundationalist picture is the *thesis of contextual determinacy*, which accepts and integrates the thesis of underdetermination while rejecting the thesis of radical indeterminacy. According to this thesis, our meanings do not live up to the standards of absolute determinacy and fixity of semantic foundationalism, but they are not radically indeterminate: they are *contextually determinate*, that is, they acquire a transitory and always imperfect, fragile and relativized form of determinacy in particular contexts of communication, given the purposes of the communicative exchanges, the background conditions and practices, the participants' perspectives, their patterns of interactions, etc.

The different significance that Wittgenstein's and Quine's indeterminacy arguments have can be further appreciated by examining the different holistic views of language that these arguments invoke. As

Quine himself has emphasized, his view of language and translation rests heavily on the holism of Pierre Duhem in the Philosophy of Science (see, e.g., Quine 1990, p. 48). This holism contends that the evidential relation between an observation statement and a theoretical hypothesis can only be determined against the background of an entire theory. According to Duhemian holism, the meaning and reference of scientific statements are always theory-relative. According to Quine, what holds for the scientific use of language also holds, *mutatis mutandis*, for everyday communication. Quine's thought seems to be that since meanings are only possible within a theory, ordinary language must contain a stock of background theories from which our words get their meaning. As Peter Hylton puts it, 'for Quine, "theory" and "language" become more or less interchangeable [. . .] and to speak a language at all is to accept a body of doctrine' (1994, p. 273). Quine urges us to think of language as a vast network of interconnected sentences, as 'a single connected fabric including all sciences, and indeed everything we ever say about the world' (1960, p. 12). Each individual speaker only masters a small portion of this vast network. This idiosyncratic portion of language is what Quine refers to as the speaker's 'web of beliefs', which contains the background theories according to which the speaker understands the sentences of his/her language. Different speakers may understand sentences according to different background theories, just as different translators may interpret utterances according to different translation manuals. And since there are no meanings independent of particular theories, meaning thus remains intrinsically and unavoidably underdetermined. But does that mean that meaning is also *radically* indeterminate? Focusing on the ordinary contexts of everyday communication, Wittgenstein's contextualism makes clear that that is not so.

Wittgenstein's indeterminacy arguments also convey a holistic point about language: namely, that meaning cannot be decontextualized and encapsulated in an interpretation. But Wittgenstein's holistic view of language reflects a contextualism that bears very little resemblance to the Duhemian holism of scientific theories. Indeed, given the anti-theoretical spirit of Wittgenstein's later philosophy, it would be very surprising if he were willing to accept the idea that ordinary language functions just like a scientific theory. Wittgenstein's arguments emphasize that meaning is crucially dependent on a particular context of language use, but this holistic point does not involve an appeal to background theories. For Wittgenstein, the context of language use is not a theoretical context; it is the context of a shared practice. Quine and Wittgenstein agree that the activities of speaking, translating and interpreting are only possible against a certain background. But they disagree about what this requisite background is: for Quine, it is a set of theories; for Wittgenstein, it is a set of techniques or common procedures, that is, the ways of doing things that competent speakers share. Thus Wittgenstein's contextualism[3] differs substantially from the theoretical holism of Quine's scientific naturalism.

There are two central differences between Wittgenstein's and Quine's holistic views of language. In the first place, Wittgenstein's view of language as a practice reflects an *action*-oriented holism that contrasts with the heavily theoretical holism of Quine. As we saw, it is precisely to emphasize the tight connection between language and action that Wittgenstein introduces the expression 'language-game'. For Wittgenstein, the most basic unit of significance, the whole within which words acquire meaning, is not a set of sentences, but a practice of use, an activity. On Quine's view, what is required in order to make sense of a sentence is that it be related to other sentences within a theoretical structure; to understand a sentence is to assimilate it into a network of interconnected sentences or a 'web of beliefs'. By contrast, for Wittgenstein, to understand a sentence is to know what to do with it, to know the role it has in a shared linguistic activity, to be able to use it appropriately in a language-game.

In the second place, Wittgenstein's contextualist holism contains a *social* component which is missing from Quine's view of language. On Wittgenstein's view, the background against which understanding takes place is something which is intrinsically social, a shared 'form of life' (cf. PI §§19 and 23). For Quine, however, the background that is constitutive of understanding is a web of beliefs, which may or may not be shared by different speakers of the same language. Quine would certainly protest against a characterization of his view in individualistic terms since he has repeatedly emphasized the social character of language. However, Quine has a very thin notion of the social. According to Quine, what the webs of beliefs of different speakers have in common is the same empirical content, the same evidential basis. He emphasizes that what communication requires is that the speakers' background theories or translation manuals be 'empirically on a par' (1990, p. 33). On this view, the social basis of language is a set of associations between words and 'publicly observable situations' (e.g. 1990, p. 38). Thus the *social* character of language is reduced to its *public* character. Quine explicitly describes sociality in terms of publicity.[4] By contrast, Wittgenstein's view of language involves a more robust notion of what is intersubjectively shared. On his view, sociality is not reduced to publicity: the social basis of language is not what is publicly accessible to potential observers; it is a set of normative standards *actually shared* by the members of a practice.[5] For Wittgenstein, language involves 'a consensus of action'; it involves shared customs and techniques. This is the core idea of Wittgenstein's contextualism, namely, that to share a language is to share 'a form of life'. As Wittgenstein puts it, what is at the bottom of our linguistic practices, the 'bedrock' of language, is 'human agreement'; and this is a practical agreement: 'not agreement in opinions but in form of life' (PI §241). In the next section I will examine how a practical agreement can be effected through training processes and in what sense it is constitutive of the linguistic competence that learners acquire.

The differences between Wittgenstein's and Quine's holistic approach to language that I have emphasized are not just differences of detail. These differences reflect opposed views of language which are at the core of incompatible philosophical positions. What animates Quine's approach is what I would call, echoing Dewey,[6] a *spectator view* of language, that is, a view that privileges the perspective of an observer engaged in theory-construction. By contrast, what informs Wittgenstein's approach is a *participant view* of language that privileges the perspective of a social agent engaged in practices. This important discrepancy between Quine's and Wittgenstein's views of language is what motivates one aspect of the dispute between their followers, Davidson and Dummett. Dummett criticizes Davidson's account of linguistic understanding as consisting in a theory that an observer constructs, as a theoretical model, to accommodate all the evidence available for the speech to be interpreted. As we saw, according to Davidson, linguistic understanding can be captured in a theory of interpretation that functions as a theory of truth for the linguistic behaviour of the interlocutor, that is, a theory that correlates two idiolects by mapping the sentences that the speaker holds to be true onto the sentences that the interpreter would utter in her idiolect to make the same truth claims. Dummett (1986) argues that the Davidsonian account overintellectualizes linguistic understanding and ignores its social and practical aspects. Echoing Wittgenstein, Dummett contends that there must be *a form of understanding that is not an interpretation*.[7] Indeed our most basic and immediate form of understanding in ordinary contexts of communication does not seem to involve explicit interpretative efforts on our part;[8] instead, it seems to be a *tacit understanding* that relies on background capacities, that is, on our mastery of language. And it is important that this mastery or competence that supports communication be understood as a practical skill, as a *know-how* (practical knowledge), rather than a *know-that* (propositional knowledge) which can be exhaustively put into words. A philosophical account of linguistic understanding must distinguish between the ability to understand speech and the ability to specify how one understands speech in a theory. If this distinction is obscured, we run the risk of missing crucial aspects of communication. In particular, from a purely theoretical perspective, the *social* and *engaged* aspects of communications are likely to be missed, whereas they are brought to the fore in accounts developed from a practical perspective. As we will see in Chapter 5 (cf. 5.1), from the detached perspective of observers and theoreticians, what is shared in communication is minimized and the social dimension of language – even the very notion of a shared language – is ultimately denied.

As Dummett's critique of Davidson suggests, on the theoretical models developed in the empiricist tradition, communication does not appear as a process of *interaction* between interlocutors. On these models, there is no genuine interaction between engaged participants in communication, there is no give-and-take, no process of communicative negotiation in which there are communicative offers and communicative reactions to them. Instead, on this picture of communication, it is all a matter of *theorizing* about linguistic behaviour. On this view, communicators do not appear as partners in conversation, as speaker and hearer engaged with each other, but rather as *eavesdroppers* who try to make sense of each other from a distance, from the detached perspective of an observer. On the Davidsonian view – and the same is true of the Quinean view – communication is not depicted as a *dialogue*, but rather, as a series of *monologues* alongside each other, as idiolects' crossing paths. Dummett's critique suggests that Davidson's view distorts communication by depicting it as a peculiar kind of eavesdropping in which the people involved are in the business of constructing second-order theories, that is, theories (or theoretical models) about each other's theories.[9] Dummett argues that this account of communication in terms of second-order theories for eavesdroppers won't do, for, unless we appeal to a more immediate first-level of linguistic understanding, we are doomed to an infinite regress of theories about theories.

It is precisely this detached and spectatorial character – this eavesdropping character – of the Quinean and Davidsonian frameworks, that leads to meaning scepticism, turning ordinary degrees of indeterminacy in everyday contexts of communication into radical indeterminacy that casts doubt on communicative exchanges. Indeed, from the perspective of an eavesdropping theory of interpretation, meaning appears to be *radically indeterminate*. It is this discrepancy between a spectator (eavesdropping) view of language and a participant view of language that led Quine and Wittgenstein to adopt different positions on the issue of indeterminacy. Radical indeterminacy arises when we look at language from the detached perspective of an observer or theoretician who abstracts from particular contexts in order to codify information. This is the theoretical perspective of Quine's linguist or radical translator (as well as that of Davidson's radical interpreter). Quine contends that this is also the perspective that we all adopt as competent speakers of a language, which allows him to conclude that radical indeterminacy is intrinsic to language use and inescapable. Wittgenstein, however, would have serious doubts as to whether the methodology of radical translation can provide an appropriate model for the explanation of linguistic competence. For, on Wittgenstein's view, the perspective of a competent speaker is not the detached perspective of an observer who theorizes about language, but rather, the engaged perspective of a participant in a practice. And from the perspective of the participants in a language-game there is no *radical* indeterminacy. Meaning becomes determinate in particular contexts of action. It is contextually defined by the techniques of use shared by the members of a practice. These techniques do not draw a sharp boundary around the meaning of our terms, but they make meaning *contextually determinate* (often as determinate as seems to be necessary in the communicative exchange in question).[10]

So, for Wittgenstein, *radical* indeterminacy is the artifact of philosophical theories that lose sight of the contextual character of language use. The upshot of Wittgenstein's indeterminacy arguments is that the use of language cannot be separated from particular activities and the concrete contexts in which they take place. These arguments show that the normativity of a language-game cannot be fully captured in a list of explicit rules or, we could add, in a network of interconnected sentences or a translation manual. The norms of even the most basic linguistic activity become wholly indeterminate when they are decontextualized. *Radical* indeterminacy arises when we detach the rules of a language-game from their technique of application. And this technique is something that necessarily remains in the background: it is not a further set of rules, it is a skilled activity, something that can only be *shown* in actions. Techniques are embodied in what practitioners do 'as a *matter of course*' (PI §238). But Wittgenstein owes us an account of how we acquire the mastery of these techniques, of how we become competent practitioners. On the other hand, Quine owes us an account of how language can be learned at all given its radical indeterminacy.

3.2 TWO PHILOSOPHICAL MODELS OF LANGUAGE LEARNING

Despite his famous critique of empiricism, Quine is deeply committed to an empiricist account of language learning. He contends that 'two cardinal tenets of empiricism remain unassailable [. . .] to this day. One is that whatever evidence there is for science is sensory evidence. The other [. . .] is that *all inculcation of meanings of words must rest ultimately on sensory evidence*' (1969, p. 75; my emphasis). For Quine, language learning is an inductive process of accumulation of evidence and theory-construction. His account of this process is based on an analogy between the epistemic position of the child learning his/her first language and that of the linguist studying an exotic language: both the child and the linguist possess no knowledge whatsoever about the target language and both face the same challenge, namely, the construction of a complex theory using sensory experience as their sole evidential basis. Quine argues that what makes this challenge a manageable task is the patterns of sensory stimulations that the child shares with the adult speakers and the linguist with his/her informants. According to Quine, the learnability and teachability of language has to be explained by appealing to salient features of the environment that stimulate our sensory receptors in a similar fashion. He insists that there must be sentences which are directly tied to these shared stimulations. As we saw, these are *observation sentences* (cf. 2.3). Quine remarks that the observation sentences that first appear developmentally in language acquisition are typically one-word sentences such as 'Mama', 'Milk', etc. Observation sentences and their stimulus meanings provide the child with the evidential basis through which he/she can have access to language; they are, in Quine's words, 'the entering wedge in the learning of language' (1990, p. 5). On the basis of this meagre evidence the child, like the linguist, will have to guess at the meaning of non-observational or 'theoretical sentences', that is, sentences which get their meaning from their interconnections with other sentences.

So, for Quine, the process of language acquisition has two distinct parts: the learning of observation sentences and the learning of theoretical sentences. The former is a process of conditioning: 'Observation sentences [. . .] become associated with stimulations by the conditioning of responses' (ibid.). On the other hand, theoretical sentences are learned through an inductive process of hypothesis formation and testing: 'the linguist [. . .] rises above observation sentences through his analytical hypotheses; there he is trying to project into the native's associations and grammatical trends rather than his perceptions. And much the same must be true of the growing child' (p. 43). With the accumulation of well-confirmed hypotheses a theoretical structure is formed that binds together the sentences one has learned into a network or web of beliefs. It is always possible to come up with alternative theoretical structures that fit the evidence equally well; that is, one's evidential basis always allows for the reorganization or restructuring of one's web of beliefs. Hence the indeterminacy of meaning.

A very different picture of linguistic competence emerges from Wittgenstein's discussions of language learning. Like Quine, Wittgenstein emphasizes that in the initial stages of language learning certain associations between words and objects are established through causal processes (PI §6). These are processes of habituation such as the following: 'the learner [. . .] utters the word ["slab"] when the teacher points to the stone. And there will be this still simpler exercise: the pupil repeats the word after the teacher' (PI §7). With these drills the pupil learns to articulate certain sounds and to utter them in the presence of certain objects. In these exercises, Wittgenstein remarks, we can see 'processes resembling language' (ibid.). These processes resemble but are not yet language, for a language involves more than articulate sounds repeated in certain contexts and after certain signals. What we have here is a *protolanguage*, a language that we extend by courtesy to the primitive behaviour of the initiate learner. But how does the child move from mere causal associations between words and objects to higher levels of linguistic competence? Wittgenstein rejects the idea that this can be achieved by means of inductive processes of hypothesis formation and testing; for these processes require sophisticated linguistic capacities that the child does not yet have. Wittgenstein warns us against accounts of first-language acquisition which appeal to learning processes that can only occur in the acquisition of a second language – that is, processes that already presuppose the mastery of a language. According to Wittgenstein, this mistake has been pervasive in the history of philosophy. We can see it, for instance, in Augustine: 'Augustine describes the learning of human language as if the child came into a strange country and did not understand the language of the country; that is, as if it already had a language, only not this one. Or again: as if the child could already *think*, only not yet speak' (PI §32).

Wittgenstein argues that the Augustinian view of language learning misrepresents the interactions between the child and the adult by describing these interactions as part of a *guessing game* in which both participants have equal cognitive competence, but one of them knows something the other does not. On this view, language acquisition is a process in which the learner exercises his/her *autonomous* cognitive capacities in an independent fashion: he/she formulates hypotheses about what words mean and confirms or disconfirms them in the light of the evidence available to him/her. Against this view, Wittgenstein insists that in first-language learning the goal is not to gather linguistic information which one is already able to employ; the goal is, rather, to learn to do things as others do, that is, to master certain *techniques of use* by imitation. According to Wittgenstein, those accounts that assimilate first-language learning to second-language learning exhibit two interrelated flaws: first, the emergence of certain basic linguistic skills is left *unexplained* in these accounts; and second, as a result, these accounts *overly intellectualize* the process of learning a first language by endowing the child with rich cognitive capacities. Quine's account of language learning seems to be open to these two objections. In the first place, Quine does not explain how the language learner makes the transition from associative processes of conditioning to inductive process of hypothesis formation and testing. Quine's account leaves us in the lurch as to how the capacity to utter certain words in the presence of certain stimuli in a parrot-like fashion can enable the learner to formulate hypotheses concerning the meaning of theoretical sentences. So this account does seem to leave the acquisition of some linguistic skills unexplained. In the second place, Quine's analogy between the child and the linguist does seem to involve a strong intellectualization of the process of language learning, for this analogy leads Quine to treat the child as a little scientist whose task is to gather evidence and to construct a theory and who has the cognitive capacities involved in the inductive processes of hypothesis formation and testing.

Wittgenstein's discussion of language learning underscores that there are certain aspects of the mastery of language that a behaviourist and empiricist account such as Quine's cannot in principle explain. Such an account cannot explain how the behaviour of the learner becomes structured by *norms*; for the norms or standards of correctness that underlie language use cannot be reduced to either behavioural dispositions or empirical generalizations. According to Wittgenstein, what is acquired in language learning is more than a set of verbal dispositions and well-confirmed hypotheses; it is a set of normative standards for the application of words. For Wittgenstein, language learning involves a process of normative structuration of behaviour that goes beyond mere conditioning. His remarks on learning suggest that this normative structuring of behaviour is accomplished through a process of *socialization or enculturation*, that is, by being trained into rule-governed practices of language use. This aspect of language learning has been underscored by the recently developed paradigm of *cultural learning* in psychology.[11] It is the cornerstone of what I call an *enculturation view* of language learning. There are two central features of this view that contrast sharply with Quine's behaviourist and empiricist view of language learning.

In the first place, according to Wittgenstein, the process of language learning is a *social* process through and through. Of course it doesn't escape Quine's attention that language learning takes place in a social environment. But on Quine's view the role of the social environment is simply to provide exposure to certain stimuli that need to be associated with certain words. On Wittgenstein's view, however, language learning is social in a stronger sense: here the process of learning is not only occasioned, but also mediated and structured, by the social environment. In other words, on

Wittgenstein's view, language is learned not just *from* another, but *through* another. In this regard, Wittgenstein remarks that learning a language-game requires 'stage-setting', that is, a context structured by norms governing the correct use of words (cf. PI §257). This normative context can only be provided by a competent practitioner who frames, selects and feeds back the learner's use of words. Wittgenstein could not stress more the importance of the guidance provided by the masters of a linguistic practice to the initiate learners. The teacher or master of a practice plays an indispensable *structuring role* in the learning process; the very process is made possible only thanks to his/her guidance.

What characterizes the early stages of language learning is the relation of cognitive dependence of the learner on the teacher. It is only against the normative background provided by the teacher as a competent language user that the learner's utterances and actions acquire a normative dimension and become significant. The normative background that the teacher brings to bear upon the behaviour of the novice is progressively made available to the learner through the training, up to the point where the learner's behaviour becomes regulated by norms without the assistance of the teacher. By interacting with masters who structure and regulate the learning environment, novices come to adopt structuring and regulatory activities of their own. The process of language learning is, therefore, a process of acquiring autonomy or gaining control in normative practices. This process consists in a gradual shift of responsibility and authority, a developmental progression *from other-regulation to self-regulation*. Language learning is thus conceived, on Wittgenstein's view, as a process of enculturation or *apprenticeship*.[12] In the training process the teacher, by virtue of his/her competence in the practice, functions as a representative of the community of practitioners; and, as such, he/she has the capacity and authority to bring the behaviour of the novice into harmony with the behaviour of the rule-following community. The goal of the training process is to bring the pupil into the practice, and this is achieved by effecting a 'consensus of action' between the pupil and the teacher and hence, by the same token, between the pupil and the community of practitioners. As Wittgenstein puts it, 'instruction effects [. . .] *agreement in actions* on the part of pupil and teacher' (1978 VI.45; my emphasis). This practical agreement in ways of doing things entails a stronger notion of intersubjectivity than the one we found in Quine's view. For Quine, language learning requires nothing more than a perceptual agreement between pupil and teacher, an agreement based on shared stimulations. For Wittgenstein, however, the intersubjectivity required for the mastery of language involves more than sharing the same sensory receptors; it involves sharing the same ways of proceeding and the normative standards that go with them.

This brings us to a second point of contrast between Wittgenstein's and Quine's views of language learning. According to Wittgenstein's enculturation view, the learner's 'entering wedge into language' is not observation, but *action*. As noted above, Wittgenstein proposes a *participatory* view of learning. On this view, mastering a linguistic practice requires the learner's active participation in the practice. Initially the novice participates in the practice by imitating others. Learning by imitation does not have the passivity of conditioning, nor the disengaged character of the inductive processes of forming and testing hypotheses. It is a process of 'learning by doing'.[13] However, this process does not take place spontaneously and without aid. It is prompted and corrected by a teacher or experienced adult. Wittgenstein remarks that if I want to train someone in a uniform activity, I show him what to do first and then I give him guidance to follow my lead: 'I do it, he does it after me; and I influence him by expressions of agreement, rejection, expectation, encouragement. I let him go his way, or hold him back; and so on' (PI §208). Wittgenstein emphasizes that in order to respond appropriately to the teacher's guidance and correction, the learner needs to exhibit certain 'natural reactions'. But these natural reactions that are prerequisite for learning are not just perceptual reactions to salient features in the environment; they are also interpersonal reactions oriented towards action. The learner needs to be sensitive and responsive to certain signs of approval and disapproval that are used to structure his/her behaviour normatively.

According to Wittgenstein's enculturation view, the process of language learning is completed when the novice starts applying the learned procedures 'as a *matter of course*' (PI §238). This involves not only the establishment of a regularity in the learner's behaviour, but also the inculcation of a *normative attitude* towards how to proceed. Through repeated practice the novice internalizes the normative standards of the linguistic community; and by the end of the learning process the novice regards the way he/she has been taught to do things as the only way to proceed. Wittgenstein emphasizes that the training process, if successful, makes the learner *blind to alternatives*: the learner is taught to follow rules *blindly*, without considering alternative courses of action as possible applications of the rules. The alternative-blindness that according to Wittgenstein is characteristic of the mastery of a technique should not be confused with the blindness of reflexes and conditioned responses. The blind rule-following of competent practitioners is not the product of causal mechanisms; it results from the internalization of standards of correctness, it is informed by normative considerations as to how things *ought* to be done. Wittgenstein describes the adoption of normative standards through training with the image of the learner going 'in a circle'. He remarks that when the pupil sees how things *must* be done, 'he has gone in a circle' (1978, VI.7). The 'circle' created by the process of training into a technique consists in the following: that what the learner is trained to do becomes the criterion that defines what he/she is doing; that is, his/her activity is circularly defined by his/her own actions: how things must be done is defined by how things are actually done according to the learned procedure.

Wittgenstein's enculturation view of language learning can be read as an account of how indeterminacy is reduced in our ordinary linguistic practices.[14] This account shows that we can have semantic determinacy in our situated language-games (although this is never the absolute determinacy imagined by semantic foundationalism). This *contextual determinacy* is achieved through a consensus of action that is established by training processes.[15] Through these processes the shared procedures and techniques of a practice become *second nature*. And this second nature that we acquire through training reduces indeterminacy. From the perspective of the competent practitioner, the use of a term in a language-game is *not radically* indeterminate. From this perspective the application of a term may even appear as *overdetermined*: it is 'overdetermined', Wittgenstein remarks, by 'the way we always use it, the way we are taught to use it' (1978, I.2 and VI.16). But, of course, what is 'overdetermined' from within will appear utterly indeterminate from without. That is, if we break the connection between language use and shared techniques of application, *radical* indeterminacy will ensue. For it is only against the background of a practical agreement in forms of life that contextually determinate meanings become possible: 'For words have meaning only in the stream of life' (1980b §687).

3.3 ENCULTURATION AND SHARED INTENTIONALITY

The enculturation view of language learning I have sketched has been recently developed in developmental and cultural psychology by Michael Tomasello and his colleagues. Like Wittgenstein, Tomasello (1999, 2003) and Tomasello, Kruger and Ratner (1993) have argued that language learning requires a *social bond*: it requires seeing others as peers engaged in a cooperative activity. Tomasello and his colleagues have distinguished three different processes of cultural learning: *imitative* learning, *instructed* learning and *collaborative* learning. The study of these different learning processes of increasing sophistication and the different cognitive mechanisms on which they rely is what the enculturation view of language learning calls for. It is interesting to note that all these processes are alluded to in Wittgenstein's remarks on language learning. These different processes are involved in the developmental progression *from other-regulation to self-regulation*, which includes the following stages: first imitation, then closely monitored instruction directed by the masters of the language, and finally advanced forms of collaboration in which the learner becomes an autonomous participant who can take the initiative and is capable of self-correction. Tomasello and his colleagues have explained this developmental progression as a social process of cultural learning.

Tomasello, Carpenter, Call, Behne and Moll (forthcoming) offer a detailed account of the social component in language learning through the notion of 'shared intentionality'. They propose that the crucial difference between human cognition and that of other species resides in the human capacity for *shared intentionality*, that is, 'the ability to participate with others in collaborative activities with shared goals and intentions' (p. 1). This notion of 'shared intentionality' elaborates an idea we have seen in the Wittgensteinian account of language learning, namely: that the process of learning is not only occasioned, but also mediated and structured, by the social environment; that language is learned not just *from* another, but *through* another. Tomasello *et al.* (forthcoming) show that participation in activities through shared intentionality involves not only especially powerful forms of intention-reading and cultural learning, but also a unique motivation to share psychological states with others. They argue that 'the result of participating in these activities is species-unique forms of cultural cognition and evolution, enabling everything from the creation and use of linguistic symbols to the construction of social norms and individual beliefs to the establishment of social institutions' (ibid.). In support of this proposal Tomasello *et al.* (ibid.) present evidence that 'human children's skills of shared intentionality develop gradually during the first 14 months of life as two ontogenetic pathways intertwine: (i) the general ape line of understanding others as animate, goal-directed, and intentional agents, and (ii) a species-unique motivation to share emotions, experience, and activities with other persons' (ibid.). The result of children's participation in collaborative activities through shared intentionality is the development of the ability to construct dialogic cognitive representations, which enable children to participate in 'the collectivity that is human cognition'. This social aspect of human cognition has also been stressed in recent research on language learning in linguistics (both in first-language and second-language acquisition).

The enculturation paradigm of language learning I have articulated following Wittgenstein is a philosophical model that has also been proven fruitful in recent research in linguistics. Marysia Johnson's *A Philosophy of Second Language Acquisition* (2004) uses this paradigm in her critical arguments against the cognitivist and experimentalist views that have dominated the research and theory in second-language acquisition. It is also this paradigm that is behind her positive proposal. This is an alternative framework for second-language acquisition theory, research and teaching that Johnson develops from Vygotsky's socio-cultural theory and Bakhtin's dialogical theory. This Vygotskian and Bakhtinian framework is highly compatible with the enculturation paradigm I have derived from Wittgenstein. In fact, what Johnson does is to apply the enculturation paradigm – through Vygotsky (1986) and Bakhtin (1981) rather than through Wittgenstein – to second-language acquisition. Johnson shows that narrow cognitivist and experimentalist approaches are not sufficient to understand the complex phenomenon of second-language acquisition, for this is a phenomenon that takes place not only in the learner's mind but also in a dialogical interaction conducted in a variety of socio-cultural and institutional settings. Therefore, Johnson argues, we have to pay attention both to the mental and the social processes involved in language learning: we have to investigate the dynamic and dialectical relationships between the interpersonal and the intrapersonal in the processes that make possible the acquisition of a second language.

Johnson's framework thus shifts the focus of second-language acquisition from abstract and formal competence to the interaction between practical competence and actual performance in socially and historically situated settings. As Johnson puts it, in her framework 'second language acquisition is viewed not in terms of competence but in terms of performance' (2004, p. 4). According to this socio-cultural and performative approach, language learning requires 'active involvement on the part of teachers, students, researchers, and theoreticians' (p. 3). On this view, the process of language learning should ultimately aim at dialogical interactions in which all the participants have equal status and authority so that there is genuine cooperation and collaborative learning. As Johnson boldly puts it, 'without a new theoretical framework that empowers all the parties involved, all our discussions about teachers' and students' greater involvement in the process of SLA [second-language acquisition] knowledge-building are futile' (ibid.). The emphasis on active participation as a constitutive element of language learning is also a crucial part of Wittgenstein's enculturation view. As we saw, this is a *participatory* view of learning in which the learner's 'entering wedge into language' is not observation, but *action*. Johnson (2004) recognizes that, along with Vygotsky and Bakhtin, Wittgenstein (and others) also held 'similar views regarding the role of society, culture, and institutions in the development of human cognition'. (p. 5). These leading thinkers are part of a lost philosophical tradition in the study of language learning that is now beginning to re-emerge. At the core of this tradition is an enculturation view: 'a dialogical and socio-cultural view of human thought, language, and communication' (ibid.).

On the enculturation view of language, communication is depicted as a *meeting of minds*, that is, as the coordination of perspectives from which shared mental structures emerge. This meeting of minds or shared intentionality is at the core of the semantic and pragmatic issues we have examined in this book: it is what makes co-reference possible and what generates the contextual determinacy of meaning. But how is shared intentionality produced and maintained beyond the learning situations in ordinary contexts of communication? Shared intentionality and its products (semantic determinacy and co-reference) are fragile and transitory achievements that always remain dependent on the negotiations and transactions of the participants in linguistic interactions. As an illustration of the production of shared intentionality in and through linguistic communication, in the next section I will discuss how the contextual determinacy of meaning is achieved through the communicative efforts and cooperation of partners in conversation. I will use this discussion to introduce the reader to the rich research on language carried out in *conversation analysis*.

3.4 CONVERSATION ANALYSIS

In linguistic interaction there are mechanisms for achieving and maintaining the contextual determinacy of meaning required by communication. These pragmatic mechanisms have been explored by researchers in conversation analysis, a framework of investigation in pragmatics developed by the pioneer work of Harvey Sacks. Drawing on ethnomethodology and especially on the work of Garfinkel,[16] Sacks (1992) studied how everyday reality is 'accomplished' and made 'observable/reportable' or 'storyable'. In his *Lectures on Conversation* he argues that we acquire 'routine ways' of dealing with scenes which enable us to understand each other. These 'routine ways' are embedded in particular communicative contexts and their normative structures; and it is by virtue of them that linguistic understanding becomes attainable in local contexts, that is, *in situ*. Sacks' pioneering work in conversation analysis, as well as subsequent research (see the different papers contained in Boden and Zimmerman, 1991), give empirical confirmation to the thesis of contextual determinacy I have developed from a Wittgensteinian perspective. In his analysis of the sequential organization of conversation Sacks (1992) identifies two central sources of contextual constraints: one *institutional* and the other *interactional*. In the first place, conversation is an integral part of activities that take place in 'appropriate' places, in institutionalized settings for linguistic interaction; and this conventionalized situatedness constrains what can be said and how to interpret what is said. In the second place, conversational exchanges are *'chained'*; and given the sequential 'chained' nature of conversation, the significance of each utterance is constrained by what has been said before and by what will be said thereafter, that is, by the *previous and future utterances* to which the utterance in question is 'chained'. The constraints arising from the institutional and interactional dimensions of conversation contribute to make meanings contextually determinate. As we saw, contextual determinacy is a fragile and transitory interpretative achievement that remains always dependent on the transactions of the participants in communication. To illustrate the contextual constraints impinging upon the interpretative negotiations between speakers, let us consider four mechanisms identified by the research in conversation analysis carried out by Sacks and his followers. These conversational mechanisms that contribute to making meanings contextually determinate are 'heckling', 'delayed interpretation', 'averting' and 'repairing'.

Sacks identifies the phenomenon of *'heckling'* in his analysis of storytelling as it appears in conversational exchanges. 'Heckling' occurs when the storyteller is interrupted and questioned about the intelligibility of his/her story. 'Heckling' can take the radical form of challenging intelligibility altogether: 'That sounds crazy', 'That doesn't make sense', 'That's nonsense', etc.; or it can take the weaker form of requesting an explicit articulation or explanation of meaning: 'What does that mean?', 'And what's the point of that?', etc. Sacks emphasizes that 'heckling' is always a possibility; and accordingly, he remarks, storytellers 'design their stories so as not to invite heckling, or to be in some way invulnerable to heckling' (1992, p. 287). This is the phenomenon of 'anti-heckling'. Among the examples of 'anti-heckling' that Sacks cites are 'This sounds crazy but . . .' and 'you may have heard this one before . . .'.

As important as the phenomenon of 'heckling', if not more so, is the fact that very often hearers refrain from asking a storyteller what something means because they expect to find out later. This is not specific to storytelling, but it is in fact a general feature of conversation. As Silverman (1998) puts it, 'in conversation we do not always expect to find out what things mean right at the start' (p. 120). Sacks explains this feature by saying that hearers follow 'a delay-interpretation rule', according to which they are not supposed to interpret the speaker's words as they are said, but rather, they are expected to accumulate 'some storage' of information until the 'chaining' of utterances provides enough context for the interpretative process to get off the ground (1992, p. 315). The phenomenon of *'delayed interpretation'* and the attitude of interpretative patience that goes with it are crucial for communication, for they allow for the full development of a contextual determinacy that is already in the making. This phenomenon involves a communicative attitude of cooperation in the construction of semantic determinacy. Hearers often exhibit a collaborative attitude that recognizes contextual determinacy in progress and tries to facilitate its construction.

A third conversational mechanism that contributes to the construction and maintenance of contextual determinacy is what we can call 'averting', that is, the act of trying to prevent misunderstandings, to discard possible misinterpretations. Attempts at averting misunderstandings are often preceded by such phrases as 'I mean . . .' or 'The point is . . .'. There are all kinds of deviant interpretations that could in principle become compelling at one point or another in the conversation. It is obviously not feasible to anticipate all *possible* misunderstandings and, therefore, speakers restrict their 'averting' to what they consider to be likely misinterpretations. Typically, 'averting' occurs only when there is some reason or indication to expect a misunderstanding. Otherwise, speakers address the instances of misinterpretation or lack of understanding of their words as they come up. This piecemeal mending or patching up of the interpretation of one's words is what Sacks calls the phenomenon of 'repairing'. According to Sacks, 'repair mechanisms' operate as mechanisms of 'local cleansing' triggered by 'remedial questions' that occur immediately after the problematic term, phrase or sentence whose intelligibility requires clarification (1992, p. 560). By default, Sacks points out, speakers are entitled to assume that their words were heard and understood in the absence of requests for clarification or 'repairing' (see 1992, p. 352).

What is most interesting about the phenomena of 'averting' and 'repairing' is that they are not just the individual duty of the speaker, but rather, the collective responsibility of all participants in communication. 'Averting' and 'repairing' are in fact very often executed through the collaboration of different partners in conversation. This shows that contextual determinacy is collectively achieved through collaborative efforts. Narrowing down interpretative possibilities and keeping meanings contextually determinate are the result of joint communicative efforts of conversational partners. Excellent illustrations of collaborative 'averting' and 'repairing' can be found in the transcripts from news interviews studied by Heritage and Greatbatch (1991). Both interviewed subjects and news anchors collaborate to facilitate the audience's understanding, in some cases by jointly 'averting' likely misunderstandings or inaccurate interpretations, and in other cases by jointly 'repairing' ambiguous phrases or terms hard to interpret in impoverished conversational contexts. I reproduce here two short excerpts from the transcript of a news interview. They come from a BBC interview of ex-Labour British Prime Minister James Callaghan, conducted by (the politician turned political journalist) Shirley Williams. The first excerpt illustrates collaborative 'averting' (or preventive 'repairing'): Callaghan's reference to education can be understood in many ways, from improving literacy to promoting social awareness; so trying to 'avert' plausible misinterpretations, Williams suggests a qualification ('You mean *political* education'). In the second excerpt there is an interesting instance of collaborative 'repairing' in which one speaker clarifies the other speaker's utterance, and the latter in turn expands on the clarification of the former; so that we go from a very vague and ambiguous reference ('a lot') to a more specific point about originality ('new ideas'), and from there to an even more specific point about the productivity of new ideas.

EXCERPT 1
Callaghan: We've neglected education. We've allowed it all to fall into the hands of the militant groups. (I mean) they do more education than anybody else.
Williams: You mean *political* education.
Callaghan: Yes, political education. (Heritage and Greatbatch 1991, p. 111)

EXCERPT 2
Callaghan: There is at the moment a gap in our thinking. I think that's got to be filled. Because a number of the things for example that uhm . . . Tony Benn says have got a lot to be be er- er- er- have got a lot in them. I mean some of his analysis has got a great deal in it.
Williams: Oh yes. He's got a great deal of er of . . . thinking. [. . .] his are new ideas.
Callaghan: He's a very fertile . . . well uh he- he- he expounds these new and fertile ideas. hhh uhm And I think that we shouldn't neglect them wherever they come from. (Heritage and Greatbatch 1991, p. 118)

The research in conversation analysis shows that meanings are not static entities, but dynamic structures that emerge from contextualized linguistic interaction. As Silverman (1998), for one, has put it, even the most apparently obvious and fixed categories 'should be viewed as an accomplishment of members' local, sequential interpretation' (p. 109). These situated interpretative interactions are orchestrated so as to produce *contextually determinate* meanings. As Wittgenstein suggests, language-games always have a *point* that normatively structures the communicative exchanges that take place in them. Wittgenstein (1975) emphasizes that it is 'immensely important' that our uses of language have 'a *point*' (p. 205), that is, that they play a role in regulating our dealings with the world and with each other, that they be integrated in our forms of life. But having a point, he remarks, is always 'a matter of degree'; and the extent to which the use of a term has a point depends on the context in which that use figures. Thus meaning becomes determinate in particular contexts. What we say and do acquires significance only against the background of a tacit agreement underlying these contexts. When our interpretations are detached from particular contexts and their underlying consensus, meanings become *radically* indeterminate: all possible interpretations become equally reasonable or belief-worthy (as the sceptical thesis of *cognitive egalitarianism* suggests). We cannot rule out *a priori* any logically possible semantic interpretation, no matter how far-fetched. But in particular linguistic contexts and activities, as we have seen, there are many constraints that restrict our interpretative negotiations, narrowing down the set of admissible interpretative possibilities significantly and deeming many logical possibilities deviant and unreasonable interpretations. For example, as I have said against Quine, rabbit-hunters do not entertain the sceptical doubt of whether the term 'rabbit' refers to rabbits, to *rabbit-stages* (temporal slices in the life of a rabbit) or to undetached rabbit-parts. The sceptic will insist that what is in question is not whether as a matter of empirical fact these alternative interpretations are considered, but rather, whether they should be. Ignoring nonstandard interpretations of our words, or pretending that they don't exist, is not acceptable if these interpretations have a legitimate claim to be considered. Our refusal to consider these interpretations out of mere stubbornness would undermine the normative validity of our claims concerning meaning. But the point of my argument in this chapter is that sceptical interpretative hypotheses are normatively excluded from local communicative contexts: for example, hunters *cannot* entertain Quinean sceptical doubts as long as they remain engaged in the activity we call 'rabbit-hunting'.

The crucial move of the argument in this chapter has been to shift the burden of proof on to the shoulders of the sceptic. Drawing on Wittgenstein and conversation analysis, my argument has consisted in contextualist considerations which show that the normative structure of our practices *excludes* certain interpretations from the meaning of our words; and this *normative exclusion* constitutes a *prima facie* reason against considering them, for their consideration runs against the tacit agreement in action underlying our practices and threatens these practices with 'losing their point'. So, with a *prima facie* reason *against* interpretations that don't fit the background consensus of a practice and in the absence of any reason *for* them, the balance tips against the sceptical semantic hypotheses and, therefore, they should be considered an illegitimate intromission in our appraisals of meaning. But it is important to note that these interpretative hypotheses are deemed unworthy of consideration, an illegitimate intromission in our semantic evaluations, *only in so far as they are mere logical possibilities*, that is, *until reasons for them are given*. It is important to note that this is a shift of the burden of proof and not a direct and final refutation of semantic scepticism. For indeed, on the contextualist view under consideration, we cannot exclude the possibility of the sceptical hypotheses (or of *any* interpretative hypothesis for that matter) becoming relevant and reasonable to entertain. To rule out these interpretative hypotheses from consideration once and for all, simply because they can threaten our consensus of action and the intelligibility of our practices, would be to say that we refuse to consider them simply because we dogmatically and arbitrarily want to stick to the current background agreement and preserve the *status quo* come what may. There is no room in the Wittgensteinian contextualism articulated in this chapter for a conservative attitude towards semantic innovations.[17] But how far can we depart from the normative agreement of linguistic communities and still make sense? In the remaining chapters we will discuss the issue of how radically we can depart from conventions and established use without losing intelligibility and falling into nonsense. What (if any) are the constraints on linguistic creativity? What (if any) are the limits of intelligibility?

CHAPTER 4

LINGUISTIC CREATIVITY AND RELATIVISM

4.1 LINGUISTIC CREATIVITY AND THE SOCIOLOGY OF LANGUAGE

At least since Humboldt philosophers of language have been concerned with the issue of *linguistic creativity*. How can we explain the inexhaustible capacity for linguistic production that competent speakers seem to have? This linguistic competence has often been described as an *infinite* generative capacity, that is, as the capacity to produce an infinite number of grammatically well-formed and meaningful sentences. Since Humboldt described linguistic competence as an infinite capacity, the mystery has been taken to be how to explain our ability to produce infinite linguistic outputs with *finite means*. The structuralists and formalists of the twentieth century tried to explain the infinite productivity of our linguistic capacities by appealing to formal mechanisms for the manipulation of signs. On this view, the production of speech consists in mechanical processes of sign manipulation, in operations on the form of signs according to rules of syntax. The foundations of this contemporary formalist account can be found in structural linguistics. The Swiss linguist and founder of the school of structural linguistics, Ferdinand de Saussure (1857–1913), conceived of language as an impersonal abstract system or *code* (*la langue*) from which spring the multifarious varieties of individual *speech events* (*la parole*). On this view, a code is more than a lexicon (a mere collection of terms); it contains a complex syntactic structure that gives form to particular linguistic performances, unifying all the instances of use of that code. Thus the syntax or grammar of language was conceived as an engine capable of producing infinite outputs with finite inputs and, therefore, the key to solving the mystery of linguistic creativity.

A more sophisticated account of linguistic competence as grammatical competence was developed by the American linguist Noam Chomsky (1965, 1972) in his theory of *generative grammar*. According to Chomsky, the production of speech involves the application of generative rules of grammar which must be there from the beginning and are, therefore, unlearned. On this view, linguistic competence consists in the possession of a universal and innate grammar, and it involves the ability to perform complex transformational operations on a natural language according to universal rules of syntax. A language learner must be able to connect his/her innate universal grammar with the grammar of the particular language to which he/she is exposed. This theory of generative grammar was developed to address a central problem concerning language learning, the *so-called problem of the poverty of stimulus*: How are children capable of identifying the grammar of a language on the basis of minimal exposure to it? How can a small and imperfect array of utterances stimulate the child to speak in a rule-governed and systematic way? Chomsky argued that we cannot solve this problem unless we postulate an innate grammatical apparatus that enables the learner to filter, systematize and generalize the scarce linguistic information that becomes available to him/her. He used this argument to refute the behaviourist account of language learning provided by Watson (1930) and Skinner (1957). Following Chomsky, Jerry Fodor (1975) argued that the transformations back and forth between universal grammar and the grammar of natural languages take place in an innate language of thought (which he termed *Mentalese*). Both Chomsky and Fodor argued that what explains the infinite productivity of our linguistic capacities is the *compositionality* and *systematicity* of language: we possess compositional rules that can be applied systematically on a finite set of signs to produce infinite combinatorial possibilities.

But were these formalist and structuralist accounts of linguistic competence on the right track? Did they formulate the problem of linguistic creativity correctly? In an interesting contextualist twist in the debate about linguisitic creativity, the French sociologist Pierre Bourdieu (1991) argued that the mystery of linguistic creativity does not concern infinite productivity, but *appropriate performance*: what is mysterious is not that we can produce an unlimited number of utterances but rather, that out of what is in principle an infinite number of possible expressions we often manage to produce one that actually fits the context of utterance, we often manage to select an expression that is appropriate to the particular speech situation we find ourselves in! How do we accomplish this feat? Arguing more specifically against Saussure and Chomsky, Bourdieu contends that the competence that actual speakers really possess is not a generative competence of infinite productivity, which is nothing more than an abstraction, but a capacity to produce expressions *à propos*: that is, the ability to come up with appropriate utterances for concrete speech situations we have never encountered before. According to Bourdieu, the mastery of language consists in a highly situated and essentially contextual ability: a 'practical sense' (*sens pratique*) that cannot be reduced to an abstract set of generative rules or algorithmic recipes for sign manipulation. This is what is instilled in linguistic training. Language learning is successfully completed when the learner has acquired a particular way of speaking and listening, a linguistic *habitus* that is exhibited in the actual and situated performances of his/her embodied speech. Our linguistic habitus is a set of dispositions that control our production of speech and our reception of the speech of others.[1] The speaker's habitus contains stable forms of sensitivity and generativity that have been laboriously manufactured through repeated performance.

According to Bourdieu's theory of the habitus, the habitual receptivity and productivity of our linguistic competence is socially and historically situated. This theory underscores that our linguistic capacities are *heavily constrained*: we are not free in our linguistic productions; we are subject to linguistic constraints that have a political and socio-economic basis. Bourdieu criticizes formal and abstract accounts of linguistic competence such as those of Saussure and Chomsky for failing to recognize linguistic constraints and for giving speakers an illusory sense of freedom and autonomy. For Bourdieu, the idea that we have absolute freedom and autonomy in our use of language is an illusion, and not an innocent one, for it has dangerous social and political ramifications. Later we will discuss the social and political dangers of denying constraints on linguistic performance and affirming linguistic freedom or autonomy (see Chapter 5). It is sufficient to note here that by ignoring linguistic constraints and their political and socio-economic basis, the formal and abstract accounts of linguistic competence are being *complicit* with the social and political forces that domesticate language use, without acknowledging these forces.

According to Bourdieu, the constitution of a language is a historical process in which socio-political and economic forces compete to
empower the modes of expression of certain classes or social groups
and to disempower those of others. Bourdieu insists that we must
take into account the power struggles that go into the formation of
a language and the power relations that are always present in its use.
This is especially clear when there is a language that has been explicitly declared 'the official language': 'The official language is bound
up with the state, both in its genesis and in its social uses' (1991, p.
45). Bourdieu argues that the political struggles that took place in
the development of modern nation–states had a crucial linguistic
dimension: they included struggles for the monopoly of language. In
other words, a crucial part of the process of political unification was
a process of linguistic unification to control people's forms of
expression. It was indispensable for the making of the nation 'to
forge a *standard* language' (p. 48). Bourdieu's historical analysis of
the development of the French language shows that for centuries
France had a wild variety of regional dialects in tension and in com-
petition with each other instead of a single national language.
Bourdieu observes that from the fourteenth century onwards 'the
common language which was developed in Paris in cultivated circles'
was 'promoted to the status of official language'; and the other side
of this historical process of instituting an official language was that
the popular and purely oral uses of all the regional dialects degen-
erated into *patois*, that is, into nonsensical, corrupted or simply
vulgar speech.[2] After the French Revolution an intellectual elite or
revolutionary intelligentsia continued this process of linguistic unification with the elaboration and imposition of an official language:
'The imposition of the legitimate language in opposition to the
dialects and *patois* was an integral part of the political strategies
aimed at perpetuating the gains of the Revolution through the production and the reproduction of the "new man"' (p. 47). As we shall
see later and in the next chapter, the process of establishing and
remodeling the configuration of a language (consolidating its rules,
its accepted usage, etc.) is a process of *identity formation*: a process
that reconfigures the identity of the linguistic community and of the
individuals in it. By shaping language in a particular way one shapes
the mentality and ideology of the people who use it. For this reason,
the consolidation of a new language was an important part of the
political struggles that the intellectuals of the French Revolution

undertook: struggles to de-authorize the old language of monarchic authority and to combat the proliferation of alternative regional languages that could compete with the new official language of the Revolution and destabilize the authority of the new central government. This is how Bourdieu describes the process of linguistic reformation and the political struggles behind it:

> To reform a language, to purge it of the usages linked to the old society and impose it in its purified form, was to impose a thought that would itself be purged and purified. [. . .] The conflict between the French of the revolutionary intelligentsia and the dialects or *patois* was a **struggle for symbolic power** in which what was a stake was the *formation* and *re-formation* of mental structures. In short, it was not only a question of communicating but of gaining recognition for a new language of authority. (1991, pp. 47–8; emphasis preserved and added)

Language has the power both to unite and to divide people: as we shall see, it can be as much the site of struggle and division as the site of social, political and cultural solidarity. So it is not surprising that language can play such a powerful role in the formation of collective identities. Bourdieu suggests that the unification of means of expression is at the same time the consolidation of a collective identity (ethnic, cultural and/or national identity). For Bourdieu, a linguistic community is always a political unit in which the socio-political and economic structures mesh in complex ways with the linguistic structures. According to Bourdieu, maintaining the linguistic unity of a community always involves (some degree of) 'linguistic domination', that is, it involves the *imposition* of a *legitimate* language, the privileging of a particular set of uses; for 'integration into a single "linguistic community"' is always 'the product of political domination that is endlessly reproduced by institutions capable of imposing universal recognition of the dominant language' (1991, p. 46). A dominant way of speaking and writing is maintained and transmitted from generation to generation by a complex network of formal and informal, public and private practices and institutions, which include schooling, the family, religion, the labour market, etc. The reproduction of the legitimate language is accomplished with the collaboration of academic, cultural and educational institutions that domesticate language and fix usage by sanctioning certain uses of language as legitimate and other as illegitimate. Bourdieu stresses in particular the decisive role that the educational system plays in the imposition of a dominant and official language by 'fashioning similarities from which that community of consciousness which is the cement of the nation stems' (p. 48). On this view, the educational system accomplishes two tasks simultaneously: producing and reproducing the official language and building 'the common consciousness of the nation' (p. 49). Bourdieu remarks that it is not surprising that the school system can play this dual role since the schoolmaster is both a *maître à parler* (teacher of speaking) and a *maître à penser* (teacher of thinking). The linguistic training that takes place in schooling contributes enormously 'to devalue popular modes of expression, dismissing them as "slang" and "gibberish" [. . .] and to impose recognition of the legitimate language' (ibid.).

According to Bourdieu's social account, a linguistic habitus is a capacity that has become stylistically marked through a *history of habituation* that is both *individual and collective*. Therefore, in order to fully understand someone's linguistic habitus, we need to elucidate the processes of habit formation that have taken place not only during the lifetime of the individual but also in the history of his/her community. The habitus is a historically produced style and cannot be taken as a given. To treat a habitus as something given, without a history, is to disregard and occlude the constitution of its normative structure and, therefore, to *misrecognize* its normative principles: that is, to leave unrecognized the power struggles that have gone into the production of this form of speech and the ones that are still ongoing, that is, the power struggles that sustain it. This is precisely the main flaw of the formal and abstract accounts of linguistic competence: they are guilty of this form of misrecognition (*méconnaissance*). Hence their complicity with the powers that be. For in these accounts the struggles for establishing what count as correct and incorrect uses of language are not simply ignored, but in fact masked and hidden by idealizations. In the first place, Bourdieu argues that structuralist accounts that study language as a *code* in a completely abstract (i.e. ahistorical and asocial) way tacitly privilege official languages: 'Saussure's *langue*, a code both legislative and communicative which exists and subsists independently of its users ("speaking subjects") and its uses (*parole*), has in fact all the properties commonly attributed to official language. [. . .] To speak of the language, without further specification, as linguists do, is tacitly to accept the official definition of the official language of a political unit' (1991, pp. 44–5). In the second place, Bourdieu argues that formalist accounts that abstract from the concrete socio-historical conditions of language use and idealize linguistic competence have dangerous political implications. But what is the danger in talking about an ideal perfect speaker with a perfect mastery of language? Linguists are indeed aware that this perfect competence is, like 'frictionless planes' in physics, an abstraction that doesn't exist; but the problem is that they don't seem to recognize the political implications of this abstraction, for which they have to take responsibility. Bourdieu argues that by grounding the legitimate and illegitimate uses of language in a universal form of competence from which they flow, linguists legitimate the symbolic power of the political institutions and authorities that regiment the social life of language. This is how he summarizes his critique of Chomsky: 'Chomsky, converting the immanent laws of legitimate discourse into universal norms of correct linguistic practice, sidesteps the question of the economic and social conditions of the acquisition of the legitimate competence and of the constitution of the market in which this definition of the legitimate and the illegitimate is established and imposed' (p. 44).

Bourdieu argues that the idealizations of formalism and structuralism are dangerous fictions that contribute to maintain the *status quo* within linguistic communities, for they create the false impression that speakers are unconstrained in their linguistic behaviour, making them blind to their linguistic oppression. And the illusion of freedom and autonomy brings with it another illusion, namely: the myth of *equality*, what Bourdieu calls 'the illusion of *linguistic communism*' (p. 43). This is the picture of language as a universal 'treasure' in which everybody can partake equally. But in actual linguistic communities there is no equal access to linguistic resources: there are differences in upbringing, in schooling, in access to higher learning and, more generally, in the social environment in which one leads one's life; and these differences result in the mastery of different vocabularies and rhetorical devices, in different pronunciations, dictions and writing styles and in different discursive competences. The overall value of one's modes of expression is what Bourdieu calls one's *linguistic capital*, which determines the *profits* that one can make in linguistic exchanges. These profits can be gains in social status and influence, but sometimes they are directly economic profits: for example, the profit of the use of language in a job interview (that is, speaking with certain diction, in a masculine or feminine way, using certain terms, etc.). It is important to note that language is not used in an abstract space of logical relations, but in a social space that is structured by power relations. Bourdieu refers to communicative contexts as *linguistic markets* to emphasize the socio-economic dimension of linguistic exchanges. There are socio-economic gains and losses in our communicative exchanges, whether directly or indirectly. In the linguistic market some people accumulate gains and accrue linguistic capital while others accumulate losses and thus become *linguistically dispossessed*. The phenomenon of 'linguistic dispossession' cannot be accommodated in formal and abstract accounts of linguistic competence, which ignore the unequal distribution of linguistic resources in actual linguistic communities. But only for those who have a good amount of linguistic capital can it make sense to abstract from the obstacles and inequalities that handicap verbal behaviour and to explain linguistic skills with ideal models of the perfect speaker. Idealized accounts of linguistic competence speak from a position of privilege; and they can only benefit those who have not suffered from exclusions and marginalization in linguistic communities. As Bourdieu suggests, it is socially and politically irresponsible to simply disregard the pervasive phenomenon of 'linguistic dispossession'. This dispossession is most patent in those whose dialects, lingos or mannerisms have been marginalized and stigmatized. But linguistic dispossession affects all speakers in so far as they cannot have full control of how language usage develops and of how different uses become valued or devalued. Even the most empowered and sophisticated academic speaker is vulnerable to linguistic dispossession to some degree: he can occasionally become linguistically dispossessed in particular contexts, for particular purposes and with respect to some linguistic subcommunities.

The idealizations of structuralist and formalist linguistics are based on the thesis of the *priority of competence over performance*. In order to undo these dangerous fictions and to uncover the political and socio-economic dimensions of linguistic competence, Bourdieu argues for a sociology of language that reverses the assumed order of priority between competence and performance. Thus he proposes the *priority of performance over competence*: it is competence that derives from performance, not the other way round. Through a process of habituation we develop our linguistic capacities: it is not an innate competence that enables us to speak, it is our speaking repeatedly in the same way that sediments a habitual capacity for language use. Against Saussurean and Chomskian linguistics, Bourdieu contends: ' *"languages" exist only in the practical state*, i.e. in the form of so many linguistic habitus which are at least partially orchestrated, and of the oral productions of these habitus' (p. 46; my emphasis). He proposes a new discipline for the study of language: the *sociology of language*, which investigates how language and linguistic competence have been socially and historically constituted, how the linguistic habitus of individuals and groups are orchestrated through social and political processes.

The central object of investigation in the sociology of language is not grammatical competence but *social acceptability*. What this discipline studies is what is (has become) socially acceptable in language use, and not just what is (has become) grammatically correct. As Bourdieu puts it, 'the competence adequate to produce sentences that are likely to be understood may be quite inadequate to produce sentences that are likely to be *listened to*, likely to be recognized as acceptable in all the situations in which there is occasion to speak. Here again, *social acceptability is not reducible to mere grammaticality*' (1991, p. 55, emphasis preserved and added). According to Bourdieu, the task of the sociology of language[3] is to investigate how certain ways of using language are *distinguished* and acquire *social value*, and how certain forms of linguistic competence and not others acquire linguistic capital: 'the legitimate competence can function as *linguistic capital*, producing a *profit of distinction* on the occasion of each social exchange' (ibid.). A crucial aspect of a linguistic habitus is that it operates and develops in a field of social distinctions that become linked to stylistic distinctions. What characterizes a linguistic market is a field of stylistic alternatives or variants that define themselves *vis-à-vis* the others. This is why one of the central concepts in Bourdieu's sociology of language is *the distinction*. According to Bourdieu, linguistic habitus or styles have an essential *contrastive* dimension: by distinguishing themselves from each other, they become valued or devalued. 'The social uses of language owe their specifically social value to the fact that they tend to be organized in systems of difference [. . .] which reproduce, in the symbolic order of differential deviations, the system of social differences' (p. 54).

Bourdieu offers a sociological account of how different habitus function in the linguistic market as different 'articulatory styles'. As he puts it, a style 'is a being-perceived which exists only in relation to perceiving subjects, endowed with the diacritical dispositions which enable them to make *distinctions* between different *ways of saying*, distinctive manners of speaking'; 'style [. . .] exists only in relation to agents endowed with schemes of perception and appreciation that enable them to constitute it as a set of systematic differences' (1991, pp. 38–9). The sociology of language must study the way in which stylistic distinctions relate to socio-economic distinctions and become embedded in a grid of power relations in linguistic markets. The distribution of linguistic capital in a community is established and maintained by a complex network of social and cultural practices and institutions. In this network intellectuals play a crucial role, for they are in charge of 'normalizing the products of the linguistic habitus' (p. 48). Members of the intellectual elite or intelligentsia of a linguistic community engage in 'literary struggles' for establishing the literary canon, that is, the texts that are going to be considered canonical in that language and will be taught to the next generations (Shakespearian plays, for example). Intellectuals fight to control the linguistic capital of a community or culture not only by selecting the classics, but also by deciding how these classical texts will be read, interpreted and taught, thus setting the parameters for language use in different contexts. Intellectuals also participate in other practices and institutions that shape the linguistic habitus of the community. For example, they are typically the members of the Royal Academies of language and those in charge of composing dictionaries. And of course, as Bourdieu points out, 'the dictionary is the exemplary result of this labor of codification and normalization' (ibid.). Finally, as we saw, the educational system also plays a decisive role in shaping the linguistic habitus of a community. And given the relationship between schooling and the labour market, the educational system establishes a direct link between one's access to linguistic resources and one's economic standing in society. These are the central socio-economic, cultural and political elements involved in the formation and reformation of a linguistic habitus.[4]

Bourdieu's account of the social processes that contribute to the perpetuation of a habitus or style and to the repression and marginalization of other habitus or styles is an account of how society tames the *linguistic creativity* of speakers. Although his theory emphasizes the unification and orchestration of the linguistic behaviour of speakers, Bourdieu recognizes that there are always stylistic changes, deviations and distinctions, even in the most rigid and homogeneous communities. For one thing, there are always stylistic changes in the passage from one generation to another. Bourdieu argues that there are always generational symbolic conflicts, no matter how subtle and tacit they may be. He talks about 'symbolic struggles' between generations in which the new generation revises the standard view of how to speak and write and negotiates how to train the next generation of speakers. According to Bourdieu, there is always and unavoidably some degree of stylistic diversity: there are always divergent discursive practices and new styles emerging. How do new ways of using language come about? We need an account of the creation of new styles, of the production of innovative uses of language. But what is the source of linguistic innovation if it is not a formal and universal infinite capacity of linguistic production? We need a *non-formal* and *non-mechanical* account of linguistic creativity that starts with situated life experiences and does not neglect the material conditions of language use. A natural place to look for such an account would be in theories of *metaphor*. Many philosophical accounts of metaphor have emphasized life experiences as the raw materials for the production of innovative uses of language. In the next section we will briefly examine the metaphorical aspects of language through Friedrich Nietzsche's radical view of metaphoricity, Paul Ricoeur's hermeneutic approach and the pragmatist and experiential account of George Lakoff and Mark Johnson.

4.2 METAPHOR

In 'On truth and lies in a non-moral sense' Nietzsche (2005) argues that *metaphoricity* is the essence of language. On his view, to speak is to play with metaphors. All words are metaphors; it is only that we *forget* about the metaphorical origin and nature of our words. We forget that our words are metaphors because we tend to reify and naturalize the metaphorical structures of language: we tend to fix the metaphors we use and to treat them as objective truths, as neutral descriptions or accurate pictures of the natural world around us. But Nietzsche asks: 'Are designations congruent with things? Is language the adequate expression of all realities?' (p. 16). He argues that linguistic diversity alone is sufficient to show that objective truth is not what guides language, that speaking is not a matter of faithful reproduction and that words are not mere replicas: 'The various languages placed side by side show that with words it is never a question of truth, never a question of adequate expression; otherwise, there would not be so many languages' (ibid.). Language involves *subjective projection*. How, for example, can the gender of words that categorize things (e.g. tables, chairs, trees, rocks, etc.) as masculine or feminine be anything but an arbitrary assignment? But we forget the arbitrary projections involved in our use of language. Nietzsche develops an account of the origin of language that tries to fight against this 'forgetfulness' which makes us the slaves of an illusory truth.

According to Nietzsche's account of the development of language, the creation of words has to be linked to sensuous experiences: 'What is a word? It is the copy in sound of a nerve stimulus' (ibid.). Nietzsche argues that truth cannot have been 'the deciding factor in the genesis of language' because many of the most basic terms in a language are directly tied to subjective stimulations. In fact, he contends, we cannot ultimately make sense of *any* meaning that is completely purified of subjective experiences: 'The "thing in itself" [. . .] is [. . .] something quite incomprehensible to the creator of language and something not in the least worth striving for. This creator only designates the relations of things to men, and for expressing these relations he lays hold of the boldest metaphors' (ibid.). Nietzsche describes the creation of words as a process of metaphorization in two stages in which an experience gives rise to an image and this in turn to a sound: 'To begin with, a nerve stimulus is transferred into an image: first metaphor. The image, in turn, is imitated in a sound: second metaphor' (ibid.). A corollary of Nietzsche's account is that there are no terms that can refer directly without the mediation of subjective experience, there are no *rigid designators*.[5] Therefore, Nietzsche concludes, all meanings are metaphorical; all the semantic domains of language are populated by metaphorical entities that are formed by our subjective projections: 'we believe that we know something about the things themselves when we speak of trees, colors, snow, and flowers; and yet we possess nothing but metaphors for things—metaphors which correspond in no way to the original entities' (pp. 16–17).

The core of Nietzsche's argument for the metaphorical nature of all terms has to be found in his account of the formation of concepts through language. This account shows that all words are metaphors in so far as they inevitably have a conceptual element, that is, in so far as they involve an element of generality:

> Every word instantly becomes a concept precisely in so far as it is not supposed to serve as a reminder of the unique and entirely individual original experience to which it owes its origin; but rather, a word becomes a concept in so far as it simultaneously has to fit countless more or less similar cases – which means, purely and simply, cases which are never equal and thus altogether unequal. Every concept arises from the equation of unequal things. (2005, p. 17)

On Nietzsche's view, concepts are always metaphorical because they involve 'the equation of unequal things'; and all terms are conceptual and hence metaphorical because they apply to many different things or to many different presentations of some thing, treating them as the same. According to Nietzsche, concepts are formed by erasing differences, by making us *forget* about them. For example, he remarks that one leaf is never completely identical to another, but we form the concept of a leaf by discarding individual differences, 'by forgetting the distinguishing aspects'. In this sense the formation of a concept always involves a *deception*: concepts are intrinsically deceptive; they deceive us about identities and differences. Nietzsche points out that philosophers have tried to resist the idea that *our words lie*; and indeed it is tempting to think of individual entities in their idiosyncrasy as imperfect instantiations of ideal things (e.g. of particular leaves as deficient copies of the ideal leaf), but in fact all that exists is the indomitable multiplicity of idiosyncratic entities. Nietzsche argues that the meanings of our words do not correspond to ideal entities (such as the ideal leaf); these ideals are nothing but fictions, for there is only wild diversity and irreducible heterogeneity in the natural world and in our experience of it.[6]

Nietzsche's account of the metaphorical essence of language results in a thoroughgoing *relativism*. On this view, there can be no objectivity in anything linguistic. Agreements are indeed enforced in linguistic communities, but Nietzsche argues that they are not backed up by anything epistemic or metaphysical that is objective –

e.g. by the epistemic force of rationality or by the metaphysical force of reality. According to Nietzsche, the enforcement of our linguistic agreements relies simply on pure brute force. On Nietzsche's view, since all the claims we make are metaphorical constructions, the distinction between truth and falsity becomes a distinction between two different kinds of metaphors. For Nietzsche, truths are *dead metaphors*: metaphors that we have forgotten are metaphors, metaphors that have become standard conventions accepted by all (or most). By contrast, lies are metaphors that society finds unacceptable. Nietzsche argues that our duty to tell the truth is simply a duty that society imposes on us, which consists in the imposition of those metaphors that find social acceptance: 'to be truthful means to employ the usual metaphors' (p. 17). But of course there is no hard and fast distinction between truth and lies on this view, for all metaphors can at one point or another be found acceptable or unacceptable (metaphors are not born in social acceptance and they can fall out of acceptance). Thus Nietzsche describes the social obligation to tell the truth as 'the duty to lie according to a fixed convention, to lie with the herd and in a manner binding upon everyone' (ibid.). We are of course not aware that when we feel obligated to tell the truth, we are being forced to lie in a particular way; and it is precisely our unconsciousness or forgetfulness about this that maintains the force of this obligation alive in us: 'man of course forgets that this is the way things stand for him'; he lies 'unconsciously and in accordance with habits which are centuries' old; and precisely *by means of this unconsciousness* and forgetfulness he arrives at his sense of truth' (pp. 17–8). In the brilliant passage that follows Nietzsche defines *truth* in a way that connects directly with the hermeneutic account of metaphor developed by Ricoeur:

> What then is truth? A movable host of metaphors, metonymies, and anthropomorphisms: in short, a sum of human relations which have been poetically and rhetorically intensified, transferred, and embellished, and which, after long usage, seem to a people to be fixed, canonical, and binding. *Truths are illusions which we have forgotten are illusions; they are metaphors that have become worn out and have been drained of sensuous force*, coins which have lost their embossing and are now considered as metal and no longer as coins. (p. 17; my emphasis)

In a similar fashion Ricoeur (1991) distinguishes between *live* and *dead* metaphors. He emphasizes that metaphors have an essential temporal dimension: they have a life, so to speak, for they are born, they mature and eventually they die. As Ricoeur puts it, metaphor is a 'diachronic phenomenon'. For Ricoeur, *dead metaphors* are not those that have fallen out of use; rather, they are those expressions in which, when we use them, we no longer experience their metaphorical character: for example, 'the neck of a bottle' or 'the leg of a table'. Metaphors become worn out and they lose their dynamic character: they become ossified. Dead metaphors are those that have become *trivial*. By contrast, *live metaphors* are those that are still shocking or at least revealing, that is, those that open our eyes to new things, to new similarities we had not recognized before. The contrast between live and dead metaphors is the contrast between novel and trivial metaphors. *Novel metaphors* are those that involve a semantic innovation, the emergence of a new meaning. A novel metaphor creates 'a new framework of connotation' by articulating meanings in a new way and calling attention to relations that had not yet been noticed. *Trivial metaphors*, by contrast, simply activate a connotation that had already been articulated; they consist in the actualization of a semantic connection so well established that it is no longer detected as a relation between heterogeneous things. The diachronic process in which the life of a metaphor consists is a movement from a novel to a trivial metaphor. The trivial metaphor has become part of the lexicon and the new similarities or semantic connections it has established are no longer noticed as new or as created (manufactured) in language, but as given and ready to use.

According to Ricoeur, what is at the core of a metaphor is a *logical and semantic paradox*: a metaphor is an attempt to *make sense with nonsense* by exploiting a semantic discrepancy or logical contradiction. The discrepancy or contradiction consists in declaring things to be *the same and different* at the same time: 'the strategy of discourse put in action in metaphor relies on the purposive creation of a semantic discrepancy in the sentence. [. . .] The function of metaphor is to make sense with nonsense, to transform a self-contradictory statement into a significant self-contradiction' (p. 78). The metaphorical statement transforms nonsensical literal meaning into an emergent new meaning. By exploiting a discrepancy or contradiction, by making us see similarities in differences, a metaphor fashions new similarities and creates a new connotation. A metaphor brings together things that were far removed; it produces 'a kind of assimilation between remote ideas' (p. 80). Following Aristotle, Ricoeur remarks that the mark of genius is 'to be intuitively aware of hidden resemblances' (ibid.). A metaphor highlights similarities without erasing differences, for what it does is to establish *sameness in spite of differences*. In fact, a live metaphor underscores the differences as much as the similarities: 'sameness and difference are not merely mixed, but remain opposed'; and, as Ricoeur points out, this 'explains the kinship between metaphor and riddle' (p. 81). A novel metaphor keeps alive the tension or clash between the heterogeneous things that are made to converge. By contrast, in a dead metaphor the tension or clash between the different things that are treated as the same is no longer noticed, and the sameness is the only thing we see, which is a testament to the force that the metaphor has acquired: it has made us forget about the differences and we are only sensitive to the similarities that the metaphor has created.

It is important to note that metaphors are semantically transformative: they rearrange language, they reconfigure the relations between our terms and concepts; they result in what Ricoeur calls 'the reallocation of predicates' (what Nelson Goodman called 'the reassignment of labels'). Ricoeur insists that metaphor is primarily a *semantic* phenomenon, and not only a *psychological* one.[7] Metaphor is not a psychological event but a discursive process; what defines metaphor is not an intuition, an instantaneous affair of subjectivity. Ricoeur argues that although poets may be intuitively aware of hidden resemblances, the 'assimilation between remote ideas is a discursive process' (p. 80). He also remarks that 'even if it is true that there is something irreducible in the grasping of similarities as a kind of sudden insight, the only progress that can be achieved by an epistemology of metaphor concerns the discursive and not the intuitive process involved in the creation of meaning' (p. 79). Through discursive processes, through language use, a metaphor creates a new connotation. The connotation may be subjective but it becomes inscribed in the meaning of the term and therefore it becomes something that is not merely psychological, but semantic, i.e. part of the system of significations invoked by the use of the expression or statement. The semantic significance of metaphors consists in the fact that they add to the connotations of words: 'some of the connotative values attached to our words are applied in a new way' (p. 79). Ricoeur uses the notion of connotation developed by

Max Black (1962) in his account of metaphor. According to this notion, a connotation or system of connotative values is 'the "system of associated commonplaces" which enlarge the meaning of our words, adding cultural and emotional dimensions to the literal values codified in our dictionaries' (ibid.). So, in short, the contribution that metaphors make is semantic and not psychological because it concerns the amount of content expressed by our words.

Ricoeur's analysis teaches us that a metaphor is not a mere trope or rhetorical device; it is more than a decorative ornament; it is 'the general process by which we grasp kinship' (p. 83). According to Ricoeur, the importance of metaphorical processes for the development of language cannot be overemphasized. Metaphor is a discursive process that is at the source of all semantic innovation, 'at the origin of all semantic fields': 'To grasp the kinship in any semantic field is the work of the metaphoric process at large' (p. 81). Metaphors have the power of creating semantic transformations and reconfiguring language: 'the power of metaphor would be to break through previous categorization and to establish new logical boundaries on the ruins of the preceding ones' (ibid.). And, Ricoeur argues, this mechanism of conceptual innovation is what we find in the restructuration of any semantic domain as well as in its original emergence: 'the dynamics of thought which breaks through previous categorization is the same as the one which generated all classifications' (ibid.). Metaphors make us aware of this process of semantic creation and restructuration because they make explicit the tension between an old and a new semantic system of significations: 'It is essential to the structure of metaphor that the old and the new are present together in the metaphorical twist' (p. 83). In a metaphorical statement we perceive both the literal meaning and the new meaning. As Ricoeur puts it, metaphors require 'stereoscopic vision': 'Several layers of meaning are noticed and recognized in the thickness of the text' (ibid.). The semantic thickness that metaphors create relates to what Ricoeur describes as the *constitutive polysemy* of words. According to Ricoeur, all words are intrinsically polysemic: no matter how univocal they happen to be at the time, they always have – in principle – a plurality of meanings; and their polysemy cannot be restricted *a priori*. On Ricoeur's view, metaphor is the central semantic mechanism for creating and extending polysemy: 'Metaphor is a clear case where polysemy is preserved instead of being screened'; 'metaphor is the procedure by which we extend polysemy' (ibid.). Ricoeur explains the two central stages involved in the extension of the polysemy of word meaning through a metaphor as follows: 'At the first stage metaphor does not belong to the lexicon. It exists only in discourse'; but 'when the tension between literal and metaphorical sense is no longer perceived, we may say that the metaphorical sense has become part of the literal sense' (p. 83).

So what in the end are metaphors for? Ricoeur argues that the central function of metaphors is epistemic or cognitive as well as metaphysical or ontological. In the first place, by rearranging language metaphors rearrange our concepts. So the primary *epistemic function* of metaphor is to change our way of looking at things. Following Black (1962), Ricoeur argues that the cognitive function of a metaphor is the same as that of a model, namely, 'to describe an unknown or a lesser known thing in terms of a better-known thing thanks to a similarity of structure' (p. 84). So a metaphor has cognitive value as a 'heuristic fiction': it is a convenient fiction (treating things as identical on the basis of a partial isomorphism) which is used as 'a way of making an object easier to handle'. But, in the second place, metaphors also have a central *ontological function*, namely, the redescription of reality. Metaphorical statements articulate the reality to which they refer in a new way; they have 'the extraordinary power of redescribing reality' (p. 84). It is by virtue of the referential function of metaphorical statements that the creative power of poetry has ontological significance:[8] 'poetry reaches the essence of things' (p. 84); 'what is changed by poetic language is our way of dwelling in the world [. . .] each poem projects a new way of dwelling. It opens up a new way of being for us' (p. 85). The opening up of possibilities is part of the *world-disclosing* function of language in general and not specific to metaphorical statements or to poetry in particular. But metaphors do make a specific contribution to the *world-disclosing* function of language: they introduce change and novelty. What metaphors do is to open our eyes to *new* possibilities, to a *new* world: 'metaphor shatters not only the previous structures of our language, but also the previous structures of what we call reality'; 'this reality, as redescribed, is a new reality' (p. 85). So Ricoeur concludes that metaphor is a 'heuristic fiction for the sake of redescribing reality' and it involves 'the metamorphosis of both language and reality' (ibid.). Like Nietzsche's (although in a less radical way), Ricoeur's account of metaphor also seems to open the door both to *conceptual* and to *ontological relativism*. To conclude this section, let me include in this discussion of metaphor a powerful experiential and ontological account developed by a linguist and a philosopher: Lakoff and Johnson.

Lakoff and Johnson (1980) emphasize the experiential and existential dimension of metaphor: with a metaphor we experience (or live) one thing in terms of another. On this view, metaphors play a crucial *structuring role* in our lives:[9] they structure not only how we speak, but also how we think, how we experience things and how we act. Consider these two alternative metaphorical conceptions of the activity of argumentation: 'Argument is war' and 'Argument is dance'. The former opens our eyes to the competitive aspects of argumentation and structures the process of argumentation as an activity in which people *defend* themselves and *attack* each other, they *shoot* reasons that may *miss the target* or be *right on target*, they *win* and *lose*, etc. The latter metaphor, by contrast, calls our attention to argumentation as an activity of cooperation in which the *moves* are directed towards achieving *harmony* or the *balance* of reasons. In this way we use metaphors to structure our concepts. But Lakoff and Johnson emphasize that the metaphorical structuring of concepts is always partial, not total. A concept can be only partially structured by a metaphor: the metaphorical structuration of a concept can only offer a partial understanding of it, highlighting some of its features while hiding others; and, therefore, with a particular metaphorical structuration a concept can be applied and elaborated or extended in some ways but not in others. Argumentation, for example, has competitive aspects that are underscored by the bellicose metaphor and can be fully articulated through it; but it also has cooperative aspects that are suppressed or occluded by this metaphor, which makes it impossible to see those cooperative elements that involve genuine mutuality and partnership: for example, in the light of the bellicose metaphor, argumentative agreement can only appear as a *compromise* or as a form of *surrendering*. But despite their partial and limited character, metaphors are *systematic*: they have the power of binding concepts into systems. Let's look at the feature of *metaphorical systematicity* and its impact on our conceptual systems.

Lakoff and Johnson's account of metaphor emphasizes that, by establishing connections between different concepts and between different aspects of our experience, metaphors contribute tremendously to the systematization of our conceptual structures and of our lives. According to Lakoff and Johnson, our conceptual systems are metaphorical in nature: they are held together by metaphorical connections, which can communicate and bind together even far-removed concepts. Thanks to the systematicity of metaphor, we are capable of travelling from one semantic domain to another with ease. Metaphors are sometimes selected because they connect previously unrelated semantic domains and this new metaphorical connection has *cognitive and explanatory power*: it enables us to structure (or restructure) one of the semantic domains in terms of the other, to understand it in a new way and to do things with it that we couldn't do before. This is arguably the case with many of the metaphors and analogies that we find in the history of science – e.g. Bohr's famous claim that the structure of the atom is like that of the solar system, with an electron revolving around an atomic nucleus in orbits like a planet or satellite. Sometimes metaphors are selected because of their *ontological significance*. According to Lakoff and Johnson, there are metaphors that are specifically ontological: they are produced to conceptualize the *reality* of something in a particular way. The target domains of an ontological metaphor are typically things or phenomena whose reality seems elusive or enigmatic to us. In this sense Lakoff and Johnson examine the ontological metaphors that have been used in Western cultures to talk about the mind: the metaphor of the mind as a machine and the metaphor of the mind as a brittle object.[10] Ontological metaphors provide models for things and phenomena in the world, highlighting certain aspects of reality (while hiding others). As Ricoeur would put it, they inaugurate 'ways of being for us', 'ways of dwelling in the world'.

However, sometimes metaphors get selected and used just because of the *sheer amount of conceptual connections* that they can produce, even if they do not involve conceptual novelty and cognitive or ontological breakthroughs. The cognitive value of these systematic metaphors lies in their capacity to increase the conceptual coherence of our conceptual systems. This kind of systematicity can be illustrated by the wide applicability of what Lakoff and Johnson call *orientational metaphors*,[11] that is, metaphors that use spatial orientations, such as up and down, in and out, front and back, etc., to organize our conceptual systems. Orientational metaphors articulate a wide variety of cultural experiences through our physical experiences of space. Thus, for example, we use the spatial concepts UP and

DOWN to structure and colour with value judgements many of our concepts and their connotations, so that HAPPY is UP and UNHAPPY is DOWN, and we talk about feeling up or down; GOOD is UP and BAD is DOWN, and we talk about looking up to and looking down on people, etc. Lakoff and Johnson argue that the fundamental values of a culture are articulated through fundamental metaphorical structures that give coherence to the conceptual system of that culture. The different ways in which metaphorical connections are used to produce cultural coherence underscores the cultural variability of conceptual structures and value systems. But Lakoff and Johnson also emphasize that there are some *universal* aspects to the metaphorical structuration of human concepts. According to them, there are metaphorical orientations that cut across all cultures: UP/DOWN, IN/OUT, ACTIVE/PASSIVE, etc. However, they argue that although these metaphors can be found in all cultures, how they are organized (which metaphors are considered primary and most fundamental) and how they are used to orient concepts can (and often does) vary from culture to culture. So Lakoff and Johnson's balanced account of the culture-specific and universal aspects of metaphor still leaves room for *conceptual and ontological relativism*, although for a much more qualified and tamed version than the ones we found in Nietzsche's and Ricoeur's accounts of metaphor. We need to examine whether there is a tenable version of *linguistic relativism* that supports the theses of conceptual and ontological relativity. Can we move from the relativity of languages and language uses to the relativity of conceptual and ontological perspectives? Is the relativity of concepts and even of worlds derivable from the linguistic diversity across cultures?

4.3 LINGUISTIC RELATIVISM

In his seminal essay 'On the very idea of a conceptual scheme' (1984) Davidson argues that we cannot make sense of the idea of there being radical conceptual differences between different languages. The target of Davidson's argument is *linguistic relativism*: the view that different languages contain incommensurable conceptual schemes. This view was first developed by the American linguists Edward Sapir (1921, 1949) and Benjamin L. Whorf (1956). They formulated the so-called *hypothesis of linguistic relativity*: the idea that we think and experience the world according to the language we speak, and that our thinking, our experience and our reality is *relative* to our language and may not be shared with speakers of other languages. According to Sapir and Whorf, substantially different languages (those with different historical roots – Indo-European languages and Native American languages, for example) contain different metaphysical systems that divide the world in different ways, that is, according to different principles of individuation that recognize different sets of entities (different ontologies). In their studies of Native American languages, such as Hopi, Sapir and Whorf found grammatical structures that could not be translated, at least not without loss or distortion of the original meanings. For example, the verbal tenses of Hopi were so different from those of Indo-European languages that, they argued, Hopi speakers seem to experience time differently and live their lives according to different temporal structures. This led Sapir and Whorf to conclude that there may be parts of a language that are untranslatable: there may be meanings that can be expressed in one language but not in others. According to Sapir and Whorf, significantly different grammars result in conceptual differences that shape speakers' minds and their conceptions of the world in different ways. On this view, two languages are untranslatable when and because their grammars and the conceptual schemes they contain are *incommensurable*, that is, because there is no overarching structure, no single set of rules and standards, which can cover both languages.

Similar relativistic ideas were also developed in the Philosophy of Science by Thomas Kuhn. In *The Structure of Scientific Revolutions* (1970) Kuhn argued that in the history of science we can recognize paradigm shifts that take place through a 'scientific *revolution*'. For example, the shift from Ptolemaic astronomy to Copernican astronomy took place through a scientific *revolution* in which the most basic concepts and norms of scientific investigation changed. The revolutionary period is a period of upheaval in which there is no longer a dominant paradigm (the old paradigm is losing its place and the emerging one is not yet fully established and accepted). In this period, Kuhn argues, scientists adhere to different paradigms, speak different languages and have different conceptions of the world. Given their different world-views, scientists within different paradigms have different ontological beliefs about the furniture of the universe: for example, chemists believed in the existence of phlogiston until the mid-eighteenth century, but they believed in the existence of oxygen and in the atomic composition of elements after Lavoisier and Dalton. Kuhn argued that pre- and post-revolutionary languages cannot be translated into one another, at least not without distortion. He generalized this unbridgeable gap between scientific paradigms and their languages with the thesis of the *incommensurability* of scientific paradigms: different scientific paradigms cannot be compared with each other objectively because they contain incommensurable standards, conceptual structures and world-views; and the languages of different paradigms are not mutually translatable. Kuhn went as far as to suggest that the scientists who speak these different languages live in different worlds – a thesis that sparked much debate and that he himself later qualified (see Kuhn, 1977). The thesis of linguistic relativity and the conceptual and ontological relativisms that result from it are highly controversial.

In 'On the very idea of a conceptual scheme' Davidson develops a *reductio ad absurdum* of the thesis of linguistic relativity. He argues that this thesis flies in the face of our actual practices of intercultural communication, which offer no evidence that the conceptual differences between speakers of different languages are *in principle* unbridgeable and incommensurable. According to Davidson, every time we are confronted with an alleged conceptual gap, we manage to bridge it in one way or another; and even if we can't bridge it, there are no good reasons to conclude that the gap is *in principle* unbridgeable. Davidson argues that conceptual differences always can and should be explained away, for any alleged conceptual difference is in principle reducible to a difference of opinion, to a factual disagreement. So, he concludes, there are no genuine conceptual differences; there cannot be. Davidson argues that there is an 'underlying paradox' in linguistic relativism and the conceptual relativism that results from it: 'Different points of view make sense, but only if there is a common coordinate system on which to plot them; yet the existence of a common system belies the claim of dramatic incomparability' (1984, p. 184). According to Davidson, this paradox is present in every formulation of linguistic and conceptual relativism, which cannot avoid but fall into a performative contradiction. That is, the very exposition of the relativist claim actually contradicts the claim: 'Whorf, wanting to demonstrate that Hopi incorporates a metaphysics so alien to ours that Hopi and English cannot, as he puts it, "be calibrated", uses English to convey the contents of sample Hopi sentences. Kuhn is brilliant at saying what things were like before the revolution using – what else? – our post-revolutionary idiom' (ibid.).

Davidson is sceptical about the very idea that gives rise to linguistic relativism: namely, the idea that there is a conceptual scheme embedded in each language. The central assumption underlying linguistic relativism is that languages contain conceptual schemes that organize our experiences and the world around us. Davidson contends that the only criterion of identity for conceptual schemes that the relativist can appeal to is the criterion of *translatability*: if two languages are intertranslatable, they contain the same conceptual scheme; and if there are differences in the underlying conceptual schemes, it must be the case that the languages in which they are embedded cannot be translated into one another, either in part or as a whole. So Davidson concludes that the only evidence we could possibly have for differences in conceptual schemes would have to come from *translation failures*, either total or partial failures of translation, depending on how different the conceptual schemes are and how deep the gap between the languages is.

Davidson's argument against the possibility of radical conceptual differences draws on the practice of translation and is developed in two stages. The first stage concerns the possibility of a complete failure in translation; the second stage the possibility of a partial failure. In the first part of the argument, Davidson contends that there cannot be an alien language that cannot be translated into ours in any way and, therefore, there cannot be an alien conceptual scheme that is totally incommensurable with ours. Davidson's argument is based on his account of translation. According to this account, all languages are *in principle* mutually translatable into one another. Davidson argues that we can only call something a language if it is in principle translatable into our language: we can only regard certain sounds as a speech and certain marks as a text if we think that it is at least in principle possible for us to understand and express their meaning. 'Translatability into a familiar tongue', Davidson claims, 'is the criterion of languagehood' (p. 186). On Davidson's view, to say that certain sounds or marks are, as far as we know, untranslatable would be to say that, as far as we know, they do not contain meanings that we can grasp and formulate in our language, and therefore that, as far as we know, they are not part of a language at all. So, for Davidson, any evidence for the untranslatability of a *language* would automatically disqualify it as a language;

on the other hand, any evidence that something is a language is auto-matically evidence that it is *in principle* translatable (even if we do not yet know how we can go about translating it). As Davidson puts it, 'nothing [. . .] could count as evidence that some form of activity could not be interpreted in our language that was not at the same time evidence that that form of activity was not speech behaviour. [. . .] a form of activity that cannot be interpreted as language in our language is not speech behavior' (pp. 185–6).

Davidson's reasoning can be put as an argument by dilemma. The first horn of the dilemma is that if sounds or marks appear to be pure noise or squiggles that seem to make no sense at all, if they are, for us, truly unintelligible and incoherent in a complete and absolute sense, we have no reason to think that they constitute a language at all. So we don't find here a case of an untranslatable *language*. The second horn of the dilemma is that if we have any reason whatsoever to think that something is a language, it must be because it is in prin-ciple translatable, because it gives us an inkling of meanings we could in principle understand and express. And here again we don't find a case of an *untranslatable* language. One could object that Davidson is assuming that the relation of translatability is a transi-tive relation, so that if A is translatable into B and B into C, we can conclude that A is translatable into C. But in fact translatability may be an intransitive relation, so that if we have a long chain of succes-sive languages in which any two contiguous languages are intertran-slatable (A–B–C– . . . –X–Y–Z), it may nonetheless be the case that two languages that are far removed from each other in this chain (say A and Z, or B and Y) may not be translatable into each other; there may be partial failures along the way in this chain, and these small failures may eventually amount to a total failure in the long run. Davidson would likely reply that the very account of the relationship between the languages in this chain shows that, ultimately, they are all translatable. In other words, in Davidson's mind, the articulation of the objection would show that there is no real failure of transla-tion because even far-removed languages that may not initially be directly translatable into each other become indirectly translatable through the mediation of bridging languages, of intermediate links in the chain: that is, A can be translated into C and C into D and so on until we reach Z. Whether the relation of translatability is tran-sitive or intransitive, Davidson's argument by dilemma contends that the relativist fails to show that there is such thing as a language that is completely untranslatable into our own. For the relativist to escape Davidson's dilemma and meet the burden of proof, he/she would have to show that the dilemma is in fact a false dilemma.

In the second part of his argument, Davidson moves from the claim that all languages are intertranslatable to the claim that all concepts expressible in language (in any language) can in principle be translated into my language. He contends that there are no alien concepts that cannot be fully captured in translation and, therefore, we cannot make sense of the possibility of something being lost in translation. Davidson's argument against untranslatable concepts is based on his *principle of charity*. According to Davidson, communication is an interpretative process regulated by the principle of charity. As we saw, what this principle says is that interpretation leaves us no option but 'to assume general agreement on beliefs'; and this, in turn, leads to a general agreement on concepts. On Davidson's view, if we were to encounter someone who didn't share our concepts and normative principles, we would have no reason whatsoever to ascribe thought or language to him/her because the sounds or marks produced by him/her would be uninterpretable. For sounds or marks to be interpretable at all, Davidson argues, we have to assume that most of the beliefs they express are like ours; and, therefore, given the assumed massive overlap of beliefs, the concepts that these sounds or marks express will appear to be like our own concepts as well – and the claim is that they cannot appear in any other way if they are to be treated as meaningful conceptual expressions. Indeed, to allow for conceptual differences is to allow for strong disparities in beliefs, for massive disagreements; and if we want to minimize belief disparities, we have no option but to assume conceptual proximity. According to Davidson, since *charity* is the condition of possibility of interpretation, we can only interpret others if we assume minimal conceptual distance between us, for significant conceptual differences or deviation would violate the principle of charity. When others think differently, we can always interpret their words so that the difference lies in isolated beliefs rather than in conceptual structures (which would affect entire clusters of beliefs). Since we maximize agreement by eliminating conceptual differences, and since the maximization of agreement is not an option, but a transcendental condition of interpretation, Davidson concludes that there are no conceptual differences that are unavoidably lost in translation. As he puts it, the overall conclusion of his argument is that conceptual relativism 'fares no better when based on partial failure of translation than when based on total failure. Given the underlying methodology of interpretation, we could not be in a position to judge that others had concepts or beliefs radically different from our own' (1984, p. 197).

Davidson's principle of charity and its implications have sparked intense debates in contemporary Philosophy of Language.[12] Instead of reviewing the arguments in these debates, in what follows I will develop a diagnosis of the blindness to conceptual differences of Davidson's view of interpretation. There are two main features of Davidson's approach that can explain why alien concepts cannot but be invisible on his view. In the first place, there is a strong *cognitive bias* in Davidson's view that leads him to focus exclusively on beliefs. According to Davidson, all there is to the interpretation of the speech of others is the examination of the sentences they hold true. But it is a mistake to think that we can reach an adequate understanding of people who are radically different from us by identifying what they believe, without taking into account the role that their beliefs play in their lives, that is, without paying attention to the practices in which those beliefs are expressed. Understanding does indeed have a holistic nature, but the background that makes understanding possible is not a system of beliefs or a network of propositions, but rather, a form of life, a life-world. This suggests that we should expect genuine conceptual differences to appear whenever we interact with people whose way of life is significantly different from ours. But these differences are bound to be invisible to us if we treat the cognitive dimension of speech as an autonomous sphere and we disregard the fact that thought and language are grounded in a way of life and informed by interests and values. This is what Wittgenstein's view emphasizes by drawing attention to the contexts of action in which we are acculturated, to the practices in which we are trained. This contextualist view overcomes the cognitive bias that renders alien concepts invisible. As Wittgenstein puts it: 'An education quite different from ours might also be the foundation for quite different concepts. For here life would run on differently. What interests us would not interest *them*. Here different concepts would no longer be unimaginable. In fact, this is the only way in which *essentially* different concepts are imaginable' (1980b, §§387–8).

Another crucial feature of Davidson's view that is responsible for the invisibility of alien concepts is the privilege of the *observer's stance* – which he inherited from Quine (see 3.2 above). According to Davidson, the perspective of the translator or interpreter is the third-person perspective of a detached observer engaged in theory-building. The interpreter observes behaviour and tries to endow that behaviour with meaning through the construction of a theory. In this process of interpretation there is only one subjectivity at work; the voice of the other becomes a set of uninterpreted noises that only the interpreter can turn into meaningful signs. On this view, the attitude of the interpreter is the attitude of a theorizing subject towards his/her object of investigation. So it is not surprising that this view renders conceptual differences invisible. For, when we adopt this attitude, the interpretative process is no longer a process of negotiation between interlocutors that can lead to a 'fusion of horizons'; when we adopt this attitude, the possibility that others may enrich our horizon of understanding is excluded. Wittgenstein's contextualism also offers an alternative to Davidson's view here. The contextualist approach encourages us to think of the relation between interlocutors as a relation between peers jointly engaged in an activity. According to this *participatory stance*, understanding other people is not a self-centred process, but rather, an intersubjective process, a process of interaction that has an I–Thou structure. There may *or may not* be a common conceptual perspective that emerges from communicative interactions; but when there is, this is a first-person plural perspective, the perspective of an emerging We. It is to a more detailed analysis and discussion of the individual and social aspects of language we now turn. This discussion as well as the discussion of identity in the last chapter will examine theses about language that connect (directly or indirectly) with the arguments about linguistic relativism considered in this section.

CHAPTER 5

SPEAKERS, LINGUISTIC COMMUNITIES AND HISTORIES OF USE

5.1 IDIOSYNCRASIES AND CONVENTIONS

As we saw, Davidson reduces communication to the encounter between idiolects. But is everything individualistic and idiosyncratic in this view? Is there *any* social aspect to communication *at all*? Can linguistic conventions be the product of the interaction between idiolects even if they are not its basis? How can a linguistic community emerge from communicative interactions? In this section we will examine how an individualistic view such as Davidson's answers these questions, and we will then contrast these answers with those offered by social accounts of communication.

Davidson (1986) argues that sharing linguistic conventions is not a precondition for successful communication: we don't need to share semantic or syntactic conventions in order to communicate successfully. He develops an argument to this effect in his discussion of *malapropisms* or *malaprops*,[1] that is, of violations of proprieties of use that typically involve mistakes in word choice, in spelling or in pronunciation: e.g. 'Lead the way and we'll precede'. The very title of Davidson's paper 'A nice derangement of epitaphs' (1986) is an instance of this phenomenon: it refers to Mrs Malaprop's idiosyncratic way of complementing a nice arrangement of epithets. To illustrate the phenomenon of malapropism, Davidson also uses the speech of popular characters in television and radio: Archie Bunker saying 'We need a few laughs to break up the *monogamy*', or Goodman Ace talking about '*monotonizing* the conversation' or 'hitting the nail right on the *thumb*'. Davidson emphasizes that these characters are perfectly well understood even though their use of language is felt as wildly idiosyncratic and, for this reason, amusing.

According to Davidson, what is interesting about malapropisms is that they 'introduce expressions not covered by prior learning, or familiar expressions which cannot be interpreted by any of the abilities' that we have acquired previously (p. 162). Malapropisms belong to a class of linguistic phenomena that call into question traditional assumptions about linguistic competence and in particular about the role of shared conventions in communication. These phenomena call attention to 'our ability to interpret words we have never heard before, to correct slips of the tongue, or to cope with new idiolects' (ibid.). For Davidson, this ability constitutes the very essence of communication and what is most characteristic of competent interpreters and communicators.

Davidson argues that if the mastery of shared conventions was essential for communication, these phenomena should be exceptional and recalcitrant cases difficult to explain, but they are not at all; they are quite frequent, in fact *ubiquitous*: ordinary linguistic deviations may not be as radical as the malapropisms of Archie Bunker and Goodman Ace; and they may not be amusing or surprising, or even noticeable; they may be simply small departures from standard pronunciation or spelling, or from standard grammar or word choice, departures so small that typically they go unnoticed. But, according to Davidson, these deviations from what is taken to be the norm and standard usage constitute a ubiquitous phenomenon. And what is most remarkable about malapropisms, Davidson contends, is that people have no problem understanding the speaker in the way intended despite the deviation from standard usage. With this contention Davidson wants to raise the following questions: What has primacy in our interpretative practices? Is it the *standard* interpretation of words or their *intended* interpretation? The meanings that come *first in the order of interpretation* are what Davidson calls *first meanings*. We need an account of how to identify first meanings; and for this we need an account of the conditions that these meanings must meet. First meanings have been traditionally assumed to be *systematic, shared* and *prepared*. Davidson's theory rejects the third feature and radically transforms the meaning of the other two.

In the first place, Davidson argues that there is no reason why first meanings have to be previously *prepared* by linguistic practice; there is no reason why a blueprint for our interpretations must exist. On Davidson's view, first meanings can be entirely *ad hoc*. According to the traditional view of interpretation, first meanings must be prefigured by established conventions or regularities of use. Davidson rejects the idea that interpretation is governed by shared practices that precede the interpretative encounter; and he tries to establish that learning social conventions and patterns of use is *neither necessary nor sufficient* for successful communication. On the one hand, the fact that conformity with previously established practice is not *necessary* for communication is made clear by the very existence of malapropisms and other deviant uses that do not prevent successful communication despite their violation of standard usage. On the other hand, Davidson argues, being grounded in prior usage is not *sufficient* for successful communication either, for having learned the conventions or regularities that govern a language does not guarantee that one will be able to apply them correctly in the interpretation of a particular speaker's verbal behaviour. More is involved in communication than the mere knowledge of linguistic conventions or of patterns of linguistic usage. The interpretation of speech also requires general intelligence and general knowledge of the world.[2]

In the second place, Davidson acknowledges that the first meanings of our interpretations must be *systematic*, but he argues that their systematicity does not require shared grammatical conventions and it can be explained without appealing to the grammar of public languages (or to the patterns contained in social practices of language use). According to Davidson, all that is required for having systematic first meanings is that they be derived from a systematic theory of interpretation, that is, a theory with a finite base and a recursive procedure. As we saw, for Davidson, a theory of interpretation for a particular speaker consists in a theory of truth for the speech of that speaker. The finite base of this theory is the collection of terms and sentences uttered or written by the speaker, and its recursive procedure is Tarski's *convention T*, which – through the specification of the truth conditions of statements – produces systematic correlations or one-to-one mappings between sentences in the speaker's idiolect and sentences in the interpreter's idiolect (see section 2.2 above).

Even more revolutionary than Davidson's account of the systematicity of meaning is his account of what is *shared* in communication. In the third place, Davidson argues that what must be *shared* in first meanings is not anything that has been learned prior to the interpretative encounter. On his view, the first meanings that emerge from interpretative encounters are determined by the communicative intentions of speakers. What must be *shared* is what the speaker is getting at, the *intended* message. But can interpretation and successful communication be fully explained in terms of speaker's intentions?

Davidson considers an objection that had been already raised against Donnellan's intentionalistic approach. We can call it the *Humpty Dumpty* objection. It was objected[3] that Donnellan shared Humpty Dumpty's theory of meaning. Donnellan's intentionalistic description of communication was said to resemble Humpty Dumpty's description of his own speech: 'When I use a word', Humpty Dumpty said, 'it means just what I choose it to mean.' In a speech of this kind – the objection goes – meanings, far from becoming determinate, actually disappear altogether, for they become completely arbitrary and random. The objection is that if your words mean whatever you want them to mean at every turn in the conversation, then they do not mean anything *in particular* and, therefore, they do not mean anything (any particular thing) *at all*. Donnellan (1968) replied that communicative intentions are not purely arbitrary and random because they are bound up with *reasonable expectations*: you can only intend to mean something by a word if you have reasons to expect that the word will be interpreted in that way by your audience. For Donnellan, as for Davidson, words are instruments or tools at the service of the intentions of the speaker, but the speaker cannot successfully use a word in a new and unexpected way unless he/she prepares the terrain for the new use, that is, unless he/she (or the context) provides sufficient clues for the intended interpretation. As Davidson puts it, 'a speaker may provide us with information relevant to interpreting an utterance in the course of making the utterance' (p. 168). And this makes it possible for interlocutors to understand semantic deviations or innovations at every turn of the conversation: 'you can change the meaning provided you believe (and perhaps are justified in believing) that the interpreter has adequate clues for the new interpretation' (p. 165). In this sense Davidson defines instances of successful communication despite malapropisms or other linguistic deviations as instances of 'getting away with it' (p. 166). Some people (like Archie Bunker, Goodman Ace or Mrs Malaprop) *get away with it* without even trying, while others do it on purpose (providing contextual clues for it) in an explicit effort to transform usage or to enrich it in new ways.

The details of a communicative context and of our negotiations in it determine how much we can *get away with*. But Davidson emphasizes that in principle there are no limits to our semantic deviations and innovations and to our *getting away with them*: 'There is no word or construction that cannot be converted to a new use by an ingenious or ignorant speaker. And such conversion [. . .] is not the only kind. Sheer invention is equally possible, and we can be as good at interpreting it (say in Joyce or Lewis Carroll) as we are at interpreting the errors or twists of substitution' (p. 167).

Davidson's argument tries to establish that the interpretative task that interlocutors face is the task of *adjusting* their theories of interpretation until they *converge*. On Davidson's view, communication is a matter of *mutual adjustment* of theories of interpretation, a process of interpretative negotiation or give and take between speakers who are constantly reinterpreting each other. To analyse this process of mutual adjustment between theories of interpretation, Davidson proposes the distinction between a *prior* theory and a *passing* theory of interpretation. According to Davidson, the kind of convergence that successful communication consists in is not the convergence between the theories that speaker and hearer have *prior* to their encounter, but rather, that between the theories of interpretation that they form during the encounter, that is, their *passing* theories. Passing theories of interpretation are those constructed *ad hoc* to fit the communicative encounter; these are the theories that 'we actually use to interpret an utterance', theories that are 'geared to the occasion' (p. 168). The speaker expects to be interpreted in a particular way, and his/her set of interpretative expectations about his/her audience constitutes his/her prior theory of interpretation, which he/she will have to adjust as the communicative exchange progresses. As Davidson puts it, 'for the speaker, the prior theory is what he *believes* the interpreter's prior theory to be, while his passing theory is the theory he *intends* the interpreter to use' (ibid.). On the other hand, 'for the hearer, the prior theory expresses how he is prepared in advance to interpret an utterance of the speaker, while the passing theory is how he *does* interpret the utterance' (ibid.). According to Davidson, utterances can always be interpreted as intended by the speaker without the interpreter having a correct theory of interpretation for them in advance. On Davidson's view, prior theories are the starting point of the interpretative process,[4] but they do not determine the success of the communicative encounter. These theories have to be mutually adjusted by the inter-locutors in the course of their communicative exchanges so as to turn them into *converging passing theories*. The core of Davidson's controversial argument is that we can always bring prior theories closer and closer together until they ultimately converge in passing theories that fit one another: no matter how far apart the prior theories of two interlocutors may be, it is always *in principle* possible to tinker with them – to adjust them and transform them – in a process of self-correction, until they converge (so that the speaker intends the hearer to interpret his/her utterance in a particular way, and the hearer uses a passing theory that interprets the utterance in just that way).

So, according to Davidson, all that matters for communication is the convergence on a passing theory. On this view, what makes com-munication possible is not a prior theory shared by all the speakers of the linguistic community.[5] What interlocutors must share (or come to share) is not a prior theory of interpretation, but a passing theory: 'What must be shared for communication to succeed is the passing theory' (p. 169). The theory the speaker intends the inter-preter to use and the theory the interpreter actually uses must coin-cide: 'Only if these coincide is understanding complete' (ibid.). As Davidson emphasizes, this articulation of the distinction between prior and passing theories of interpretation undermines the 'com-monly accepted account of linguistic competence and communica-tion' in terms of shared conventions. For, on this view, 'what interpreter and speaker share, to the extent that communication suc-ceeds, is not learned and so is not a language governed by rules or conventions known to speaker and interpreter in advance' (p. 172). So, given that the theory of interpretation that speaker and hearer must share is only a *passing* theory, Davidson concludes that the meanings that come first in the order of interpretation are *transient meanings*: first meanings are transitory meanings constructed for the purpose of a particular communicative exchange and there is no reason to think that they will survive that exchange. According to this view, the meanings that matter for the purpose of communica-tion have no semantic stability whatsoever: on the one hand, sharing previously learned meanings is not a necessary and sufficient part of communication; and, on the other hand, the semantic sharing pro-duced in communication is not a durable product that will necessar-ily outlive the situation in which it is obtained. On the Davidsonian picture, the sharing of meaning is contingently produced by a communicative exchange, but there is no reason to expect that this contingent fruit of communication will survive beyond the communicative exchange and that it can be extrapolated outside the specific context in which it emerges.

Davidson's account of meaning and communication in terms of converging passing theories leads to a radical redescription of the traditional notions of language and linguistic competence. As Davidson puts it, his account gives new content to 'the idea of two people "having the same language" by saying that they tend to converge on passing theories' (p. 173). On this view, speaking *the same language* becomes a matter of degree to be measured according to the tendency to converge on passing theories: 'degree or relative frequency of convergence would then be a measure of similarity of language' (ibid.). But this seems to relativize and ultimately dissolve *the very notion of a language*, for 'any theory on which a speaker and an interpreter converge is a language' and 'then there would be *a new language for every unexpected turn in the conversation*' (ibid., my emphasis). Thus, on Davidson's view, the notion of a shared language becomes *philosophically irrelevant*; it is simply not needed for a philosophical theory of communication and communicative competence. A philosophical theory of interpretation that tries to specify the necessary and sufficient conditions for communication does not need to indulge in the social fiction of a shared language, for speaking the same language – sharing linguistic conventions – is neither necessary nor sufficient for communication. For Davidson, being a competent participant in communication does not require having learned rules or conventions for the signs being used. He defines linguistic competence as 'the ability to converge on a passing theory from time to time'; and he emphasizes that this ability does not involve the mastery of rules or conventions: 'For there are no rules for arriving at passing theories, no rules in any strict sense, as opposed to rough maxims and methodological generalities' (p. 173). With this account 'we have abandoned not only the ordinary notion of a language, but we have erased the boundary between knowing a language and knowing our way around in the world' (ibid.). Davidson concludes his argument with the provocative claim that 'there is no such thing as language':

> I conclude that *there is no such thing as language*, not if a language is anything like what many philosophers and linguists have

supposed. There is therefore no such thing to be learned, mastered, or born with. We must give up the idea of a clearly defined shared structure which language-users acquire and then apply to cases. [. . .] we should give up the attempt to illuminate how we communicate by appeal to conventions. (1986, p. 174; my emphasis)

On Davidson's thoroughgoing individualistic view, the social aspects of language and communication are not essential. On this view, the social is reduced to the fleeting encounters between mutually independent idiolects, to the contingent crossing of paths of the languages of solitary and autonomous individuals. Against this view Dummett (1986) has argued that to repudiate the role of conventions completely, as Davidson does, is to deny that language is a social practice, for conventions are 'what constitute a social practice' (p. 474). And indeed Davidson rejects the idea that words have meaning by virtue of a social practice, that they can have meaning independently of particular speakers in particular communicative situations. Davidson's thoroughgoing individualism disregards the crucial ways in which speakers are mutually dependent, that is, the crucial ways in which the members of a linguistic community rely on one another for their communicative exchanges. In particular, this view is unable to explain the phenomenon of 'the *division of linguistic labor*' identified and explained by Putnam (1975a). According to Putnam, we divide the semantic labour of articulating the meaning of our terms in the light of what is known to us by relying on experts in different semantic fields. On Putnam's view, spelling out the meanings of terms is not the individual responsibility of every speaker who uses them, but the social responsibility of the linguistic community as a whole. On this view, meanings are not to be determined by the communicative intentions of individual speakers, but rather, by the best knowledge available in the community, that is, by the experts in different fields within the community who are the last authority of the corresponding semantic domain. Thus, for example, Putnam (1975a) argues that 'water' means 'H_2O' in our linguistic community for all the individuals who use the term, even if they have no knowledge of the chemical composition of the liquid called by that name, because it has been so determined by the relevant experts – the chemists who are in charge of studying that substance.

Davidson's account of communication in terms of passing theories is indeed *socially thin*, but it is *individually thin* as well, for the notion of a *passing* theory also deflates the notion of an *idiolect*. According to Davidson's account, successful communication does not require the same language or the same theory of interpretation either across speakers or across temporal slices of the same speaker, that is, in the same speaker over time. If everything prior to the communicative encounter becomes ultimately irrelevant, the prior theory of the speaker and the previous stages of his/her idiolect drop out of consideration: all that matters for successful communication is the present convergence of contemporaneous slices of idiolects; and those ephemeral slices are what passing theories consist in. Thus Davidson's view results not only in a thoroughgoing individualism, but also in a thoroughgoing *presentism*. Can the Davidsonian view, despite its thinness, do justice to the communicative phenomena we are familiar with? Is Davidson's highly influential and highly controversial account of interpretation ultimately adequate for our linguistic practices? In what follows we will identify three areas in which the Davidsonian account seems to fare poorly; we will then examine Davidson's possible reply to these considerations as well as further objections that will take us beyond the Davidsonian framework.

In the first place, the Davidsonian account is incapable of explaining the *social costs of linguistic deviations*. Davidson leaves out of account the social consequences that malapropisms have. It is not at all clear that speakers really *get away with it*, as Davidson claims, for there are typically important consequences to their deviations. Speakers' departures from standard usage affect how they are socially perceived in communicative exchanges and the social status they acquire through their verbal behaviour. For indeed conformity with standard conventions and canonical ways of speaking are rewarded, while deviations are punished. As we saw in section 4.1, this is discussed and explained in detail in Bourdieu's account of the process of *linguistic unification* and the establishment of a *legitimate language*. By leaving out the social and political dimension of language, Davidson's account disregards the crucial disadvantages that speakers' transgressions of linguistic conventions bring with them. This is not surprising since Davidson focuses on the formal conditions of communication and intelligibility. As we saw in 4.1, Bourdieu criticizes the social and political short-sightedness of formalism and emphasizes the dangers and costs of disregarding the socio-economic and political dimension of language use. Bourdieu's indictment of formalism for its complicity with the symbolic domination that it fails to acknowledge is based on an account of communication that emphasizes the crucial role that power relations play in linguistic exchanges: 'One must not forget that the relations of communication *par excellence* – linguistic exchanges – are also *relations of symbolic power* in which the power relations between speakers or their respective groups are actualized' (1991, p. 37; emphasis preserved and added). According to Bourdieu, speakers always have a particular *style*; and their *style*, which he defines as 'individual deviation from the linguistic norm' (p. 38), always operates in a determinate social space where it is perceived in a particular way. These social perceptions create and reinforce linguistic *distinctions* which are at the same time social *distinctions*: some styles become *distinguished* while others become *vulgar*. Our linguistic exchanges do not take place in neutral spaces, such as the formal space of theory-comparison and theory-adjustment suggested by Davidson, but in socio-economic spaces. As we saw, Bourdieu describes these spaces as 'linguistic markets' in order to emphasize that linguistic exchanges result in gains and losses, and that through them some people accumulate *linguistic capital* while others become *linguistically dispossessed*. A good example of someone who does not seem to have a lot of linguistic capital is precisely Archie Bunker; and his malapropisms certainly contribute to his linguistic dispossession: they become emblematic signs of his inferior status as a social and economic agent. Archie Bunker's deviant style as a speaker has a crucial impact on his social and economic performance (on how well he can perform in a job interview, for example); and therefore it is a crucial factor in his limited access to jobs, social relations and other opportunities, contributing tremendously to his depressed socio-economic position. So does he really *get away with it*?

Davidson presents a picture of communication in which the identity of speakers is sharply separated from their identity as social agents. Bourdieu criticizes the formal accounts of communication that are based on this sharp separation. He argues that 'the use of language, the manner as much as the substance of discourse, depends on the social position of the speaker' (1991, p. 109); and that we cannot understand the social position of a speaker unless we situate it *vis-à-vis* linguistic conventions and accepted proprieties of use. Bourdieu conceptualizes communication as 'an encounter' between 'the socially constructed dispositions of the linguistic habitus, which imply a certain propensity to speak and say determinate things', and 'the structures of the linguistic market, which impose themselves as a system of specific sanctions and censorships' (p. 37). On this view, speech acts are essentially and unavoidably social acts; and we cannot fully understand their intelligibility unless we understand their social constitution. By contrast, Davidson's account disregards the social conditions of communication and its social consequences, giving speakers a *false sense of freedom*. By emphasizing that speakers are free to say whatever they like, Davidson paints an unrealistic picture of the linguistic agency that real people actually have. This illusory linguistic freedom, this fictitious autonomy, does a disservice to socially situated speakers (that is, to real people), especially to those who have been linguistically marginalized, for it hides their linguistic oppression and the obstacles they face in their communicative practices. We will examine some of these obstacles in the final section of the concluding chapter.

In the second place, Davidson's account of communication in terms of converging passing theories seems ill-equipped to explain the *unintended connotations* of words which are beyond the conscious control of speakers. But unintended connotations seem to be an important part of the meanings expressed and understood in communicative exchanges. This seems particularly clear when we use emotionally charged terms that can provoke a strong emotional reaction in others even if not intended by the speaker. For example, terms with racist, sexist or homophobic connotations can hurt people even if the speaker does not intend to use them in a racist, sexist or homophobic way – in fact, these connotations can injure people even if the speaker is unaware of them. We can thus combine this problem area with the previous one (about social consequences) and look at oppressive or injurious connotations that harm and disempower some speakers while empowering others. Are verbal attacks always under the control of the communicative intentions of the speaker?

In *Excitable Speech* (1997) Judith Butler offers a performative and non-intentionalistic account of hate speech.[6] According to this account, what makes certain words function as weapons is not simply the intentions of particular speakers who use them, but their *history of use*, which gives words the particular force that they have and the power to injure. As suggested by Butler's account, even when a verbal attack is intentional, the term used (e.g. a racial slur) does not function as a weapon simply by virtue of the communicative intention of the speaker or his/her passing theory, but by virtue of a social practice of use that has given force to the word and has made certain subjects vulnerable to it. A crucial part of Butler's account of hate speech concerns the *vulnerability* of linguistically constituted identities. We can only understand the phenomenon of verbal abuse if we understand the processes through which linguistic identities are formed and the specific powers and vulnerabilities that speaking subjectivities develop. Hate speech and other verbal attacks do not derive from the agency of a sovereign subject who is in full control of the power of his/her words and the impact that they will have on others. The phenomenon of verbal abuse exceeds the individualistic dimension of speech and seems to be tied to social meanings developed through histories of use. It is through social practices of use that words acquire particular connotations and forces and the subjects exposed to them develop certain vulnerabilities. How can these social phenomena be explained as resulting from the interaction between idiolects?

Davidson's account of communication as idiolectical exchange cannot account for either the phenomenon of verbal abuse, or for how certain speaking subjectivities become vulnerable to verbal attacks and injurious connotations while others do not. This inability seems to derive from the fact that the account ignores the role that the social aspects of language play in the formation of subjects and groups, of individual and collective identities. Davidson's individualism and presentism simply presuppose a neutral notion of individual identity that takes too much for granted, depicting speakers as autonomous subjects. This view will be indirectly criticized in the next chapter when we discuss the linguistic formation of identity. In this discussion we will examine the mutual dependence between speaking subjects and linguistic communities, which results in individual and collective identities being bound up with each other.

In the third place, by dismissing the importance of linguistic differences and of the very notion of a language, Davidson's account seems unable to shed light on the *problematic relationships between languages and between dialects*. If what constitutes a language is of no significance and of no consequence, linguistic struggles become fully mysterious. But these struggles often shape and structure our communicative exchanges and the contexts in which they take place;

and we cannot simply disregard the linguistic communities to which our interlocutors belong and the social status and recognition (or lack thereof) of the languages or dialects they speak. Given the Davidsonian claim that 'there is no such thing as language', how can we make sense of people's investment in their languages or dialects and of the social and cultural battles fought for them? If a shared language is an illusion, it is a very powerful illusion that we take for granted not only in philosophy and linguistics, but also in ordinary life. If the concept of a language is a fiction, it is not only a theoretical fiction, but also a practical and social fiction with enormous force in our actual human communities and traditions. As suggested by Dummett in his critique of Davidson, it seems socially and politically irresponsible to simply declare that languages do not exist. Is there nothing at stake when oppressive regimes try to suppress minority languages, when 'teachers punish children for speaking those languages in the playground'? Dummett writes:

> In India crowds demonstrate against the proposal to make Hindi the sole official language. Bretons, Catalans, Basques and Kurds each declare that language is the soul of their culture. The option does not seem to be open to us to declare that such governments and such peoples are under an illusion that there is anything they are suppressing or cherishing (1986, p. 465).

Languages are powerful social realities: sometimes, when they are used as tools for the oppression of certain groups, they are the site of cultural and ethnic violence; but sometimes they constitute the site of cultural solidarity and liberation, that is, the channel for the cultural self-affirmation of a people who articulate their experiences, needs, interests and values in and through a language that becomes bound up with their identity, so that taking pride in their language becomes an essential part of taking pride in their identity. There is an intimate relationship between languages and collective identities; and this too will be examined in some detail below when we examine the linguistic formation of subjects and communities and the inter-relations between language and identity in the next chapter.

What could the Davidsonian philosopher say about the three areas of linguistic phenomena that we have identified as being left out of the account of communication as the passing encounter between idiolects? Can he explain the social costs of linguistic deviations, the existence of unintended connotations and the battles between languages and between dialects? The Davidsonian philosopher is likely to reply that these empirical areas belong to the sociology of language, but they are not part of the proper object of study of a philosophical theory of communication. A philosophical theory, it has been argued, does not have to get into these practical matters, for it involves only a transcendental and *a priori* inquiry into the conditions of possibility of communication. Even if we were to accept Bourdieu's claims that language exists 'only in the practical state' (1991, p. 46) and that there is no communication without power relations, the Davidsonian philosopher could nonetheless insist that his/her theory is not a theory for the empirical reality of communication and language, but rather, an idealized model of communication which does not aim at empirical adequacy. Such an idealized model is not based on empirical facts about language use, but on idealizations concerning how communication could, in principle, be accomplished. Taken literally, these idealizations are fictions, but they are expected to shed light on our understanding of how we communicate with one another, just as the fiction of frictionless planes in physics contributes to our understanding of motion on real planes with plenty of friction.

The objection that the Davidsonian account leaves out the social and political dimension of language and communication is likely to be dismissed as an irrelevant empirical objection that misses the point of this philosophical account of communication. Davidson replied to Dummett in just this way, stressing that the interest of his theory 'was not to describe actual practice, but to decide what is necessary to linguistic communication' (1994, p. 6).[7] But is there a sharp separation or division of labour between the philosophical and the empirical study of language? According to Davidson, it is only the latter that must study the empirically contingent social norms and conventions of language use, while the former can abstract from them and concern itself exclusively with the necessary and sufficient conditions of communication. It is worth noting that this is a very traditional conception of the philosophical study of language, one that seems to betray the naturalistic orientation of the Quinean framework in which Davidson develops his views, and one that many contemporary philosophers of language reject. Bourdieu and Butler would certainly protest against drawing any sharp distinction between the socio-political and the purely linguistic or communicative, relegating the former to the realm of the empirical and the latter to the realm of the *a priori* and transcendental; and we have already seen Bourdieu's arguments for this (cf. 4.1), which include a political argument (the charge of complicity with the established authorities and the powers that be).[8] But let's consider Davidson's account of the formal conditions of intelligibility in its own terms, and let's move to a more internal critique, to less empirical and more traditionally philosophical objections that call into question whether this account offers tenable transcendental conditions, that is, coherent conditions of possibility for communication and linguistic understanding. Given that Davidson is willing to concede the empirical inefficacy of his theory, we need a stronger objection against him, one that shows that the kind of idealized model of communication he proposes is flawed, that is, that his theory – understood in its own terms – rests on bankrupt and self-undermining idealizations. Influential philosophers of language, including Dummett (1986), have criticized the viability of Davidson's idealizations from a social perspective, arguing that communication becomes possible only thanks to a social practice of language use. According to this social perspective, Davidson's account of communication in terms of converging passing theories, by destroying the essentially social dimension of language, also destroys the kind of genuine sharing required by communication. These considerations are inspired by the Philosophy of Language of the later Wittgenstein, and more specifically his celebrated *Private Language Argument*. In the next section I will briefly examine this argument and will connect it with Derrida's view of language and a more general discussion of the sociality and temporality of language use.

5.2 COMMUNITIES, DECONSTRUCTION AND HISTORIES OF USE

In order to bring our discussion of the individualistic and social aspects of language to a close, let's examine what is perhaps the most famous and influential argument on this issue: Wittgenstein's *Private Language Argument*. This is an argument against the possibility of a *private* language, *private* – that is – in a *radical* sense: *not* in the sense of being merely *solitary* or contingently used by only one speaker, but in the more radical sense of being in principle *incommunicable*. A radically private language, in Wittgenstein's sense, is a language that is not teachable or sharable. As Wittgenstein puts it, 'the individual words of this language are to refer to what can only be known to the person speaking; to his immediate private sensations. So another person cannot understand the language' (PI §243). Wittgenstein tries to show that this language of absolute and irreversible privacy is an illusion, what he calls a *philosophical fiction or myth*. Wittgenstein's *Private Language Argument* tries to establish two points: first, that there cannot be a form of *normativity* that is radically private; and second, that there cannot be a radically private *reference* to which speakers' meanings can be reduced.

In the first place, drawing on the rule-following discussion that precedes it, Wittgenstein's *Private Language Argument* develops the point that a radically private language makes no room for normativity, for a distinction between *correct* and *incorrect*, because there cannot be such a thing as an *absolutely autonomous* source of correctness. Can language use be the *absolutely autonomous* practice of a single individual?[9] Wittgenstein's argument is that our normative distinctions between what is correct and what is incorrect cannot get a foothold in a radically private language where there is no difference between what *seems* correct and what *is* correct. No one can question what *seems* correct to the speaker since he/she is the only one around, and not just contingently: he/she is the only one who can be around to make a normative assessment about the use of the term because he/she is, by definition, the only user. Wittgenstein's argument suggests that the difference between *seeming* correct and *being* correct requires the possibility of negotiation and mutual correction; and for this there must be different centres of normative assessment any one of which could in principle be wrong. If the possibility of being wrong is eliminated, the possibility of being correct becomes empty: being correct is no longer a genuine possibility that may or may not happen, but a default status that attaches to everything one does and means nothing. Rather than securing correctness infallibility actually destroys it because being correct loses its force when the possibility of being incorrect has disappeared. Wittgenstein already established this point in the rule-following discussion, which suggests that there cannot be a radically private language-game because the rules of the game collapse when what counts as correct cannot be contested (see esp. PI §201). In this sense the *Private Language Argument* can be understood as an elaboration and application of ideas already suggested in the rule-following discussion, where Wittgenstein contended that '"obeying a rule" is a practice. And to think one is obeying a rule is not to obey a rule. Hence it is not possible to obey a rule "privately": otherwise thinking one was obeying a rule would be the same thing as obeying it' (PI §202).

In the rule-following discussion Wittgenstein argued against the illusion of absolutely autonomous or self-grounding practices. According to Wittgenstein, nothing can guarantee its own intelligibility and correctness. A practice cannot have itself as its own measure of correctness, for, as he puts it, having oneself as the only measure of correctness is like vindicating the validity of what is reported in a newspaper by checking it against multiple copies of the same newspaper (PI §265). We can pretend that our speech acts are self-justifying: imagine someone saying 'But I know how tall I am! I am *this* tall!', while 'laying his hand on top of his head to prove it' (PI §279). But on closer examination, that kind of autonomous normativity turns out to be mere show; the performance is an empty gesture. When everything is correct, when there is no such thing as the possibility of making a mistake, that means that we cannot draw a distinction between correct and incorrect in practice and at that point normativity has disappeared: it has collapsed. Thus absolute autonomy instead of making normativity unassailable annihilates it. There cannot be a radically private language because there cannot be a language-game with a purely internal and infallible normativity, with self-justifying rules that make invalidity impossible; when the possibility of contestation is eradicated, when there is no possibility of mistake, we are no longer dealing with a normative activity. Insofar as it is a normative activity, a language-game must contain the possibility of being *correct* and *incorrect* and the possibility of *normative negotiations*: a dialectical process of contestation and justification, of raising challenges and meeting them, of critique and advocacy.

It is important to note that Wittgenstein's argument about normativity applies to communities as well as to individuals. It is in fact irrelevant whether the infallible and autonomous source of normativity we posit is individual or collective. As suggested by Blackburn's essay 'The individual strikes back' (1984), the community is in the same predicament as the individual when it is taken as the sole and ultimate authority that can single-handedly establish what counts as correct, for then there is no distinction between what *seems* right to the community and what *is* right. For this reason,

Wittgenstein's argument should not be taken (as some have)[10] to point in the direction of *collectivism*, but rather, in the direction of *relationalism*. Wittgenstein's rejection of individualism should not be understood as an endorsement of the thesis that correctness is determined by the collective will of the community or the opinion of the majority;[11] rather, it should be taken as suggesting, simply, that normativity is a relational matter that binds subjects together and involves an intersubjective process of negotiation. Because of its relational nature what is normative – what can be deemed correct or incorrect – cannot be reified and localized anywhere in particular, especially not in the mind of an individual as accounts of *mental reference* had tried to do. And this brings us to the second point that the *Private Language Argument* tries to establish.

In the second place, Wittgenstein argues against the postulation of *private referents* to which the incommunicable meanings of a speaker can be reduced: for example, radically private mental episodes corresponding to sensation terms such as 'pain'. According to his argument, private reference accomplishes nothing – it is semantically irrelevant: the *idle wheel*[12] of semantic theory – for private referents play no normative role whatsoever in our communicative practices and our elucidations of meaning. To illustrate this point Wittgenstein develops the famous thought experiment of the *beetle in the box*. He writes:

> Now someone tells me that *he* knows what pain is only from his own case! Suppose everyone had a box with something in it: we call it a 'beetle'. No one can look into anyone else's box, and everyone says he knows what a beetle is only by looking at *his* beetle. Here it would be quite possible for everyone to have something different in his box. One might even imagine such a thing constantly changing. But suppose the word 'beetle' had a use in these people's language? If so it would not be used as the name of a thing. *The thing in the box has no place in the language-game at all*; not even as a *something*: for the box might even be empty. No, one can 'divide through' by the thing in the box; it cancels out, whatever it is. That is to say: if we construe the grammar of the expression of sensation on the model of 'object and designation' *the object drops out of consideration as irrelevant*. (PI §293; emphasis preserved and added)

Thus Wittgenstein attacks the reification of meanings in mental entities in which individualistic semantic theories have indulged. According to Wittgenstein, it is not the presence of a private mental object associated with a term or a private communicative intention accompanying the use of the term that guarantees its meaning and provides the normative standard for its correct use. Similar deflationary considerations against the reification of meaning can be found in the writings of Jacques Derrida. Derrida's arguments (perhaps more clearly than Wittgenstein's) undermine individual *and* collective reifications of meaning, showing that meanings cannot be fixed once and for all either by the speaker's intentions or by the shared conventions of the linguistic community. In 'Signature, event, context' (1982) Derrida develops an argument to this effect through an analysis of the *structural repeatability* of signs. Derrida emphasizes that what turns sounds or marks into signs is their repeatable structure, but he argues that we cannot understand the iterability of signs in terms of *presence* as the philosophical tradition has tried to do. The target of his critique is the traditional view of communication in terms of *presence*: the presence of the object talked about, of the audience addressed and especially the presence of the communicative intention of the speaker or writer. Derrida argues that philosophers have traditionally appealed to these communicative presences as the foundation of communication in order to explain the intelligibility of signs, including *written* signs, which is specially surprising since in reading and writing the absence of the communicative elements is the norm, rather than the exception: the audience is typically absent when we write, the author is typically absent when we read and the objects talked about in writing are rarely in the neighbourhood.

According to Derrida (1982), in traditional philosophical accounts of the written language (of which Condillac's is a paradigmatic example) absence is treated as 'a modification of presence', that is, as something derivative and secondary to presence, in fact as a proxy for a presence, which is always recoverable and remains that which animates communicable meanings. In these traditional accounts, Derrida argues, the manipulation of written marks in reading and writing is described as the 'tracing and retracing' of absences so that they are rendered present. Reading, for example, is depicted as traveling back to a presence, namely, the presence of the intention of the author that animated the text when it was written and has to be recovered for the text to be understood. According to Derrida, the intrinsic repeatability of written signs shows that this account of the written language is bankrupt: that signs are repeatable means that their intelligibility must subsist after the presence of the different communicative elements disappear. Derrida argues that the intelligibility of a written mark cannot be subordinated to the presence or even the existence of any particular speaking subjectivity that uses the term or to the presence or existence of any objective reality to which the term is associated: it cannot be tied to the presence of the object or referent because this may be destroyed, or to the presence of the interlocutors addressed because they may disappear, or to the presence of the speaker and his/her intentions because the written sign outlives the speaker and his/her intentions.

Derrida's claim is that a sign must survive the absence or *death* of every communicative element. So what characterizes the intelligibility of a sign is not presence but absence. On Derrida's view, what turns a mark or a noise into an intelligible sign is precisely its detachment from any presence: separation, discontinuity, *death*; the absence of referents, interlocutors and authors. And, for Derrida, this is an *absolute* absence, that is, an absence that cannot be thought of as a form of presence. This is what Derrida calls *différance*: 'this distance, division, delay, *différance* must be capable of being brought to a certain absolute degree of absence for the structure of writing' (1982, p. 315). *Différance* is the radical, unavoidable and irreparable absence or death that all signs have by virtue of their structural iterability. This is how Derrida puts the point with respect to the absolute absence or death of the addressee (similar things could be said about the absolute absence or death of the author or of the referent):

> A written sign is proffered in the absence of the addressee. [. . .] But is not this absence only a presence that is distant, delayed, or, in one form or another, idealized in its representation? [. . .] My 'written communication' must, if you will, remain legible despite the absolute disappearance of every determined addressee in general for it to function as writing, that is, for it to be legible. It must be repeatable – iterable – in the absolute absence of the addressee or of the empirically determinable set of addressees. [. . .] *A writing that was not structurally legible – iterable – beyond the death of the addressee would not be writing.* (1982, p. 315; emphasis added)

So, on Derrida's view, for a sign to be legible it has to be iterable beyond the death of every communicative presence. In other words, the radical separation from or annihilation of every presence is consubstantial to the legibility of the written sign. Derrida draws various consequences from his account of the written language in terms of absolute absence or *différance*. One of these consequences is that there cannot be such a thing as a *secret* language or code. Derrida develops an argument that strongly resembles Wittgenstein's *Private Language Argument*. The main difference is that what Derrida's argument rejects is not the possibility of a language that is the private property of a single individual, but rather, the possibility of a language that is the exclusive property of a pair of individuals. He writes: 'Let us imagine a writing with a code idiomatic enough to have been founded and known, as a secret cipher, only by two "subjects". Can it still be said that upon the death of the addressee, that is, of the two partners, the mark left by one of them is still a writing?' (p. 315). He answers that the mark is legible only to the extent that it is iterable in their absence and in the absence of whoever uses the code. So Derrida concludes:

> This implies that there is *no code* – an organon of iterability – *that is structurally secret*. The possibility of repeating, and therefore of identifying, marks is implied in every code, making of it a communicable, transmittable, decipherable grid that is iterable for *a third party*, and thus for *any possible user in general*. All writing, therefore, in order to be what it is, must be able to function in the radical absence of every empirically determined addressee in general. And this absence is not a continuous modification of presence; it is a break in presence, 'death', or the possibility of the 'death' of the addressee, inscribed in the structure of the mark. (1982, pp. 315–16; my emphasis)

Other important consequences of the Derridian analysis of signs are the *indeterminacy* of meaning and the *deauthorization* of linguistic rules and communicative contexts. As Derrida puts it, his view leads to: 'the disruption, in the last analysis, of the authority of the code as a finite system of rules; the radical destruction, by the same token, of every context as a protocol of a code' (p. 316). Given the infinite iterability of signs, a radical departure from whatever has been previously established in language is always waiting in the wings. And this unavoidable possibility invites the destabilization of any context of use and underscores the instability of meaning. The structural phenomenon of *différance* underscores a real '*crisis* of meaning' (p. 319). Since the identity of a sign is dispersed in an infinite chain of possible repetitions, strictly speaking, there are no such things as self-identical signs that remain the same over time, for 'the very iterability which constitutes their identity never permits them to be a unity of self-identity' (p. 318). On Derrida's view, the infinite iterability of signs entails their eternal 'drifting' in the sea of language. This 'drifting' raises the ever present possibility of destabilizing contexts and *deconstructing* any meaning and history of use by rearranging the word's past and its projection into the future. But in the midst of so much indeterminacy and instability how do we manage to *do things with words*? Derrida himself raises this question in his critique of Austin.

Derrida criticizes Austin for describing the context in which a speech act takes place as a '*total* situation', for communicative contexts are never complete and self-contained; they are always temporally extended and characterized by their·'structural nonsaturation' (p. 310). On Derrida's view, speech acts never acquire closure at the moment of their production and in the context in which they are carried out, for they are always reshaped in other contexts in which they are *cited*. For example, a marriage ceremony, the making of a promise and an act of christening are all speech acts that can be cited in different ways in the future and the chain of citation may decide how they are to be regarded. Speech acts can always be *cited* in new ways, that is, *reinscribed* in new contexts. On this view, there can be no such thing as a final and fully secure performative success, because no matter how well established a performative success may seem to be, it can always be overturned in the future: a marriage may be declared null, a baptismal act ineffective, a promise fraudulent. Performative successes have to be positively sanctioned by future uses and certified in future contexts; and, therefore, they are always unfinished and contingently dependent on the agency of future language users. This underscores the precariousness and arbitrariness of performatives, of their illocutionary forces and of the linguistic institutions to which they are associated.

On Derrida's view, performatives are artificial historical constructions that can be brought down at any point. According to Derrida, it is *infelicity*, rather than felicity, that characterizes our speech acts:

they are always *on the verge of failing*; and even when they succeed, their felicity is precarious because it can be invalidated at any moment. In ordinary life, however, we are blind to the precariousness and arbitrariness of performative successes. But why does this artificiality pass unnoticed in everyday affairs? Perhaps because we want to believe that we are married, sincere, loyal, faithful, etc., as if these were final qualities of our actions and our character, while in fact they are constantly open to reinterpretation. Marriage, sincerity, loyalty, faithfulness, etc., are all artificial constructions sustained only by what we say and keep saying in *citational* chains. What our speech acts amount to is determined by how they are *cited*. On Derrida's view, it is *citation* or *reinscription* that determines the significance and nature of speech acts: 'a general citationality – or rather, a general iterability – without which there would not even be a "successful" performative' (1982, p. 325). It is in this sense that Derrida claims that 'a successful performative is necessarily an impure performative' (ibid.), criticizing and yet echoing Austin, who recognized that there is no 'pure' performative that can guarantee its own success.[13] In particular, Derrida criticizes the role that Austin and other Speech Act theorists have given to the presence of communicative intentions in fixing performatives. Derrida argues that communicative intentions become irrelevant in the chains of citation in which speech acts are integrated. Whether or not certain intentions accompany the production of speech acts is irrelevant because speech acts can always be cited or reinscribed in new ways; and the original intentions of the authors are lost in these citational chains, in these infinite possibilities of reinscription. In this context Derrida describes *différance* as 'the irreducible absence of intention' (p. 327). He now talks about structural iterability and structural *différance* as essential features of *all signs*, not only of written signs, thus generalizing his account of the written language to *all language use*. He emphasizes that *différance* belongs to the general structure of communication, even face-to-face communication. Against the Davidsonian account of conversational exchanges that we discussed in the previous section, Derrida would argue that, in order to be intelligible (legible), the signs used must survive the passing encounters of idiolects, and their meanings cannot be tied to the fleeting exchanges between particular interlocutors. Indeed Davidson's claim about the transient nature of meanings violates the structural *iterability* of signs that Derrida analyses. Davidson's view reduced intelligibility to presence in a radical way, so that meanings could subsist only in the *passing* theories of particular moments (corresponding to time-slices of idiolects). In sharp contrast with the Davidsonian view, the Derridian view suggests that it is not the presence but the absence of communicative intentions that defines the use of signs and their meaning.

Through Derrida's critique of Austin we learn that the notion of *différance* should be understood as the 'essential absence of intention' or 'structural unconsciousness' that 'prohibits every saturation of a context' (p. 327). So *différance* leads to a *loss of context*; and it is this kind of decontextualization that makes possible what Derrida calls *deconstruction*. Deconstruction is the disruption – without complete neutralization – of the normative force of any conceptual system that animates language and of the opposition that that system establishes between what is intelligible and what is nonsensical. In deconstruction we do not simply reject a conceptual system of meanings, but we problematize it from the inside by bringing in possibilities of signification that have been left outside the system, that is, by putting side by side the recognized and the unrecognized, the accepted and the rejected. As Derrida puts it,

> Deconstruction cannot limit itself or proceed immediately to a neutralization: it must, by means of a double gesture, a double science, a double writing, practice an overturning of the classical opposition and a general displacement of the system. [. . .] Deconstruction does not consist in passing from one concept to another, but in overturning and displacing a conceptual order, as well as the nonconceptual order with which the conceptual order is articulated. (1982, p. 329)

Derrida's negative insights can be supplemented with a more positive outlook on meaning. For the indeterminacy of context can be understood as having both a negative and a positive significance: as underscoring the ever present possibility of *deconstruction* as well as the ever present possibility (and perhaps necessity) of *reconstruction*. The elasticity and openness of iterable chains of use make room not only for decontextualization and deconstruction, but also for recontextualization and reconstruction. So let's now look critically at the deconstructive view to see if we can draw different conclusions from the indeterminacy of meaning and the instability of communicative contexts.

As we have seen, with his notion of *citation* or *reinscription* Derrida (1982) argues that the use of language in new communicative contexts, far from relying on a process of contextualization that ties the new use to prior usage, consists, in fact, in a process of *decontextualization* that always involves a departure from previous contexts. Derrida contends that the performative force of a speech act is derived from its *break* with prior contexts. Accordingly, he refers to the force of the performative as 'breaking force' (*force de rupture*). Derrida's view accentuates the relative autonomy of speech acts with respect to their contexts of use. This *contextual freedom* is based on the model of written communication. Derrida's account assimilates all language use, all speech acts, to the paradigm of decontextualization that is allegedly found in the written language. As Butler (1997) puts it, for Derrida, 'performative utterances operate according to the same logic as written marks [. . .] which, as signs, carry a force that breaks with its context [and this] breaking force (*force de rupture*) is not an accidental predicate but the very structure of the written text' (p. 148). Derrida calls our attention to the gaps or intervals between instances of use and argues that they are a constitutive feature of the iterability of signs: as iterable structures, signs are marks *cut off* from their putative originating contexts. Against the Austinian emphasis on the *continuity* between contexts of use Derrida underscores the *discontinuity* between contexts. But are our speech acts *cut off* from prior usage or *tethered* to it? Things are far more complicated than this debate between polarized positions on performativity makes it seem. If we want to do things with words, do we have to contextualize or decontextualize these words? Do they acquire force by complying with norms or by breaking them, by being faithful to previous contexts of use or by departing from them? As I have argued elsewhere,[14] the polarized dichotomy between rigid contextualization and unconstrained decontextualization is a false dilemma and both of its horns should be rejected. On the one hand, the strict conventionalism ascribed to Austin involves a rigidified contextualization that can only be obtained if discursive contexts are glued together by absolutely fixed and stable norms or conventions. But it is illusory to think that there is an absolute continuity between contexts of use, as if they cascaded with a perfect flow in an unrelenting succession of congruous slices. On the other hand, the Derridian paradigm of decontextualization proposes an illusory freedom from historical contexts. This contextual freedom is illusory because historical contexts of communication do indeed constrain – even if they do not determine – the range of acts that can be successfully performed at any given time and their domain of significance. There are no radical breaks or absolute gaps between discursive contexts; and, therefore, it is misleading (at best) to characterize language use as the capricious decontextualization of signs. Radical continuity and discontinuity are impossible ideals or illusions that do not capture at all the normative relations that exist between actual contexts of communication. In what follows I will briefly discuss Butler's notion of *resignification* and my own notion of *echoing* to explain the interrelations between contexts, or what is called the phenomenon of *intercontextuality*.

Following Derrida, Butler emphasizes the deferred and unsaturated nature of communicative contexts – what Derrida calls 'the *illimitability* of contexts'. But she argues that from the illimitability of contexts we should not infer the context-independence of our speech acts. *Pace* Derrida, the illimitiability of discursive contexts does not call for the *decontextualization* of signs and speech acts, but for their *repeated contextualization*, for an ongoing and never-ending contextualization. As Butler puts it:

> The 'illimitability' of contexts simply means that any delineation of a context that one might perform is itself subject to a further contextualization, and that contexts are not given in unitary forms. This does not mean [. . .] that one should cease any effort to delineate a context; it means only that any such delineation is subject to potentially infinite revision (1997, pp. 147–8)

Butler uses the notion of *resignification* to develop an account of the infinite process of revision and modification of communicative contexts and the uses of language that take place in them. *Resignification* is the centrepiece of Butler's performative account of the instability and plasticity of meaning. According to this account, meanings develop and change in and through transformative *citational* chains which consist in speech acts that cite previous ones and at the same time take up their meaning in a new direction. On Butler's view, the meanings of our signifiers have a temporal structure built into them: they are *constrained* by past uses, but they remain *open* to future uses. The future of a signifier depends on a 'citational chain', that is, a chain of signification that operates through an insistent citing of the signifier. Butler explains the *openness* of signifiers in terms of the semantic *excess* of our speech acts, which cite or invoke indefinitely many past and future speech acts. As Butler puts it, any speech act in a performative chain has 'a condensed historicity: it exceeds itself in past and future directions, an effect of prior and future invocations that constitute the instance of utterance' (1997, p. 3). The excessive *resignification* of a performative consists in 'a repetition that fails to repeat loyally, a reciting of the signifier that must commit a disloyalty [. . .] in order to secure its future' (p. 220). Although Butler's account is more deconstructive than reconstructive, her view also points in the direction of the rearticulation of meanings and the formation of new meanings through changing citational chains. It is this aspect of the Butlerian account that I have developed through the notion of *echoing*, one of the core notions of my *polyphonic contextualism* – a view of language that draws on philosophers as different as Bakhtin, Dewey and Wittgenstein.[15]

I have articulated and defended a contextualist view of language that depicts communicative contexts as containing an irreducible multiplicity of voices and perspectives that constitute possible paths or bridges to other contexts. In other words, on my view, communicative contexts are essentially *polyphonic*, and their polyphony is *indomitable*: it cannot be constrained because the multiplicity of voices and perspectives that a context can contain remains – at least in principle – always open and ever growing. My polyphonic contextualism offers an account of intercontextuality that underscores the crucial normative relations of dependence between contexts that speak to each other or *echo* one another, while at the same time emphasizing the openness of the performative chains that can be found across contexts. I describe the complex relations between multiple voices and perspectives in and across contexts through the notion of *echoing*, which is my reformulation (through Wittgenstein and Dewey) of the Butlerian notion of resignification through repetition: echoing voices speak to another by repeating the use of signs in a variety of ways (sometimes very similar, sometimes wildly different), having a wide range of effects depending on the kind of interaction involved in the echoing – echoing voices can reinforce each other, reproduce each other, modify each other, correct each other and even reverse each other. On my view, communicative contexts are not insulated and sealed off from one another; they are in dialogue, and these intercontextual dialogues exhibit diverse and heterogeneous tendencies that can be exploited in many ways. On my view, there is no such thing as absolute contextual determination or absolute contextual freedom. My contextualism emphasizes that the discursive agency of language users is hybrid: it is constituted by a mixture of freedom and constraint; it is determined and not determined, free and not free; it is creative but limited.

The *echoing* phenomenon is a form of semiotic *repetition* that fuels a constant dynamism in the temporal life of meaning. Semantic connections are forged by the echoing of one context in other contexts. In using the same term as in previous contexts something is added to or subtracted from these prior contexts. And, in turn, the contribution that one context makes to the meaning of a term is subsequently modified and transformed in other contexts. By echoing each other, the semantic interventions or resignifications of language users constantly reshape the meaning of signs – sometimes broadening and enriching meaning, sometimes narrowing and impoverishing it. As I have argued elsewhere, how much echoing the use of a term produces is a good measure of how well entrenched it is in the linguistic community. Echoing thus functions as a mechanism of normalization: the more a use is echoed, the more consolidated it becomes. But echoing can also function as a mechanism of deviation and semantic innovation: the more an eccentric use of language is echoed, the more the standard use is destabilized and the more room there is for new uses and new meanings. And indeed it is the phenomenon of echoing that explains how a new use of language acquires intelligibility; for the echoing shapes the performative chains of repetitions in which word meanings are gestated. The echoing involved in every use of language supplies us with an opportunity for semantic disruption and subversion, an opportunity that we may decide to exploit or not; and this is a decision (typically implicit and tacit) that we are constantly confronted with in our discursive performances. Both my view and Butler's thus emphasize the *discursive responsibility* we have as speakers and writers: the responsibility we must assume for our use of language, for how we echo others and contribute (or fail to contribute) to their resignifications, for starting new lines of resignification and for continuing or discontinuing existing lines.

Meanings are always being modified in new contexts of use. And as active members of linguistic practices and makers of language, we contribute to these transformations: we participate in the reworking of language, in the reconstruction of meaning through the continuation or discontinuation of the use of terms in particular ways. For this we have to take responsibility. We are always confronted with new contexts and new possible ways of speaking and signifying; and, as speakers and writers, we have to take responsibility for opening or closing possibilities in our practices. But in order to understand the agency of language users and their discursive responsibility, we need to understand how we are formed as *subjects* in and through language. It is to the process of subject formation in linguistic interaction and the interrelations between language and identity that I now turn.

CHAPTER 6

LANGUAGE AND IDENTITY

6.1 INTERPELLATION AND CENSORSHIP

Louis Althusser (2001) has offered a powerful account of the formation of identity through the address of the other. The centrepiece of this account is the notion of *interpellation*. Althusser characterizes the phenomenon of interpellation as a kind of hailing that has the formative power of configuring one's identity in a particular way and of making one accept this concrete configuration as what one is. The interpellations to which individuals are subject are determined by the dominant ideology: 'all ideology hails or interpellates concrete individuals as concrete subjects' (2001, p. 117; emphasis omitted). As an illustration Althusser offers his celebrated example of an act of hailing in the street by a policeman who says 'Hey, you there!' He remarks that 'the hailed individual will turn around' and 'by this mere one-hundred-and-eighty-degree physical conversion, he becomes a *subject*' (p. 118). By turning around the passerby responds to the address and assumes an identity projected on him/her; and in this way the other's recognition becomes the normative framework that defines the subjected individual. The voice of the interpellated subject is thus subordinated to the voice that interpellates him/her: the agency of the former is under the yoke of the latter, always taking the form of a response to the interpellating voice, which sets the terms of the interaction.

Althusser argues that interpellation turns individuals into *subjects*; and he describes the process of *subjectification* as a process of *subjugation* or *submission* to the dominant ideology that is behind the categories of interpellation. On this view, to be a subject is to be *subjected to* the normative expectations of an ideological system.

But of course the *ideological* nature of subjectivity is never made explicit when it is being constituted through interpellations. Interpellation involves an ideological imposition whose ideological character is *hidden*.[1] Besides its concealed ideological character, Althusser emphasizes another important feature of interpellation: its *inescapability*. This feature has different aspects. In the first place, interpellation is inescapable in the sense that it cannot be evaded if it is felt at all: once it is registered, there is no escape, for trying to ignore it or evade it – for example, literally running away from the policeman who says 'Hey, you there!', or not turning back when someone calls you using a derogatory term such as 'bitch' or 'faggot' – is also a reaction to the address and it leaves a mark in the subjectivity of the individual interpellated. In the second place, interpellation is inescapable because it is part of the very constitution of the subject and, in that sense, it precedes the appearance of the subject. As Althusser puts it, *'individuals are always-already subjects'*; they are 'always-already interpellated by ideology as subjects' (p. 119). Interpellation is the condition of possibility of subjectivity; it is what sets the stage or prepares the scene for the appearance of the subject. This is illustrated by Althusser's remarks about the familial ideology (paternal/maternal/fraternal) 'in which the unborn child is expected' (ibid.). This ideological preparation of the arrival of the new member of the family includes talk about the child's gender, name, position in the family, etc.: 'Before its birth, the child is therefore always-already a subject, appointed as a subject in and by the specific familial ideological configuration in which it is "expected" once it has been conceived' (ibid.) – and, we could add, even before it has been conceived (e.g. people's talk about their interest in conceiving, adopting, etc.).

Bourdieu's social theory expands the account of the ideological formation of the subject by including the *unconscious* and *corporeal* aspects of the formation of identity through the address of the other. This account can be read as broadening the Althusserian notion of interpellation to cover also *subliminal* and *nonlinguistic* forms of address. Bourdieu emphasizes that the social imposition of an identity is accomplished through *insinuations* that often take the form of subliminal messages that are not consciously registered by the recipient and do not even have to be verbalized. These tacit forms of address include 'ways of looking, sitting, standing, keeping silent, or even of speaking ("reproachful looks" or "tones", "disapproving glances" and so on)' (1991, p. 51). This is how identity categories and structures of subjectivity are transmitted from generation to generation in a linguistic community, by shaping people's sense of what they can say and do and of what they are. This is what Bourdieu describes as 'the power of suggestion', which 'instead of telling the child what he must do, tells him what he is, and thus leads him to become durably what he has to be' (p. 52). It is 'the power of suggestion' that produces our unconscious sensitivity and predisposition to be responsive to certain interpellations. According to Bourdieu, the submission to symbolic power prefigured in the habitus of speakers is established through *suggestions* or *insinuations* (glances, tones, postures, etc.),[2] which are a more subtle and powerful form of *intimidation* than the one present in explicit forms of interpellation or hailing, as well as prior to them.

According to Bourdieu's account, our communicative performances are full of subliminal messages that mould the subjectivity of the new individuals who are brought into language; they 'are *full of injunctions* that are powerful and hard to resist precisely because they are *silent and insidious, insistent and insinuating*' (1991, p. 51; my emphasis). On Bourdieu's view, the most important feature of these performative impositions of symbolic power is their *elusiveness*. These implicit impositions involve a very peculiar kind of *intimidation*, an intimidation that takes place *without an act of intimidation*. About this form of intimidation Bourdieu observes: 'a symbolic violence which is not aware of what it is (to the extent that it implies no *act of intimidation*) can only be exerted on a person predisposed (in his habitus) to feel it, whereas others will ignore it' (ibid.). But even though this insidious intimidation is invisible to the subjects who endure it, these subjects *actively* participate in it without knowing it. Symbolic subjugation is neither chosen, nor passively and mechanically imposed; it involves the *active complicity* of the individuals subjected to it. Speakers are not simply the passive recipients of symbolic domination; but they do not choose to participate in their own subjection either. On Bourdieu's view, the active complicity in symbolic domination inscribed in the habitus consists in an unconscious readiness to be interpellated, to be responsive to the voices of others, which resides in bodily dispositions. Symbolic domination takes place with the cooperation of the dominated subjects. This is how Bourdieu describes the speakers' complicity in their own domination:

All symbolic domination presupposes, on the part of those who submit to it, a form of *complicity* which is neither passive submission to external constraint nor a free adherence to values. The *recognition* of the legitimacy of the official language has nothing in common with an explicitly professed, deliberate and revocable belief, or with an intentional act of accepting a 'norm'. It is *inscribed, in a practical state, in dispositions* which are impalpably inculcated, through a long and slow process of acquisition, by the sanctions of the linguistic market. (1991, pp. 50–1; my emphasis)

The suggestions or insinuations that produce the sensitivity and readiness to respond to symbolic power are typically issued and received unconsciously, escaping the knowledge and control of speakers. Bourdieu describes them as 'insidious', as 'silent' and 'invisible', for, unlike the explicit address or name-calling of interpellation, these 'suggestions' do not involve any explicit statement or representation, and they take place without the appeal to convention and without the citation of coined terms. These sensitivity-shaping and readiness-forming 'suggestions' are 'all the more absolute and undisputed for not having to be stated' (1991, p. 52). These formative insinuations involve an 'invisible, silent violence'. This insidious violence exerted by symbolic power is very hard to avoid and resist because it is unrecognized, or rather, as Bourdieu puts it, *misrecognized*: symbolic power is a silent and invisible power that is *misrecognized* as such and thus tacitly and unconsciously *recognized* as legitimate. Bourdieu uses the terms 'recognition' (*reconnaissance*) and 'misrecognition' (*méconnaissance*) to convey that the exercise of power through symbolic interaction involves the sedimentation of background conceptualizations and beliefs. These conceptualizations and beliefs are embodied and unconscious symbolic formations that come alive in and through our symbolic performance. While avoiding the cognitivism and voluntarism of the philosophy of the subject, Bourdieu's account of symbolic domination through symbolic interaction still rests on a dialectic of recognition. But this dialectic proceeds through unknowing and uncontrollable forms of recognition that are inscribed in the unconscious dispositions of the body. This is a dialectic of recognition that is full of misrecognitions: of oneself, of one's peers and of the powers that structure our symbolic interactions. One's misrecognitions of symbolic power can work in spite of one's own interests and situate one's agency in a field of conflict and contradiction.

Bourdieu's account of the formation of the linguistic habitus through subliminal suggestions and insinuations has had a significant impact on the contemporary literature on identity and especially on Butler's account of the performative constitution of identity. On Butler's view, interpellations are essentially performative. As she explains it, the act of interpellation is not descriptive, but 'inaugurative': 'It seeks to introduce a reality rather than report on an existing one; it accomplishes this introduction through a citation of existing convention' (1997, p. 33). According to Butler's performative account, insinuations and subliminal forms of address – what Bourdieu called 'the power of suggestion' – function as forms of *censorship* which, once internalized, operate as *self-censorship* in the subject. Let's look at the central ideas concerning identity formation in Butler's view of performativity and censorship. Like Bourdieu, Butler also broadens the Althusserian account of subject formation beyond explicit forms of address. In particular, she emphasizes that social interpellation goes beyond voices: 'the discourse that inaugurates the subject need not take the form of a voice at all' (p. 31); 'the interpellative name may arrive without a speaker – on bureaucratic forms, the census, adoption papers, employment applications' (p. 34). According to Butler's account, the names one is called are coined forms of address which interpellate the individual in particular ways; they have the capacity to 'animate the subject into existence' and to configure different aspects of his/her identity such as gender, sexuality, race and ethnicity. Names constitute one socially, but Butler emphasizes that 'one's social constitution takes place without one's knowing' (p. 31). This insight leads Butler to develop an important revision of Althusser's view of subjection, which requires the subject's explicit acknowledgement and appropriation of the interpellation in order to make it effective and constitutive of the subject's identity. Arguing against this cognitivist remnant of the dialectic of recognition inherited from the philosophy of the subject, she writes: 'The subject need not always turn around in order to be constituted as a subject' (ibid.); 'interpellation can function without the "turning around", without anyone ever saying, "Here I am"' (p. 33).

In *Excitable Speech* (1997) Butler extends the Althusserian account of interpellation to elucidate the use of common nouns and names to address the subject. Developing an analysis of discrimination and hate speech, she is especially interested in terms that have a pejorative and denigrating use such as 'faggot', 'spic', 'nigger', etc. The broadening of the notion of social interpellation beyond voices and even beyond the verbal realm is crucial for Butler's analysis of hate speech. She argues that racist speech, for example, 'neither begins nor ends with the subject who speaks or with the specific name that is used' (p. 34). Linguistic forms of agency piggyback on nonlinguistic ones. According to Butler's account, symbolic domination is parasitic on other (nonverbal) forms of domination: nonverbal violence is mimicked by our discursive agency and continued in the symbolic domain; that is, it is symbolically reproduced through performative chains that *cite* (or *echo*, I would say) – and thus recreate – the violence in question. A name can be used to denigrate because it is linked to a social injury and a traumatic experience, so that its iterability is a repetition of the injury and the trauma. As Butler puts it, hate speech involves 'the restaging of injury through signs' (p. 36). Injurious names are those that involve a traumatic performativity, that is, those in which a trauma is not simply remembered, but relived (cf. pp. 36–7).

Butler also explores the ways in which interpellation can be *resisted*. How is resistance possible in the social constitution of the subject? How can individuals fight the names they are called and the ways in which their identity is depicted by others? Interpellation is inescapable and demands a response (conscious or unconscious) from the subject; but an interpellation can be answered with a repudiation or disavowal, with a refusal to accept the address in its own terms: 'That is not me, you must be mistaken!' And yet, as Butler points out, it is easy to 'imagine that the name continues to force itself upon you, to delineate the space you occupy, to construct a social positionality. Indifferent to your protests, the force of interpellation continues to work' (p. 33). But following Bourdieu, Butler argues that although the social constitution of identity through interpellation does not require the conscious and explicit acknowledgement of the subject, it still depends on the subject's *complicity*. As in Bourdieu, this complicity is not a chosen and self-aware form of collaboration, but an unconscious form of complicity established *prior* to the explicit interpellations that require explicit responses. For a hailing to be an identity-constituting interpellation, the interpellated individual must have already been subjected; that is, he/she must have already yielded to the authority of the interpellating voice and have thus become ready to succumb to its call.[3]

What Butler identifies as the readiness to symbolic domination or subjugation is precisely the kind of complicity that Bourdieu sees inscribed in the habitus. Butler understands this complicity as a form of *self-censorship*, which she explains with the psychoanalytic notion of *foreclosure*. This notion derives from the Lacanian psychoanalysts Jean Laplanche and J.-B. Pontalis, and it designates 'a primary form of repression, one that is not performed by a subject but, rather, whose operation makes possible the formation of the subject' (1998, p. 255). Butler emphasizes that 'foreclosure is not a singular action, but a reiterated effect of a structure' (ibid.). 'The action of foreclosure does not take place once and for all, but must be repeated to reconsolidate its power and efficacy' (p. 256). So, foreclosure is the consequence of a repeatable structure that has to be continually sustained, the effect of the collective censoring of the things we say and do that is constantly reinforced in the community through performative chains that exceed any particular individual and set the stage for the intelligibility of any action or utterance. In 'Ruled out: vocabularies of the censor' (1998) Butler develops an analysis of foreclosure as part of her general performative account of censorship.

Butler (1998) argues against traditional accounts that depict censorship as something purely *negative and constraining*, while in fact censorship has also a *positive and enabling* side. For Butler, censorship is simultaneously constraining and enabling because by telling subjects what they cannot say, it delimits the space of what can be said. Censorship establishes 'what must remain unspeakable for contemporary regimes of discourse to continue to exercise their power' (p. 255). Butler encourages us to think of censorship as a *productive* form of power. She describes censorship – 'the exclusion of certain sites of enunciation' – as a productive force that shapes admissible speech as well as the subjectivity of those who can speak. On this view, censorship is, therefore, *doubly productive*: it produces speech and it produces speakers; it has the creative force of moulding both language and identity simultaneously. So an account of the *productivity* of censorship must involve an 'account of how power constrains and forces the production of speech' as well as an 'account of how the speaking subject is produced' (ibid.). On the one hand, 'censorship is what permits speech by enforcing the very distinction between permissible and impermissible speech'; it 'produces discursive regimes through the production of a domain of the unspeakable' (ibid.). On the other hand, censorship, understood as foreclosure, is what produces the identity of speakers and the agency they can have in language: 'If the subject is produced in speech through a set of foreclosures, then it is this founding and formative limitation that sets the scene for the agency of the subject' (p. 256).

Butler also criticizes another misconception of the received view of censorship: the idea that censorship typically operates through *explicit prohibitions*. On the traditional view censorship is thought of on the model of explicit regulations that are enforced from a position of power. On this view, censorship arises as a reaction to offensive or inadmissible speech; it comes, so to speak, after the fact, that is, after the threat of inadmissible speech has already appeared in the scene. Butler, by contrast, wants to call attention to more fundamental forms of censorship: *implicit* forms of censorship that are *prior* to the production of speech and found our sense of what can and cannot be said, inaugurating the boundaries of admissible speech before they are overstepped. On the received view, 'censorship appears to come after speech has been uttered: the speech has already become offensive, and some recourse to a regulatory agency has been made' (p. 248). But in Butler's alternative view of censorship as productive of speech, that *temporal relation is inverted*: 'Censorship precedes the text (by which I include "speech" and other cultural expressions), and is in some sense responsible for its production' (ibid.). The intrinsic *selectivity* of language is already, according to Butler, a primordial and constitutive kind of censorship present in every instance of language use, for there cannot be language without selectivity, that is, without a process of selection and articulation of intelligible possibilities that relegates other possibilities to the realm of the unintelligible. Selectivity involves a *structural* kind of censorship: we compose a message or formulate a communicative content by selecting, out of an infinite number of possibilities, those that we can treat as intelligible, those that can convey meaning for us. And, as Butler asks, 'would there be meaningful speech at all were it not for the prior foreclosures and operative principles of selectivity that form the field of linguistic intelligibility?' (ibid.).

Butler's performative account of censorship involves the reconceptualization of the *power* that speakers have in their use of language. On the received view, censorship is depicted as the phenomenon in which a centralized or even sovereign power unilaterally represses speech. This view takes as paradigmatic the case of *state censorship*. The paradigm of a state with absolute power controlling the speech of its citizens strongly suggests that we can think of the symbolic or discursive power of the censor in terms of *sovereignty* and *autonomy*. Besides the sovereign conception of the symbolic power of institutionalized authorities, there is also the sovereign view of individual speakers as being in full control over the language they speak. On this traditional view of speaking subjectivities, sovereignty and autonomy are transferred from the state to the citizen. This is what Butler calls 'the sovereign conception of the speaking citizen' that is often invoked in contemporary democracies: 'the subject is described according to the model of state power, and although the locus of power has shifted from the state to the subject, the unilateral action of power remains the same' (p. 255). Butler forcefully argues that the sovereign view is mistaken: the sovereign conception of symbolic power is not adequate either for institutional authorities or for individual subjects, for neither institutions nor speakers are sovereign and autonomous. She argues that the unconstrained notion of sovereignty is rendered unrealizable by the structural censorship that inaugurates speech: 'If implicit censorship makes speech possible, then the sovereignty of the citizen becomes questionable'; 'agency in speech is conditioned by the workings of implicit censorship' (p. 248). Butler insists that neither a central or institutionalized authority nor the individual subject can be said to have full control over language. As an alternative to the received view, Butler offers *a postsovereign conception of speaking subjects* according to which speakers do not have absolute power over their speech, but only a limited, conditioned power: the power to *resignify*, to contribute to citational chains. There is no absolute power in language, but only the resignifying powers of postsovereign subjects. And given that speech is never fully under anyone's control, the *censorship* as well as the *liberation* of speech always remain *necessarily incomplete*.

On the one hand, Butler argues that *censoring a text is necessarily incomplete*. A text can never be fully constrained by censorship because the censoring powers can never anticipate all the meanings that can possibly be contained in it or read into it. This uncontrollable polysemy of language is what Butler calls the *excessive* dimension of speech. In some sense a text always escapes censorship, for there is always something about the text being censored that exceeds the reach of the censor. Butler admits that there are kinds of censorship that are more complete than others, but she insists that there is no censorship that can be absolutely complete, foolproof and final. According to Butler, explicit prohibitions and regulations are the most vulnerable forms of censorship: 'Censorship is exposed to a certain vulnerability precisely through becoming explicit' (p. 250). The special vulnerability that explicit censorship has derives from the fact that, in order to declare *something* outside the boundaries of admissible speech, that *something* must be *cited*. An explicit prohibition cannot take place without a conjuring of the very act prohibited; and a verbal prohibition must cite the very term that is being banned from language; and thus 'the effort to constrain the term culminates in its proliferation': explicit prohibitions require 'rehearsing and proliferating the very terms that they seek to bar from discourse' (ibid.). Explicit censorship is 'compelled to repeat what it seeks to constrain, and so invariably reproduces and restages the very text that it seeks to silence' (p. 249). As an illustration of this point, Butler (1997, 1998) examines the consequences of the US congressional statute passed in October 1994 that put into law the 'don't ask, don't tell' policy on homosexual self-declaration in the military. Butler argues that the statute has in fact contributed to the proliferation of references to homosexuality 'not only in its supporting documentation but also in the public debates fostered on the issue' (1998, p. 250). The proliferation in the use of a term triggered by explicit censorship is what Butler calls the phenomenon of *redoubling* (a special kind of *echoing*, I would say): 'Regulation of the term "homosexual" is thus no simple act of censorship or silencing; on the contrary, the statute redoubles the term it seeks to constrain and can only effect this constraint through this paradoxical redoubling' (ibid.).

On the other hand, Butler also argues that *uncensoring a text is necessarily incomplete*, for 'no text can remain a text – that is, remain readable – without first being subjected to some kind of censorship (p. 248). Every text is 'produced through a process of selection that rules out certain possibilities, and realizes others' (ibid.). The process of selection often appears to be under the control of the decisions made by the author of the text. But Butler argues that this appearance of control is illusory, for 'the author does not create the rules according to which selection is made' (ibid.). In order to become readable or legible, a text must be subject to a structural kind of censorship that is inescapable: 'no text can be fully freed from the shackles of censorship because every text or expression is in part structured through a process of selection' (p. 253). One cannot lift this form of censorship completely, for 'to oppose censorship fully is to oppose the conditions of intelligibility' (ibid.). So how can we oppose censorship at all? How can we fight all these different forms of censorship, explicit and implicit, that constrain our speech and shape us as subjects within language? Butler emphasizes the 'political salience of impossible speech', that is, of silences and of apparently nonsensical forms of expressions, because they can be indicative of symbolic oppression: they may indicate ways of being in language that could be liberated and expressed if certain censorships were lifted. Butler offers an account that acknowledges the inescapability of censorship and yet makes room for critical and subversive processes of liberation in our symbolic performance. Symbolic domination can undergo change; its course is not set in stone; it can take many different turns. The performative reiteration of symbolic violence can be disrupted and even subverted. Symbolic domination can be resisted. The paths of symbolic domination are not predetermined, but performatively developed through the symbolic interaction of speakers; they depend on our agency and we have in principle the power to change them, although this is a very limited and constrained power. For censoring and uncensoring language are not phenomena that can be brought under the complete control of anybody or anything, of any individual or any institution. As Butler's discussion of censorship makes clear, there is no such thing as absolute liberation: we cannot escape all forms of symbolic domination. But any given form of symbolic domination can in principle be resisted and could eventually be escaped or overcome.

According to Butler, the limited possibilities for resistance and liberation open to us as speakers spring from 'the agency of a postsovereign subject whose sphere of discursive operation is delimited in advance but is also open to a further and unexpected delimitation' (1998, p. 256). Butler's postsovereign view of speaking subjects brings with it a qualified notion of *responsibility* which concerns (not linguistic creation *ex nihilo*, but) our capacity to redirect speech by repeating histories of use differently.[4] As discussed above (cf. 5.2), a speaker must take responsibility for his/her resignifying powers: 'The speaker assumes responsibility precisely through the citational character of speech. The speaker renews the linguistic tokens of a community, reissuing and reinvigorating such speech. *Responsibility is thus linked with speech as repetition, not as origination'* (1997, p. 39; my emphasis). Postsovereign subjects are those who do not have sovereignty or autonomy but have the power to *resignify*; that is, they don't have full control over the language they speak, but they have a say in the evolution of this language and can contribute to its destiny. The resignifying powers of speakers often contribute to the perpetuation of foreclosures, but they can also contribute to their displacement or transformation. This is how Butler describes the mutual dependence between foreclosure and our postsovereign resignifying agency:

> The subject who speaks within the sphere of the speakable implicitly reinvokes the foreclosure on which it depends. This reinvocation, however, is neither mechanical nor sure. One speaks a language that is never fully one's own, but that language only persists through repeated occasions of that invocation. The speech act maintains temporal life only in and through the utterances that reinvoke and restructure the conditions of its own possibility. (1998, p. 256)

Subjects can occupy radical positions in discursive practices, so radical that they can violate even the most fundamental forms of implicit censorship or foreclosure. But we must remember that 'to move outside of the domain of speakability is to risk one's status as a subject' (1998, p. 253). For, as Butler's account of foreclosure shows, the rules of intelligibility that establish boundaries between the intelligible and the nonsensical are 'rules that govern the inception of the speaking subject through its differentiation from an unspeakable Other' (ibid.). With this account Butler reminds us that resignification can be a dangerous business, especially for those subjects who inhabit dark places beyond the boundaries of admissible language, or for those who do not have recognizable linguistic identities and inhabit the interstices between languages. There are speakers who have been marginalized and stigmatized, speakers with *abject identities*, with subjectivities produced through interpellations that result in abjection. Among these abject subjectivities are those that Gloria Anzaldúa calls *frontier subjects* or *border people*: those who live in the space between linguistic communities and speak a *border tongue*. The identity and predicament of these subjects will be the topic of the next section. Butler's performative account of censorship underscores the *disempowerment* of these abject subjects: 'One can live in a polity without the ability to translate words into deeds, and this is a relatively (though not absolutely) powerless way to live: it is to live on the margins of the subject or, rather, as its margins' (p. 248). Abject subjects run high risks in the lives they lead, but at the same time the risks that endanger their lives can be productive, for they are creative opportunities for redrawing the normative boundaries established in language: 'A subject who speaks at the border of the speakable risks redrawing the distinction between what is speakable and what is unspeakable' (p. 256).

6.2 TONGUES UNTIED

Drawing on the work of Gloria Anzaldúa, in this concluding section I will elucidate the relationship between language and identity through a discussion of diversity and polyphony in linguistic communities. In this elucidation I will use the Bakhtinian notion of *polyphony*,[5] of a choral dialogue of multiple and heterogeneous voices, to articulate a pluralistic view of linguistic and cultural identity. With this notion I will elucidate the overlapping and criss-crossing dialogues of heterogeneous voices that go into the formation of a linguistic community. According to my polyphonic view, not only are bilingual and plurilingual societies polyphonic, but every linguistic community (even if monolingual and apparently homogeneous) contains a plurality of voices. The central thesis of the polyphonic view I will articulate is that *communities and cultures always speak in many voices*. I will suggest – as a conclusion to this chapter and to the book – that we need to keep the cultural dialogues between linguistic communities as open as possible, without constraining and disciplining their constitutive diversity, that is, the plurality and heterogeneity of their voices. In other words, we need to keep our dialogues *polyphonic*. We have to be prepared to fight *homogenizing* and *normalizing* tendencies that erase differences.

As we saw in the previous section and in the discussion of Bourdieu in 4.1, the social shaping and unification of a language and the domestication of the identities of its speakers go hand in hand. Coercive social and cultural forces and institutions (from school to the family and the media) are responsible for the standardization of language and the homogenization of mainstream identities, as well as for the marginalization of languages and identities that are considered deviant. These coercive forces – which can come from inside one's own group or community as well as from other social units – limit the self-expression of individuals and groups. They often restrict, handicap and even preclude the emergence and development of alternative identities that can be subversive and transformative. A crucial part of this social and cultural process of disciplining identities and taming their polyphony is the attempt to subdue and domesticate new languages and dialects that people develop to express their experiences, ideals, values, needs, interests, etc. These new linguistic formations (new language-games) can facilitate the rearticulation or reconstruction of established communities or cultural groups and the creation of new ones. Therefore, keeping *tongues untied* and cultural dialogues open are prerequisites for the flourishing of new identities. But how does one resist the taming of one's tongue?

Of special interest here are *frontier identities* and *border languages*. These are the languages and identities of those who live at the limits or borders between communities or cultures – *en la frontera*.[6] Frontier identities and border languages are studied in the pioneer work of Gloria Anzaldúa. In *Borderlands/La Frontera* (1987, 1999) Anzaldúa examines the development of her own language and her own identity growing up between two cultures along the US–Mexico border. She tells us that at the core of her Chicana identity is a cultural and linguistic duplicity that makes her a stranger even to the members of the cultural group to which she belongs. Those who have frontier identities often display signs of cultural otherness in their faces and bodies, in their manners and comportment and in their speech. These are signs that often come under attack, being subject to the domesticating social and cultural forces that conspire to erase them. Our bodies and habits are disciplined; our tongues are tamed. In this respect, Anzaldúa talks about the concerted efforts 'to get rid of our accents', which she describes as a violent attack on one's identity and basic rights: 'Attacks on one's form of expression with the intent to censor are a violation of the First Amendment. *El Anglo con cara de inocente nos arrancó la lengua.* Wild tongues can't be tamed, they can only be cut out' (1999, p. 76).

It is important to note that the efforts to tame one's tongue do not come only from outside one's group or family. Anzaldúa poignantly remarks that her Chicana tongue is not only tamed – and ultimately 'cut out' – by the Anglos, but also by other Hispanics. Chicano Spanish is not recognized and respected by many other Spanish speakers: 'Even our own people, other Spanish speakers, *nos quieren poner candados en la boca.* [. . .] Chicano Spanish is considered by the purist and by most Latinos deficient, a mutilation of Spanish' (pp. 76–7). And this scorn and disciplining effort come not just from other Spanish speakers, but from Chicanas and Chicanos themselves, who have internalized the alleged inferiority of their language and, ultimately, of their identity. 'Chicanas who grew up speaking Chicano Spanish have internalized the belief that we speak poor Spanish [. . .] we use our language differences against each other' (p. 80). Thus Chicanos are left speaking 'an orphan tongue':

> *Deslenguadas. Somos las del español deficiente.* We are your linguistic nightmare, your linguistic aberration, your linguistic *mestisaje*, the subject of your *burla*. Because we speak with tongues of fire we are culturally crucified. Racially, culturally, and linguistically *somos huérfanos* – we speak an orphan tongue. (Anzaldúa 1999, p. 80)

The domestication of a border language such as Chicano Spanish leaves its speakers *tongue-tied*, speechless, indeed as if their tongues had been cut out, for they are rendered unable to express themselves in their own ways. The social stigmatization and cultural orphanage of their forms of expression amount to the marginalization of their very identities:[7] 'If a person, Chicana or Latina, has a low estimation of my native tongue, she has also a low estimation of me. [. . .] I am my language. Until I can take pride in my language, I cannot take pride in myself' (pp. 80–1). This moment of self-empowerment through one's tongue is a moment of cultural pride and cultural affirmation. It involves a demand for *cultural solidarity*, for the formation of a proud linguistic community liberated from self-hatred, a community in which the marginalized tongue finds a home and a family and is no longer orphan. Anzaldúa makes this point in very Wittgensteinian terms, calling for the construction of a 'We' – *un 'Nosotras'* – around a common tongue that corresponds to a shared form of life. She writes: 'Chicano Spanish is a border tongue which developed naturally. [. . .] *Un language que corresponde a un modo de vivir.* Chicano Spanish is not incorrect, it is a living language' (p. 77). On Anzaldúa's view, language must be adequate to the life experiences of the people who speak it; there is no sense in calling Chicano Spanish deficient just because it does not conform to some canonical rules (whose rules?). She remarks that this language 'sprang out of the Chicano's need to identify ourselves as a distinct people': 'for a people who cannot entirely identify with either standard (formal, Castillian) Spanish nor standard English, what recourse is left to them but to create their own language? A language which they can connect their identity to, one capable of communicating the realities and values true to themselves. [. . .] We needed a language with which we could communicate with ourselves, a secret language' (ibid.).

Anzaldúa emphasizes that language can be both unifying and divisive: we often use our linguistic differences against each other, but we also develop language as a site of solidarity for the formation of group identity. The relations between cultural and linguistic differences do not have to be necessarily antagonistic and oppressive; these relations can also be productive. Anzaldúa's account recognizes that cultural borders and the cohabitation of different forms of life can have a special kind of linguistic productivity: 'at the juncture of cultures, languages cross-pollinate and are revitalized; they die and they are reborn' (p. 20). A border tongue can be characterized for its special kind of creativity. As Anzaldúa's discussion suggests, language can be an ethnic home or a cultural cradle. As she puts it, 'for some of us, language is a homeland closer than the Southwest' (ibid.). It is for this reason that she finds it impossible to separate her language from her ethnic identity: 'Ethnic identity is twin skin to linguistic identity. (p. 81)

As Anzaldúa teaches us, a common tongue that can express people's 'realities and values' makes possible the cultural process of community formation around a shared form of life. Through a common tongue people can articulate their shared experiences, problems, needs, interests, values, etc.; and thus cultural solidarity becomes possible. For this reason, Chicano Spanish deserves recognition and respect from the members of the Hispanic family as well from other cultural groups. For this reason also, we ought to acknowledge the special cultural productivity of *border tongues* in general, for they make possible the articulation of new experiences and new forms of identity, facilitating the diversification of cultural norms and cultural expectations. The task of cultural self-affirmation through language is a complex and always ongoing task. It is extremely complex because it has to be constantly diversified, making sure that no voices are left out. As Anzaldúa points out, 'there is no one Chicano language just as there is no one Chicano experience' (p. 80). Even for a single individual, taking pride in one's tongue is typically not a single, unified task, but a plurality of tasks, with multiple fronts, for we speak in many tongues: 'because we are a complex, heterogeneous people, we speak many languages' (p. 77). For this reason, because of the unavoidable and indomitable diversity of human experience, there is no sense in talking about the *purity* of a language or the *purity* of an identity. Languages and identities are not only intrinsically diverse, but also necessarily open to change. The development of language and identity constitutes a never-ending task, for languages and cultural identities are *living* things that are always changing.

Keeping tongues untied is a pressing task for which we are all collectively responsible, as individuals and as communities. But it is indeed not an easy task. In and through cultural dialogues we need to secure recognition and respect for all languages and expressions of identity but especially for those that have been silenced, for those subjects and groups left without a voice, for those whose experiences depart from normalized cultural expectations and whose identities do not fit into the established cultural moulds available to them. There are cultural identities that need a new language to express themselves and the creation of a supportive community in which to flourish, identities that – without special attention and care – are doomed to isolation and silence because they will remain marginalized and tongue-tied. Keeping tongues untied, keeping cultural dialogues polyphonic, involves a process of constant interrogation and challenge, a process of *radical but immanent critique* of our linguistic and cultural practices and the ways in which they include and exclude people. We need to destabilize whatever cultural borders or frontiers are erected, whatever relations of inclusion and exclusion are established in our linguistic communities. We need to allow for alternative cultural spaces and alternative cultural practices. We have to make it possible for people to develop their own ways of expressing themselves and of articulating their experiences, problems, interests, etc. We have the individual and collective responsibility to do everything we can to keep cultural dialogues open and to allow for the identities of groups and individuals to be *polyphonic*, that is, to contain a (diverse and heterogeneous) plurality of voices. We must keep tongues untied. We must make our cultural dialogues polyphonic. Of course, open and polyphonic dialogues do not guarantee cultural solidarity, social justice, the mitigation of oppression and the flourishing of happier cultural groups. The achievement of these goals is never guaranteed. But what untying tongues and having polyphonic dialogues can do is to increase the capacity that groups and individuals have to negotiate their languages and the symbolic articulations of their experiences.

When tongues are untied, we do not know what they will say, or even in what language they will speak; but we know at least this: that they will be able to talk. 'I will have my voice [. . .]. I will have my serpent's tongue – my woman's voice, my sexual voice, my poet's voice. I will overcome the tradition of silence' (Anzaldúa 1999, p. 81).

NOTES

1: COMMUNICATION AND SPEECH ACTS

1 See esp. Jakobson (1990).
2 There are, of course, those who argue that all speech acts are *essentially* representational and assertoric (i.e. can be reduced to or analysed into assertions) because in all of them what is essential, from the point of view of the theory of meaning, is their representational assertoric content. This kind of *assertionalism* that privileges the representational function of language will be discussed in the next chapter.
3 See, e.g., Habermas (1992), p. 79.
4 For the debate between Habermas and his critics, see Kelly (1994). For sympathetic expositions of Habermas' theory of communicative action and its social and political implications, see McCarthy (1978) and White (1988).
5 Jakobson first formulated his famous account of the elements of communication and of communicative functions in an essay written in 1956 and published in 1976 in his *Selected Writings* with the title 'Metalanguage as a linguistic problem' (the paper that was his Presidential Address to the Linguistic Society of America). I am using here a more refined version of his exposition of the six elements and functions of communication in 'The speech event and the functions of language' (1990).
6 The cognitive significance of the metalingual function as a crucial component of communicative competence explains Jakobson's life-long research interests in pathological phenomena relating to aphasia, for, as he puts it, aphasia can be 'defined as a loss of ability for metalingual operations' (1990, p. 76).
7 He also emphasizes that it would be a mistake 'to confine poetry to the poetic function' (1990, p. 76) and to ignore the role that the other communicative functions of language play in poetry: 'The particularities of diverse poetic genres imply a differently ranked participation of the other verbal functions along with the dominant poetic function. Epic poetry, focused on the third person, strongly involves the referential

function of language; the lyric, oriented towards the first person, is intimately linked with the emotive function; poetry of the second person is imbued with the conative function and is either supplicatory or exhortative' (1990, p. 77).

8 This expression has been widely used in the Heideggerian tradition. See Heigdegger (1962, 1971).

9 See especially Goodman (1978).

10 Austin's discussion suggests that we check whether the sincerity condition is met or violated not by trying to detect the presence or absence of some inner act, but by the other things that the speaker says and does before and after his/her act of promising. Some have read this Austinian way of going about assessing felicity as involving a commitment to behaviourism and verificationism.

11 See Chapter 3 of Medina (forthcoming).

12 'In using the imperative ["Shut the door"] we may be ordering you to shut the door, but it just isn't made clear whether we are ordering you or beseeching you or inciting you or tempting you, or one or another of many other subtly different acts' (Austin 1979, p. 244).

13 As Austin observes, 'since apparently we don't approve of insulting, we have not evolved a simple formula "I insult you"' (1979, p. 245).

14 In his usual style, Austin's distinctions and classifications undo themselves to give rise to new insights. I have analysed elsewhere (Medina, forthcoming) how Austin's texts depart from the traditional argumentative line from premises to conclusions and consist in a complex labyrinth of performative doings and undoings, which leave nothing (no concept or categorization) fixed and stable but proceed, instead, by constant destabilization and critical questioning.

15 It is unclear whether cryptic expressive speech acts such as 'Hooray!', 'Shame!' and 'Damn!' can be said to contain any locutionary content at all. But they can be said to relate to certain facts and to imply certain contents such as that there is something cheerable, or that there is someone worth castigating or cursing. Semantic relations of implication will be discussed below and in the next chapter.

16 Traditionally, in all their different versions, Truth-Conditional Semantics, Verificationism and Assertibilism have identified a sentence's meaning with its propositional or locutionary content, disregarding matters concerning the illocutionary and perlocutionary aspects of utterances.

17 After a thorough examination of the different solutions that have been proposed, Lycan (2000), for one, concludes that 'Cohen's problem about the truth conditions of sentences that contain explicit performative prefaces has not been solved' (p. 184).

18 See Geis and Zwicky (1971).

19 See esp. Grice (1968), but also (1969).

20 See Martinich's 'A theory for metaphor' (in Martinich (1985), pp. 427–39) for a fully developed pragmatic theory of metaphor based on Gricean principles.

21 Of course this example can have quite different analyses in different contexts. The context may weaken the implicature substantially and a much

weaker intended meaning may be suggested: perhaps all I am trying to say is that I have no basis to judge Peter's intellectual competence and the quality of his philosophical work. The context or background I share with my interlocutor can make this clear: for example, if it is towards the beginning of the term and we both know that our familiarity with the work of this first-year graduate student is likely to be limited.

22 This idea will be further elaborated and radicalized by Donald Davidson (1986 and 1994) who, as we shall see, argues that semantic conventions and coined meanings shared by a linguistic community are neither necessary nor sufficient conditions for communication. Following this line of argument, Davidson goes as far as to claim that 'there is no such thing as language' but only particular speakers with particular ways of talking ('idiolects') which interact with each other in complex ways regulated by very abstract *a priori* principles of interpretation. See also Davidson (1984 and 2001). Davidson's theories will be discussed in sections 2.2, 4.3, and 5.1.

23 As a cure for this, Davis (1998) suggests the methodological attitude of pretending that we do not already know the meanings that are normally implicated by the utterances we examine, looking at these utterances with the fresh eyes of the uninitiated hearer who tries to hit upon the clues available in the conversational context to figure out the speaker's intended meaning.

24 It has been suggested that there may be a deep-seated narratological assumption about conjunctions that explains how the causal relations and temporal connections that remain implicit in them are forged. This is the explanation offered by Sperber and Wilson (1986), who have developed a line of research in pragmatics called *Relevance Theory*, which departs from Gricean principles in important respects.

25 In Relevance Theory (see Sperber and Wilson (1986) and previous footnote) researchers have suggested an intermediate kind of case between conversational and conventional implicature called 'explicature'. This is a kind of conveyed meaning that is cancellable but should be counted as said rather than merely implicated if left uncanceled. For example, it is argued that 'A woman walked to the cliff's edge and jumped' *says* that the woman jumped off the cliff unless the speaker explicitly cancels the explicature by adding 'not off the cliff, but just up and down near the edge'. Recanati (1989), for one, contends that if the speaker does not cancel the explicature, he/she will be counted as having said, and not merely implicated, that the woman jumped off the cliff. As Lycan (2000) points out, the research programme of Relevance Theory is now thought of 'as a competitor rather than a development of Grice's model' (p. 195).

26 Even conventional implicatures that are often taken to be completely straightforward are actually very complex semantic phenomena that need to be empirically investigated and philosophically elucidated more thoroughly. It is important to note that it is not an easy thing to explain how conventional implicatures are established, for they do not spring automatically from stipulations, but are slowly sedimented through the cumulative effects of language use over extensive periods of time.

27 Indeed, not all the negated sentences resulting from (1), (2) and (3) seem to carry their corresponding semantic presupposition with the same strength. While the repudiation of the semantic presupposition appears to be almost contradictory for the negation of (1) and (2) – 'Peter didn't realize that he had no money and he had some', 'John didn't stop harassing Mary and he was never doing it' – this does not seem to be the case for the negation of (3): 'It wasn't Grandma who ate the ice-cream and no one did' (e.g. because the ice-cream melted away, was never bought, or whatever). However, the conversational context can turn these apparently contradictory sentences into perfectly sensible statements, for example as a reply to and correction of a previous statement: 'Of course Peter didn't realize that he had no money; he had some', 'Of course John didn't stop harassing Mary; he was never doing it', 'Of course it wasn't Grandma who ate the ice-cream; no one did'.

2: MEANING, SENSE AND INTERPRETATION

1 See, for example, Millikan (1987) and especially (2004).
2 See McDowell (1994).
3 For a full discussion of this idea see Rorty (1979).
4 See Lafont (1999), Chapter 1, for a discussion of the contribution of these authors to the Philosophy of Language.
5 Different aspects of the Humboldtian contrast between language as *ergon* and language as *energeia* have been elaborated in linguistics through Saussure's distinction between 'langue' and 'parole' and Chomsky's distinction between 'competence' and 'performance'. We will come back to these distinctions in our discussion of linguistic creativity in section 4.1.
6 See the various formulations that Frege gives to this principle in *Begriffsschrift* (1879), p. 67, and *The Foundations of Arithmetic* (1884), pp. 90, 108–9 and 127 (translations of both of these works are contained in Frege 1997).
7 It is worth noting that for Frege reference comes in two flavours: terms can designate *objects* or *concepts*. As Frege explains in 'On concept and object', concepts are unsaturated entities or structures that are completed by objects, just as a function is an unsaturated structure (as indicated by the variable or dummy that accompanies it) and is completed when it is assigned a specific value. On the basis of this distinction Frege differentiates between two kinds of referential expressions: names, which designate objects, and conceptual or predicative expressions, which designate concepts. A combination of a name and a conceptual expression, which depicts a conceptual structure being completed or saturated by an object, is required for a complete assertoric content, for saying something of something. Despite this distinction, the primary examples Frege uses in 'On sense and reference', and the ones I am using here, are names that refer to objects. However, when I talk about the reference of terms in general I use the more general expressions 'thing' or

'entity', which should be understood as covering both objects and concepts.

8 Propositional attitudes are mental attitudes or states such as belief, desire, doubt, expectation, etc., which people have with respect to contents that can be expressed in propositions.

9 Frege's inferentialism shaped the holistic views of Wittgenstein and the members of the Vienna Circle. For a discussion of the relations between the inferentialist views of Frege, Wittgenstein and the logical positivists, see Medina (2002) Chapters 3 and 4.

10 See esp. Brandom (1994).

11 This label (whose literal translation is 'conceptual notation') is the name Frege gave to his logical notation as well as the title of the essay in which he introduced it.

12 See esp. Weiner (1990) and (1999).

13 Alexius Meinong (1853–1920) was an Austrian philosopher and psychologist who founded the so-called *Gegenstandstheorie*, the theory of (existent and non-existent) intended objects.

14 See Russell (1985).

15 This is of course the case only if the description is *purely* referential, that is, used *merely* as a tool to pick out someone and not as an essential part of the description of the speaker's object of desire. But if, for example, the speaker is drawn to martini drinkers in particular, it is plausible to think that his/her attraction could in fact diminish when he/she realizes that the man he/she was referring to was drinking water.

16 See Carnap (1947).

17 This pattern may include stimulations of all kinds: visual, tactile, olfactory, auditory, etc. The relevant visual stimulations, for example, would compose a complex pattern of chromatic irradiation of the eye.

18 Quine also gives a more sophisticated example of the role that background knowledge can play in the native's verbal reactions to the query 'Rabbit?' or 'Gavagai?': 'There may be a local rabbit-fly, unknown to the linguist, and recognizable some way off by its long wings and erratic movements; and seeing such a fly in the neighborhood of an ill-glimpsed animal could help a native to recognize the latter as a rabbit' (1960, p. 37).

19 'Occasion sentences whose stimulus meanings vary none under the influence of collateral information may naturally be called observation sentences, and their stimulus meanings may without fear of contradiction be said to do full justice to their meanings' (1960, p. 42).

20 See esp. Quine (1960), Chapter 2, pp. 26ff.; 'Epistemology naturalized' (1969), esp. pp. 80ff; and Quine (1990), Chapter 3, pp. 37ff.

21 In *Word and Object* Quine states his 'principle of indeterminacy of translation' as follows: 'The thesis is then this: manuals for translating one language into another can be set up in divergent ways, all compatible with the totality of speech dispositions, yet incompatible with one another' (1960, p. 27).

22 Quine also describes and defends this thesis under the heading of 'ontological relativity'. See (1969) Chapter 2, esp. pp. 45ff; and (1990) Chapter 2, esp. pp. 33–6.

23 Quine writes: 'I have directed my indeterminacy thesis on a radically exotic language for the sake of plausibility, but in principle it applies even to the home language' (1990, p. 48).

24 See especially Davidson's essay 'Radical Interpretation', in Davidson (1984), pp. 125–39.

25 See especially Davidson's discussions in 'Belief and the basis of meaning', in Davidson (1984), pp. 141–54.

26 For a full discussion of this point and a detailed exposition of the relationship between the notions of meaning and truth, see Davidson's essay 'Truth and meaning', in Davidson (1984), pp. 17–36. In that essay the reader can find Davidson's account of how to construct a theory of interpretation as a theory of truth, following Tarski. This is briefly discussed in the next paragraph in the text.

27 See Tarski (1956).

28 This is not a theory that explains what truth means in that idiolect, but rather (as observed above), a theory that interprets the idiolect by taking truth as a primitive notion that requires no explanation. In short, for Davidson, a theory of interpretation for a language or idiolect is a theory of truth that can correlate any arbitrary assertion in that language with a sentence in our language; in other words, it is a theory that shows how to construct T-sentences, that is, how to apply Tarski's *convention T* so as to correlate that language with ours through one-to-one mappings between sentences.

29 This was first recognized in the nineteenth century by the German philosopher Friedrich Schleiermacher (1768–1834), a post-Kantian idealist and father of modern theological and religious studies.

30 Gadamer explains this points as follows: 'the interpreter's own thoughts have also gone into the re-awakening of the meaning of the text. In this the interpreter's own horizon is decisive, yet not as a personal standpoint that one holds on to or enforces, but more as a meaning and a possibility that one brings into play and puts at risk, and that helps one truly to make one's own what is said in the text' (1989, p. 350).

31 This is the famous phrase coined by Nagel (1986). This absolute perspective has been traditionally invoked by metaphysical realism. For thorough discussions of this view as well as alternatives to it in the Philosophy of Language, see Putnam (1975b, 1978, 1981, 1988, 1995 and 2001).

32 See esp. Habermas (2005) and also McDowell (2005).

3: INDETERMINACY AND LANGUAGE LEARNING

1 Cf. e.g. Paul Roth (1987). There have been exceptions to this trend in the recent literature. A notable one is Meredith Williams (1999), Chapter 8, pp. 216–39.

2 For a full analysis and discussion of Wittgenstein's indeterminacy arguments in the *Philosophical Investigations*, see Medina (2002) Chapter 6.

3 For an account of how this *contextualism* is developed in Wittgenstein's philosophy, see Medina (2002) and Chapter 1 of Medina (forthcoming).

4 'Language is a social art. In acquiring it we have to depend entirely on intersubjectively available cues' (1960, p. ix). '[Language] is a social art which we all acquire on the evidence solely of other people's overt behaviour under publicly recognizable circumstances' (1969, pp. 26–7).

5 All *social* practices are public (that is, in principle accessible to potential observers), but not all *public* phenomena are social (that is, dependent on the actual consensus of a community).

6 I am referring to the famous expression Dewey coined to describe the target of his critique, namely, 'the spectator theory of knowledge'. See Dewey (1988).

7 See Wittgenstein's remarks in PI §201.

8 As Dummett puts it, 'when the hearer does not have to search for the speaker's meaning, but takes for granted that he is using words in just the way with which he is familiar, there is, as Hacking says, no process of interpretation going on' (1986, p. 464).

9 Dummett does not deny that this peculiar kind of eavesdropping can take place or that we may find a use for these sophisticated second-order theories: 'There is certainly a place for second-order theories, since eavesdroppers, as well as speakers and hearers, need to engage in interpretation' (1986, p. 466). Dummett's complaint, though, is that Davidson treats this rare and sophisticated case as the paradigmatic case of communication that should be used to explain every instance of linguistic understanding.

10 The degrees of determinacy required in linguistic interaction vary according to the purposes of particular activities. For example, whether the term 'rabbit' refers to rabbits, to rabbit-stages or to undetached rabbit-parts is a doubt that simply does not enter into the minds of hunters who use this term to coordinate their actions.

11 See Tomasello (1999, 2003); Tomasello, Kruger and Ratner (1993); and Tomasello, Carpenter, Call, Behne and Moll (forthcoming).

12 For a detailed account of learning through apprenticeship, see Tomasello, Kruger and Ratner (1993).

13 This practical view of learning derives from Dewey (1988) in the pragmatist tradition and from Vygotsky (1986) in the tradition of cultural psychology. There are interesting points of convergence between these two traditions and Wittgenstein's later philosophy.

14 For a full discussion of this point see Williams (1999), 'The etiology of the obvious: Wittgenstein and the elimination of indeterminacy', pp. 216–39.

15 See Medina (2002), Chapter 6, and (forthcoming), Chapter 1.

16 See Garfinkel (1967) and Garfinkel and Sacks (1970).

17 As I have argued elsewhere (Medina, 2002), Wittgenstein's view of language emphasizes meaning change, but it also underscores the constraints to which semantic changes are subject. Our linguistic practices can always be extended in different ways, but these possible extensions are constrained by contextual factors. Joseph Margolis' account of predication (1996, 1999) offers an explanation of this point. In the application of a term to new contexts, Margolis points out, we are confronted with a 'choice among various lines of extension amid an indefinite run of

such possibilities'; but our learned linguistic skills make this choice manageable by narrowing down the set of relevant possibilities: 'our aptitude
for discerning relevant similarities in a run of would-be cases – any cases
– signifies our mastery of the same *sittlich* practices within whose bounds
such similarities obtain or are reasonably extended' (1999, p. 64).

4: LINGUISTIC CREATIVITY AND RELATIVISM

1 Despite his critique of structural linguistics, there is a structural component in Bourdieu's theory of the habitus. Bourdieu describes the habitus
   as 'a structured structure', which brings inside the individual a normative organization that mediates his/her experiences and reactions; but
   also as 'a structuring structure', which makes that internal organization
   productive in guiding and organizing the agency of the individual. As 'a
   structured and structuring structure' (1984, pp. 170–1), the habitus is
   simultaneously a receptive and a generative capacity. A habitus is a particular *mode of generation and appreciation* inscribed in the body of the
   agent, a complex set of dispositions that make possible the articulation
   and interpretation of symbolic (or signifying) behaviour.
2 The historical change in meaning of the very term 'patois' is instructive.
   As Bourdieu observes, 'patois [. . .] ceased to mean "incomprehensible
   speech" and began to refer to "corrupted and coarse speech", such as
   that of the common people' (1991, p. 47).
3 This is how Bourdieu describes the object of study of the sociology of
   language: 'A structural sociology of language, inspired by Saussure but
   constructed in opposition to the abstraction he imposes, must take as its
   object *the relationship between the structured systems of sociologically
   pertinent linguistic differences and the equally structured systems of social
   differences*' (1991, p. 54).
4 It is not surprising, therefore, that the thinkers of the French Revolution
   were so invested in the production of dictionaries and the establishment
   of a new educational system.
5 This is the expression that Kripke (1972) made famous in his metaphysical account of direct reference. A similar account can be found also in
   the metaphysical realism of Putnam's early philosophy (see Putnam,
   1973 and 1975a).
6 Nietzsche argues that we are tempted to postulate the ideal model of a
   class of entities outside the realm of our experience of the natural world,
   either in our minds or in some Platonic heaven (as suggested by Plato's
   theory of forms). He describes this philosophical fiction as 'the idea that,
   in addition to the leaves, there exists in nature the "leaf": the original
   model according to which all the leaves were perhaps woven, sketched,
   measured, colored, curled, and painted—but by incompetent hands, so
   that no specimen has turned out to be a correct, trustworthy, and faithful likeness of the original model' (2005, p. 17).
7 In 'What metaphors mean' (1984) Davidson rejects the idea that metaphor is a special semantic phenomenon. Arguing against Max Black's

semantic analysis of metaphor (see Black, 1962), Davidson contends that metaphors mean what they say (literally, so to speak) without intimating any special meaning. He argues that there are no hidden or metaphorical meanings. According to Davidson, metaphors do not create new meanings and therefore they should not be considered a semantic phenomenon in Black's sense (or Ricoeur's for that matter). He argues that metaphorical statements do not require special instructions for interpretation, that they should be interpreted exactly in the same way as literal statements. Davidson recognizes that making and understanding a metaphor are creative endeavours, but he argues that so are the composition and interpretation of any speech or text, for creativity is an intrinsic feature of speaking and understanding. For an elucidation of Davidson's theory of interpretation, see 2.2 above and 5.1 below.

8 For an account of the poetic uses of language in ontological terms, see Heidegger (1971).

9 For a structural account of metaphor as a cognitive mechanism, see Gentner (1988) and (1989). Gentner explains metaphor as a *structure-mapping engine* that is one of the central learning mechanisms in the development of human cognition. See also my articles with her (Gentner and Medina, 1997 and 1998) for a wider discussion of structure-mapping in language learning and cognitive development.

10 See Lakoff and Johnson (1980), Chapter 6.

11 See Lakoff and Johnson (1980), Chapter 4.

12 See Lepore (1986) and Lepore and McLaughlin (1985). For a Wittgensteinian argument against Davidson's *charity* and his conceptual monism, see my 'On being "other-minded": Wittgenstein, Davidson, and logical aliens' (Medina, 2003a).

5: SPEAKERS, LINGUISTIC COMMUNITIES AND HISTORIES OF USE

1 The term derives from Mrs Malaprop, a character in Sheridan's *The Rivals* (1775).

2 For Davidson, as for Quine, there is no principled distinction between linguistic knowledge and empirical knowledge of the world. For a discussion of this point, see section 2.2 above.

3 This objection can be found in Alfred Mackay's article 'Mr. Donnellan and Humpty Dumpty on referring' (1968).

4 This is how Davidson describes this process from the speaker's perspective: 'Let's look at the process from the speaker's side. The speaker wants to be understood, so he intends to speak in such a way that he will be interpreted in a certain way. In order to judge how he will be interpreted, he forms, or uses, a picture of the interpreter's readiness to interpret along certain lines'; 'the speaker's view of the interpreter's prior theory is not irrelevant to what he says, nor to what he means by his words; it is an important part of what he has to go on if he wants to be understood' (1986, p. 168).

5 Davidson explicitly rejects the possibility of being able to explain linguistic understanding in terms of a shared prior theory available to all the members of the linguistic community. He considers the use and interpretation of proper names from this angle. Davidson conjectures that if we lived in a semantic paradise in which everyone knew the names of everyone else, people would have ready in advance a theory that, without adjustment or correction, could interpret the names employed in every case. But the important point, as Davidson observes, is that 'even this semantic paradise will be destroyed by each new nickname, visitor, or birth' (1986, p. 168).

6 According to Butler, hate speech *performs* violence: 'oppressive language does more than represent violence; it is violence' (1997, p. 5). Butler conceptualizes the linguistic violence performed by words and symbols as the injury (even the destruction) of an identity and its social location. She describes the victim of hate speech as being lost, in a state of disarray: 'To be injured by speech is to suffer a loss of context, that is, to not know where you are' (p. 4).

7 In his reply to Dummett Davidson clarifies his position, emphasizing that he does not deny the contingent existence of learned social conventions that regulate language use, but he does deny that sharing such conventions is either necessary or sufficient for communication. He writes: 'Of course I did not deny that in practice people usually depend on a supply of words and syntactic devices which they have learned to employ in similar ways. What I denied was that such sharing is sufficient to explain our actual communicative achievements, and more important, I denied that even such limited sharing is necessary' (1994, p. 2).

8 Indeed it is difficult to avoid the political suspicion that the Davidsonian claim that 'there is no such thing as language' springs from (and makes sense only for) a position of privilege in which *language* can be declared irrelevant, that is, the position of those who do not have to fight for their language, those who are not linguistically handicapped, those unaffected by linguistic oppression. But of course this kind of consideration is typically dismissed as *ad hominem*.

9 Autonomous practices are those whose normativity does not depend on anything outside themselves: actions and utterances are normatively autonomous if they can guarantee their own correctness. Wittgenstein's rule-following discussion as well as his *Private Language Argument* try to establish that there cannot be absolute normative autonomy.

10 See, for example, Wright (1987).

11 For a full discussion of this point, see Medina (2002 Chapter 6), esp. pp. 185–94.

12 This is 'a wheel that can be turned though nothing else moves with it' and, therefore, a wheel that is not really 'part of the mechanism' (PI §271).

13 See my discussion of the debate between Derrida and Austin in Medina (forthcoming), Chapter 3.

14 See Medina (forthcoming), Chapter 3.

15 See Medina (forthcoming).

6: LANGUAGE AND IDENTITY

1 As Althusser puts it, interpellation involves 'the practical *denegation* of the ideological character of ideology by ideology: ideology never says, "I am ideological"' (2001, p. 118). This important feature of interpellation, its *concealed* ideological character, is discussed in more detail below in the examination of Bourdieu's account of symbolic impositions.

2 'There is every reason to think that the factors which are most influential in the formation of the habitus are transmitted without passing through language and consciousness, but through *suggestions inscribed in the most apparently insignificant aspects* of the things, situations and practices of everyday life' (1991, p. 51; emphasis added).

3 On Butler's view, interpellation is only efficacious as part of an ongoing subjugation, not by itself, and not as the first step in this process of symbolic domination either. Prior to the acts of interpellation to which the individual is subjected and as a condition for their efficacy, we find in him/her a predisposition, that is, a 'certain readiness to be compelled by the authoritative interpellation' (1997, p. 32). In this sense Butler insists that interpellation is a mechanism whose efficacy cannot be reduced to the moment of enunciation.

4 This qualified notion of discursive responsibility is similar to what I have described elsewhere as *echoing* responsibility, see Medina (forthcoming). See also the final pages of section 5.2 above to see how this notion of responsibility emerges from Butler's notion of resignification and from my notion of echoing.

5 See Bakhtin (1981).

6 As I have argued in Medina (2003b), all of us have multiple identities and are members of multiple groups. As Gomez-Peña (2000) puts it, 'we are all members of multiple communities, at different times and for different reasons. Most communities in the 90s are fragmented, ephemeral, dysfunctional, and insufficient. They can only contain and "include" selected aspects of ourselves' (p. 277). So *frontier identities* and *border tongues* simply make explicit and perspicuous the tensions and problems that to some degree affect all languages and identities.

7 This silencing is certainly gender-specific. As Anzaldúa notes, in the case of Chicanas, the silencing of their ethnic voices converges with the silencing of their female voices. In this sense she describes how she was raised, as a woman, in a 'tradition of silence': '*Ser habladora* was to be a gossip and a liar, to talk too much. [. . .] *Hocicona, repelona, chismosa* [. . .] are all signs of being *mal criada*. In my culture they are all words that are derogatory if applied to women – I've never heard them applied to men' (1999, p. 76). This double oppression and marginalization as woman and Chicana that Anzaldúa describes reminds us that there are multiple and converging fronts of oppression. The phenomenon of *multiple oppression* has been discussed and theorized by Lugones (2003). It is also the topic of Medina (2003b).

REFERENCES

Althusser, L. (2001), *Lenin and Philosophy and Other Essays* (New York: Monthly Review Press).

Anzaldúa, G. (1987, 1999), *Borderlands/La Frontera: The New Mestiza* (San Francisco: Aunt Lute Books).

Austin, J. L. (1975), *How to Do Things with Words* (Cambridge, MA: Harvard University Press).

— (1979), 'Performative utterances', in *Philosophical Papers* (third edition) (Oxford and New York: Oxford University Press), pp. 233–52.

Bach, K. and Harnish, R. M. (1979), *Linguistic Communication and Speech Acts* (Cambridge, MA: MIT Press).

Bakhtin, M. M. (1981), *The Dialogic Imagination*, edited by M. Holquist (Austin: University of Texas Press).

Black, M. (1962), *Models and Metaphors* (Ithaca, NY: Cornell University Press).

Blackburn, S. (1984), 'The individual strikes back', *Synthese*, 58, 281–301.

Boden, D. and Zimmerman, D. H. (1991), *Talk and Social Structure: Studies in Ethnomethodology and Conversation Analysis* (Berkeley and Los Angeles: University of California Press).

Bourdieu, P. (1984), *Distinction* (Cambridge, MA: Harvard University Press).

— (1991), *Language and Symbolic Power* (Cambridge, MA: Harvard University Press).

Brandom, R. (1994), *Making It Explicit* (Cambridge, MA: Harvard University Press).

Bühler, K. (1933), 'Die Axiomatik der Sprachwissenschaft', *Kant Studien*, 38, 19–90.

— (1934), *Sprachtheorie* (Jena: Gustav Fischer).

Butler, J. (1997), *Excitable Speech. A Politics of the Performative* (New York and London: Routledge).

— (1998), 'Ruled out: vocabularies of the censor', in R. Post (ed.), pp. 247–59.

Carnap, R. (1947), *Meaning and Necessity* (Chicago: University of Chicago Press).

Chomsky, N. (1965), *Aspects of a Theory of Syntax* (Cambridge, MA: MIT Press).
— (1972), *Language and Mind* (New York: Harcourt).
Cohen, L. J. (1964), 'Do illocutionary forces exist?', *Philosophical Quarterly*, 14, 118–37.
Cresswell, M. J. (1973), *Logics and Languages* (London: Methuen).
Davidson, D. (1984), *Inquiries into Truth and Interpretation* (Oxford: Clarendon Press).
— (1986), 'A nice derangement of epitaphs', in R. E. Grandy and R. Warner (eds), pp. 157–74.
— (1994), 'The social aspect of language', in B. McGuinness and G. Oliveri (eds), *The Philosophy of Michael Dummett* (Dordrecht: Kluwer Academic Press), pp. 1–16.
— (2001), *Subjective, Intersubjective, Objective* (Oxford: Clarendon Press).
Davis, W. (1998), *Implicature* (Cambridge: Cambridge University Press).
Derrida, J. (1982), *Margins of Philosophy* (Chicago: University of Chicago Press).
Dewey, J. (1988), *John Dewey. The Later Works, 1925–1953* (Carbondale: Southern Illinois University Press).
Dilthey, W. (1989), *Introduction to the Human Sciences. Selected Works, Volume 1* (Princeton: Princeton University Press).
— (1996), *Hermeneutics and the Study of History. Selected Works, Volume 4* (Princeton: Princeton University Press).
Donnellan, K. (1966), 'Reference and definite descriptions', *Philosophical Review*, 75, 281–304.
— (1968), 'Putting Humpty Dumpty together again', *Philosophical Review* 77, 203–15.
Dummett, M. (1986), 'A nice derangement of epitaphs: comments on Davidson and Hacking', in E. Lepore (ed.), pp. 459–76.
Fodor, J. (1975), *The Language of Thought* (Cambridge, MA: Harvard University Press).
Frege, G. (1952a), 'On concept and object', in M. Black and P. Geach (eds), *Translations from the Philosophical Writings of Gottlob Frege* (Oxford: Blackwell).
— (1952b), 'On sense and reference', in M. Black and P. Geach (eds).
— (1997), *The Frege Reader*, edited by M. Beaney (Oxford: Blackwell).
Gadamer, H.-G. (1989), *Truth and Method* (New York: Continuum).
Garfinkel, H. (1967), *Studies in Ethnomethodology* (Englewood Cliffs, CO: Prentice Hall).
Garfinkel, H. and Sacks, H. (1970), 'On formal structures of practical actions', in C. McKinney and E. A. Tiryakian (eds), *Theoretical Sociology* (New York: Appleton-Century-Crofts), pp. 338–66.
Geis, M. and Zwicky, A. (1971), 'On invited inferences', *Linguistic Inquiry*, 2, 561–6.
Gentner, D. (1988), 'Metaphor as structure-mapping: the relational shift', *Child Development*, 59, 47–59.
— (1989), 'Mechanisms of analogical learning', in S. Vosniadou and A.

Ortony (eds), *Similarity and Analogical Reasoning* (Cambridge: Cambridge University Press), pp. 199–241.

Gentner, D. and Medina, J. (1997), 'Comparison and the development of cognition and language', *Japanese Journal of Cognitive Science*, 4, 112–49.

— (1998), 'Similarity and the development of rules', *Cognition*, 65, 263–97.

Gomez-Peña, G. (2000), *Dangerous Border-Crossers* (New York: Routledge).

Goodman, N. (1978), *Ways of World-Making* (Indianapolis, IND: Hackett).

Grandy, R. E. and Warner, R. (1986), *Philosophical Grounds of Rationality* (Oxford: Oxford University Press).

Grice, H. P. (1957), 'Meaning', *Philosophical Review*, 66, 377–88.

— (1968), 'Utterer's meaning, sentence-meaning, and word-meaning', *Foundations of Language*, 4, 225–42.

— (1969), 'Utterer's meaning and intentions', *Philosophical Review*, 78, 147–77.

— (1975), 'Logic and conversation', in D. Davidson and G. Harman (eds), *The Logic of Grammar* (Encino, CA: Dickenson), reprinted in A. P. Martinich (ed.) (1985), pp. 156–67.

Habermas, J. (1992), *Postmetaphysical Thinking: Philosophical Essays* (Cambridge, MA: MIT Press).

— (2005), 'Richard Rorty's pragmatic turn', in Medina and Wood (eds), pp. 109–29.

Heidegger, M. (1962), *Being and Time* (New York: Harper & Row).

— (1971), *Poetry, Language, Thought* (New York: Harper & Row).

Herder, J. G. von (1772/2002), 'On the origin of language', English translation in M. Forster (ed.), *Herder: Philosophical Writings* (Cambridge: Cambridge University Press).

Heritage, J. and Greatbatch, D. (1991), 'On the institutional character of institutional talk: the case of news interviews', in Boden and Zimmerman (eds), pp. 93–137.

Humboldt, W. v. (1988), *On Language. The Diversity of Human Language-Structure and its Influence on the Mental Development of Mankind* (Cambridge: Cambridge University Press).

Husserl, E. (1970), *Logical Investigations* (London: Routledge).

Hylton, P. (1994), 'Quine's Naturalism', *Midwest Studies in Philosophy*, 99, 261–82.

Jakobson, R. (1990), *On Language* (Cambridge, MA: Harvard University Press).

Johnson, M. (2004), *A Philosophy of Second Language Acquisition* (New Haven, CONN: Yale University Press).

Kelly, M. (1994), *Critique and Power. Recasting the Foucault/Habermas Debate* (Cambridge, MA: MIT Press).

Kripke, S. (1972), *Naming and Necessity* (Cambridge, MA: Harvard University Press).

— (1982), *Wittgenstein on Rules and Private Language* (Cambridge, MA: Harvard University Press).

Kuhn, T. (1970), *The Structure of Scientific Revolutions* (second edition) (Chicago: University of Chicago Press).

— (1977), *The Essential Tension: Selected Studies in Scientific Tradition and Change* (Chicago: University of Chicago Press).

Lafont, C. (1999), *The Linguistic Turn in Hermeneutic Philosophy* (Cambridge, MA: MIT Press).

Lakoff, G. and Johnson, M. (1980), *Metaphors We Live By* (Chicago: University of Chicago Press).

Laudan, L. (1990), 'Demystifying underdetermination', *Minnesota Studies in the Philosophy of Science*, 14, 267–97.

Lepore, E. (ed.) (1986), *Truth and Interpretation* (Oxford: Blackwell).

Lepore, E. and McLaughlin, B. (eds) (1985), *Actions and Events: Perspectives on the Philosophy of Donald Davidson* (Oxford: Blackwell).

Lugones, M. (2003), *Pilgrimages/Peregrinajes: Theorizing Coalition against Multiple Oppression* (New York: Rowan and Littlefield).

Lycan, W. (2000), *Philosophy of Language. A Contemporary Introduction* (London and New York: Routledge).

MacKay, A. (1968), 'Mr. Donnellan and Humpty Dumpty on referring', *Philosophical Review*, 77, 197–202.

Malinowski, B. (1953), 'The problem of meaning in primitive languages', in C. K. Ogden and I. A. Richards (eds), *The Meaning of Meaning* (New York: Harcourt), pp. 296–336.

Margolis, J. (1996), 'The politics of predication', *Philosophical Forum*, 27, 195–219.

— (1999), *What, After All, Is a Work of Art?* (University Park: Pennsylvania State University Press).

Martinich, A. P. (ed.) (1985), *The Philosophy of Language* (Oxford: Oxford University Press).

McCarthy, T. (1978), *The Critical Theory of Jürgen Habermas* (Cambridge: Cambridge University Press).

McDowell, J. (1994), *Mind and World* (Cambridge, MA: Harvard University Press).

— (2005), 'Towards rehabilitating objectivity', in Medina and Wood (eds), pp. 130–45.

Medina, J. (2002), *The Unity of Wittgenstein's Philosophy* (Albany, NY: SUNY Press).

— (2003a), 'On being "other-minded": Wittgenstein, Davidson, and logical aliens', *International Philosophical Quarterly*, 43 (4), 463–75.

— (2003b), 'Identity trouble: disidentification and the problem of difference', *Philosophy and Social Criticism*, 29 (6), 657–82.

— (forthcoming), *Speaking from Elsewhere. A New Contextualist Perspective on Meaning, Identity, and Discursive Agency* (Albany, NY: SUNY Press).

Medina, J. and Wood, D. (eds) (2005), *Truth: Engagements across Philosophical Traditions* (New York: Blackwell).

Millikan, R. G. (1987), *Language, Thought, and Other Biological Categories: New Foundations for Realism* (Cambridge, MA: MIT Press).

— (2004), *Varieties of Meaning: The 2002 Jean Nicod Lectures* (Cambridge, MA: MIT Press).

REFERENCES

Nagel, T. (1986), *The View from Nowhere* (Oxford: Oxford University Press).

Nietzsche, F. (2005), 'On truth and lies in a non-moral sense', in Medina and Wood (eds), pp. 14–24.

Post, R. (ed.) (1998), *Censorship and Silencing* (Indianapolis, IND: Getty Research Institute).

Putnam, H. (1973), 'Meaning and reference', *Journal of Philosophy*, 62, 699–711.

— (1975a), 'The meaning of "meaning"', in *Mind, Language and Reality: Philosophical Papers, Volume 2* (Cambridge: Cambridge University Press), pp. 215–71.

— (1975b), *Mind, Language, and Reality* (Cambridge: Cambridge University Press).

— (1978), *Meaning and the Moral Sciences* (London: Routledge).

— (1981), *Reason, Truth, and History* (Cambridge: Cambridge University Press).

— (1988), *Representation and Reality* (Cambridge, MA: MIT Press).

— (1995), *Words and Life* (Cambridge, MA: Harvard University Press).

— (2001), *The Threefold Cord* (New York: Columbia University Press).

Quine, W. v. (1951), 'Two dogmas of empiricism', *Philosophical Review*, 60, 20–43.

— (1960), *Word and Object* (Cambridge, MA: MIT Press).

— (1969), *Ontological Relativity and Other Essays* (New York: Columbia University Press).

— (1990), *Pursuit of Truth* (Cambridge, MA: Harvard University Press).

Recanati, F. (1989), 'The pragmatics of what is said', *Mind and Language*, 4, 295–329.

Ricoeur, P. (1991), 'Word, polysemy, metaphor: creativity in language', in M. J. Valdés (ed.), *The Ricoeur Reader* (Toronto: University of Toronto Press), pp. 65–85.

Rorty, R. (1979), *Philosophy and the Mirror of Nature* (Princeton: Princeton University Press).

Roth, P. (1987), *Meaning and Method in the Social Sciences* (Ithaca, NY: Cornell University Press).

Russell, B. (1905), 'On denoting', *Mind*, 14, 479–93.

— (1985), *The Philosophy of Logical Atomism* (La Salle, IL: Open Court).

— (1993), 'Descriptions', in his *Introduction to Mathematical Philosophy* (London: Dover), pp. 167–80.

Sacks, H. (1992), *Lectures on Conversation. Volumes 1 and 2* (Oxford: Blackwell).

Sapir, E. (1921), *Language: An Introduction to the Study of Speech* (New York: Harcourt).

— (1949), *Selected Writings* (Berkeley: University of California Press).

Searle, J. (1965), 'What is a speech act?', in M. Black (ed.), *Philosophy in America* (Ithaca, NY: Cornell University Press), pp. 221–39.

— (1969), *Speech Acts* (Cambridge: Cambridge University Press).

Silverman, D. (1998), *Harvey Sacks: Social Science and Conversation Analysis* (New York: Oxford University Press).

Skinner, B. F. (1957), *Verbal Behavior* (New York: Appleton-Century-Crofts).

Sperber, D. and Wilson, D. (1986), *Relevance: Communication and Cognition* (Cambridge, MA: Harvard University Press).

Strawson, P. (1950), 'On referring', *Mind*, 59, 320–44.

Tarski, A. (1956), 'The concept of truth in formalized languages', in J. H. Woodger (ed. and trans.), *Logic, Semantics, and Mathematics* (Oxford: Clarendon Press).

Taylor, C. (1985), *Human Agency and Language* (Cambridge: Cambridge University Press).

Tomasello, M. (1999), *The Cultural Origins of Human Cognition* (Cambridge, MA: Harvard University Press).

— (2003), *Constructing a Language: A Use-Based Theory of Language Acquisition* (Cambridge, MA: Harvard University Press).

Tomasello, M., Carpenter, M., Call, J., Behne, T. and Moll, H. (forthcoming), 'Understanding and sharing intentions: the origins of cultural cognition', *Behavioral and Brain Sciences*.

Tomasello, M., Kruger, A.C. and Ratner, H.H. (1993), 'Cultural learning', *Behavioral and Brain Sciences*, 16, 495–552.

Vygotsky, L. (1986), *Thought and Language* (Cambridge, MA: MIT Press).

Watson, J. (1930), *Behaviorism* (New York: Norton).

Weiner, J. (1990), *Frege in Perspective* (Ithaca, NY: Cornell University Press).

— (1999), *Frege* (Oxford: Oxford University Press).

White, S. (1988), *The Recent Work of Jürgen Habermas* (Cambridge: Cambridge University Press).

Whorf, B. L. (1956), *Language, Thought and Reality* (Cambridge, MA: The Technology Press of Massachusetts Institute of Technology).

Williams, M. (1999), *Wittgenstein, Mind and Meaning* (New York: Routledge).

Wittgenstein, L. (1958), *Philosophical Investigations* (Oxford: Blackwell).

— (1975), *Wittgenstein's Lectures on the Foundations of Mathematics* (Chicago and London: University of Chicago Press).

— (1978), *Remarks on the Foundations of Mathematics* (Oxford: Blackwell).

— (1980a), *Remarks on the Philosophy of Psychology, Volume II* (Chicago: University of Chicago Press).

— (1980b), *Zettel* (Chicago: University of Chicago Press, 1980).

Wright, C. (1987), *Realism, Meaning, and Truth* (Oxford: Blackwell).

FURTHER SUGGESTED READING

Alston, W. (1963), 'Meaning and use', *Philosophical Quarterly*, 51, 107–24.

Ayer, A. J. (1946), *Language, Truth, and Logic* (London: Victor Gollancz).

Bach, K. (1999), 'The myth of conventional implicature', *Linguistics and Philosophy*, 22, 327–66.

Bakhtin, M. M. (1984), *Problems in Dostoevsky's Poetics*, edited and translated by C. Emerson (Minneapolis: University of Minnesota Press).

Bennett, J. (1971), *Linguistic Behaviour* (Cambridge: Cambridge University Press).

Benveniste, E. (1971), *Problems in General Linguistics* (Coral Gables, FL: University of Miami Press).

Bilgrami, A. (1992), *Belief and Meaning* (Oxford: Blackwell).

Blackburn, S. (1984), *Spreading the Word* (Oxford: Clarendon Press).

Bourdieu, P. (1977), *Outline of a Theory of Practice* (Cambridge: Cambridge University Press).

— (1990), *The Logic of Practice* (Stanford: Stanford University Press).

Brandom, R. (ed.) (2000), *Rorty and his Critics* (Oxford: Blackwell).

Brown, W. (1998), 'Freedom's silences', in R. Post (ed.), pp. 313–27 (see References).

Burge, T. (1973), 'Reference and proper names', *Journal of Philosophy*, 70, 425–39.

— (1974), 'Demonstrative constructions, reference and truth', *Journal of Philosophy*, 71, 205–23.

Butler, J. (1990), *Gender Trouble: Feminism and the Subversion of Identity* (New York: Routledge).

— (1993), *Bodies that Matter: On the Discursive Limits of 'Sex'* (New York and London, Routledge).

— (1997), 'Merely cultural', *Social Text*, 52/53, 265–77.

Cavell, S. (1976), *Must We Mean What We Say?* (Cambridge: Cambridge University Press).

— (1979), *The Claim of Reason* (Oxford: Oxford University Press).

Crary, A. and Read, R. (eds) (2000), *The New Wittgenstein* (London and New York: Routledge).

Dascal, M. (1984), *Pragmatics and the Philosophy of Mind* (London: John Benjamins Publishing Co.).

— (2003), *Interpretation and Understanding* (London: John Benjamins Publishing Co.).

Davidson, D. (1984), 'Communication and convention', *Synthese*, 59, 3–18.

— (1992), 'The second person', *Midwest Studies in Philosophy*, 17, 255–67.

Devitt, M. (1981), *Designation* (New York: Columbia University Press).

Devitt, M. and Sterelny, K. (1987), *Language and Reality* (Cambridge, MA: MIT Press).

Diamond, C. (1991), *The Realistic Spirit. Wittgenstein, Philosophy, and the Mind* (Cambridge, MA: MIT Press).

Donnellan, K. (1970), 'Proper names and identifying descriptions', *Synthese*, 21, 335–58.

— (1974), 'Speaking of nothing', *Philosophical Review*, 83, 3–31.

— (1979), 'Speaker reference, descriptions, and anaphora', in P. French, T. Uehling and H. Wettstein (eds), *Contemporary Perspectives in the Philosophy of Language* (Minneapolis: University of Minnesota Press).

Dummett, M. (1973), *Frege: Philosophy of Language* (New York: Harper & Row).

— (1975), 'What is a theory of meaning?', in S. Guttenplan (ed.), *Mind and Language* (Oxford: Oxford University Press).

— (1978), *Truth and Other Enigmas* (Cambridge, MA: Harvard University Press).

— (1994), 'Reply to Davidson', in B. McGuinness (ed.), *The Philosophy of Michael Dummett* (Dordrecht: Kluwer).

Evans, G. (1982), *The Varieties of Reference* (Oxford: Oxford University Press).

Evans, G. and McDowell, J. (eds) (1976), *Truth and Meaning* (Oxford: Oxford University Press).

Felman, S. (1983, 2002 – New Edition), *The Literary Speech Act: Don Juan with J. L. Austin, or Seduction in Two Languages* (Ithaca, NY: Cornell University Press).

Fodor, J. (1994), *The Elm and the Expert* (Cambridge, MA: MIT Press).

Fodor, J., and Lepore, E. (1992), *Holism* (Oxford: Blackwell).

Fogelin, R. (1988), *Figuratively Speaking* (New Haven, CONN: Yale University Press).

Foucault, M. (1972), 'The discourse on language', in *The Archeology of Knowledge and the Discourse on Language* (New York: Pantheon), pp. 215–37.

Frege, G. (1956), 'The thought', *Mind*, 65, 289–311.

French, P., Uehling, T. and Wettstein, H. (eds), (1979), *Contemporary Perspectives in the Philosophy of Language* (Minneapolis: University of Minnesota Press).

Gadamer, H.-G. (1976), *Philosophical Hermeneutics* (Berkeley: University of California Press).

Geach, P. (1962), *Reference and Generality* (Ithaca, NY: Cornell University Press).

Goodman, N. (1970), 'Seven strictures on similarity', in L. Foster and J. W. Swanson (eds), *Experience and Theory* (Amherst: University of Massachusetts Press).

— (1981), 'Twisted tales; or story, study, and symphony', *Synthese*, 46, 331–50.

Habermas, J. (1984), *The Theory of Communicative Action, Volume 1* (Boston: Beacon Press).

— (1987), *The Theory of Communicative Action, Volume 2* (Boston: Beacon Press).

— (1990), *Moral Consciousness and Communicative Action* (Cambridge, MA: MIT Press).

— (1994), 'Actions, speech acts, linguistically mediated interactions and the life-world', in G. Floistad (ed.), *Philosophical Problems Today* (Amsterdam: Kluwer), pp. 45–74.

Horwich, P. (1990), 'Wittgenstein and Kripke on the nature of meaning', *Mind and Language*, 5, 105–21.

Humphrey, J. A. (1999), 'Quine, Kripke's Wittgenstein, simplicity, and skeptical solutions', *The Southern Journal of Philosophy*, 37, 43–55.

Keenan, E. L. (ed.) (1975), *Formal Semantics of Natural Language* (Cambridge: Cambridge University Press).

Lance, M. N. and O'Leary-Hawthorne, J. (1997), *The Grammar of Meaning. Normativity and Semantic Discourse* (Cambridge: Cambridge University Press).

Lepore, E. and Van Gulick, R. (eds) (1991), *John Searle and his Critics* (Oxford: Blackwell).

Lewis, D. (1986), *On the Plurality of Worlds* (Oxford: Blackwell).

Linsky, L. (1977), *Names and Descriptions* (Chicago: Chicago University Press).

Loar, B. (1976), 'The semantics of singular terms', *Philosophical Studies*, 30, 353–77.

Loewer, B. and Rey, G. (eds) (1991), *Meaning in Mind. Fodor and his Critics* (Oxford: Blackwell).

Luria, A. R. (1976), *Cognitive Development: Its Cultural and Social Foundations* (Cambridge, MA: Harvard University Press).

Lyotard, J-F. (1984), *The Postmodern Condition* (Minneapolis: University of Minnesota Press).

— (1988), *The Differend* (Minneapolis: University of Minnesota Press).

Margalit, A. (ed.) (1979), *Meaning and Use* (Dordrecht: Reidel).

Medina, J. (2003), 'Wittgenstein and nonsense: psychologism, Kantianism, and the *Habitus*', *International Journal of Philosophical Studies*, 11, (3), 293–318.

— (2004), 'Pragmatism and ethnicity: critique, reconstruction, and the New Hispanic', *Metaphilosophy*, 35 (1/2), 115–46.

Munitz, M. and Unger, P. (eds) (1974), *Semantics and Philosophy* (New York: New York University Press).

Nye, A. (ed.) (1998), *Philosophy of Language: The Big Questions* (Oxford: Blackwell).

Ortony, A. (ed.) (1979), *Metaphor and Thought* (Cambridge: Cambridge University Press).

Pears, D. (ed.) (1975), *Bertrand Russell* (Garden City, NY: Anchor Books).

Peirce, C. S. (1934), *Collected Papers of Charles Sanders Peirce* (Cambridge, MA: Harvard University Press).

— (1991), *Peirce on Signs: Writings on Semiotics* (Chapel Hill: University of North Carolina Press).

Quine, W. v., (1953), *From a Logical Point of View* (Cambridge, MA: Harvard University Press).

Ricoeur, P. (1976), *Interpretation Theory: Discourse and the Surplus of Meaning* (Austin: Texas Christian University Press).

— (1981), *The Rule of Metaphor: Multi-Disciplinary Studies of the Creation of Meaning in Language* (Toronto: University of Toronto Press).

Ricoeur, P. and Thompson, J. B. (eds) (1981), *Hermeneutics in the Human Sciences: Essays on Language, Action, and Interpretation* (Cambridge: Cambridge University Press).

Rorty, R. (1989), *Contingency, Irony, and Solidarity* (Cambridge: Cambridge University Press).

— (1991), *Objectivity, Relativism, and Truth* (Cambridge: Cambridge University Press).

— (1998), *Truth and Progress* (Cambridge: Cambridge University Press).

Russell, B. (1957), 'Mr. Strawson on Referring', *Mind*, 66, 385–9.

Salmon, N. (1981), *Reference and Essence* (Princeton: Princeton University Press).

Schatzki, T. R. (1987), 'Overdue analysis of Bourdieu's theory of practice', *Inquiry*, 30, 113–35.

Scheman, N. and O'Connor, P. (eds) (2002), *Feminist Interpretations of Ludwig Wittgenstein* (University Park: Penn State University Press).

Searle, J. (1985), *Expression and Meaning: Studies in the Theory of Speech Acts* (Cambridge: Cambridge University Press).

— (1986), 'Meaning, communication, and representation', in R. E. Grandy and R. Warner (eds), pp. 209–26 (see References).

— (1998), *Mind, Language, and Society* (New York: Basic Books).

Sedgwick, E. K. (1990), *Epistemology of the Closet* (Berkeley and Los Angeles: University of California Press).

Sellars, W. (1963), 'Some reflections on language games', in *Science, Perception, and Reality* (London: Routledge).

— (1974), 'Meaning as functional classification', *Synthese*, 27, 417–37.

— (1997), *Empiricism and the Philosophy of Mind* (Cambridge, MA: Harvard University Press).

Shusterman, R. (ed.) (1999), *Bourdieu: A Critical Reader* (Oxford: Blackwell).

Sosa, E. (1970), 'Propositional attitudes de dicto and de re', *Journal of Philosophy*, 67, 883–96.

Stalnaker, R. (1970), 'Pragmatics', *Synthese*, 22, 272–89.

Strawson, P. (1964), 'Intention and convention in speech acts', *Philosophical Review*, 73, 439–60.

— (1970), *Meaning and Truth* (Oxford: Clarendon Press).

Unger, P. (1983), 'The causal theory of reference', *Philosophical Studies*, 43, 1–45.

Vygotsky, L. (1978), *Mind in Society* (Cambridge, MA: Harvard University Press).

Williams, M. (1991), 'Blind obedience: rules, community and the individual', in K. Puhl (ed.), *Meaning Scepticism* (Berlin: Walter de Gruyter), pp. 93–125.

Wittgenstgein, L. (1958), *The Blue and Brown Books* (Oxford: Blackwell).

— (1969), *On Certainty* (Oxford: Blackwell).

— (1980), *Culture and Value* (Chicago: University of Chicago Press).

Young, I. M. (1997), *Intersecting Voices. Dilemmas of Gender, Political Philosophy, and Policy* (Princeton: Princeton University Press).

Ziff, P. (1960), *Semantic Analysis* (Ithaca, NY: Cornell University Press).

— (1967), 'On H. P. Grice's account of meaning', *Analysis*, 28, 1–8.

INDEX

INDEX